CULTIVATING ~~VIRTUE:~~

Self-Mastery with the Saints

Translated from the Italian by

A Member of the Order of Mercy

Mt. St. Joseph's Seminary

Hartford, Connecticut

Albatross Publishers

Naples, Italy

2019

Originally published in New York in 1891 by
P.J. Kenedy as *A Year With the Saints*.

ISBN 978-1-946963-26-0

To Mary, Our Lady of Mercy, under the title of Queen of All Saints, this translation is affectionately dedicated in the hope that through her advocacy it may conduce to the growth of sanctity in numerous souls.

Contents

Translator's Preface

In presenting this work for the first time in English dress, the translator would take the opportunity of drawing the attention of the devout American reader to one or two peculiarities in its structure, which have already won for it a wide recognition among readers of books of its class in Europe.

In the first place, the allotment of separate months to individual virtues agrees well with a practice of self-examination much recommended by many spiritual writers, who advise us to take different virtues in turn as the objects of special effort. Nothing certainly could be better fitted to assist us in the acquisition of a virtue than these selections from the writings of the most eminent masters of spiritual science which portray its beauties, declare its necessity or explain its various degrees and the methods of its attainment.

In the second place, the few words of exhortation or instruction which open the reading for each day are followed by the best of all commentaries—that of action. A great part of the book

is composed of examples which, while they have the interest of anecdote, furnish at the same time the strongest proofs of the possibility of carrying out in real life precepts and principles which might otherwise seem too high and heavenly for our everyday existence.

In the hope then that these exotic flowers may flourish and blossom in many an American garden, they are offered to the lovers of spiritual excellence and beauty by

THE TRANSLATOR.

JANUARY

Perfection

---

*Be ye perfect as your Heavenly
Father is perfect.*—MATT. 5:48

---

1   Consider all the past as nothing, and say, like David:
Now I begin to love my God.

—ST. FRANCIS DE SALES

It was in this manner that the Apostle St. Paul acted; though,
after his conversion, he had become a vessel of election, filled
with the spirit of Jesus Christ, yet, to persevere and advance in
the heavenly way, he made use of this means, for he said in his
Epistle to the Philippians: "Brethren, I do not count myself to
have apprehended. But one thing I do: forgetting the things that
are behind, and stretching forth myself to those that are before,
I press towards the mark, to the prize of the supernal vocation of
God in Christ Jesus." [PHIL. 3:13–14].

Thus the glorious St. Anthony went from day to day, stimulating himself to virtue. St. Anastasius said of him that he always looked upon himself as a beginner, as if every day were the first in which he was serving God, and as if in the past he had done nothing good and were but just setting foot in the way of the Lord and taking the first steps on the road to Heaven. And this was the very last admonition he left to his monks at his death: "My sons," he said to them, "if you wish to advance in virtue and perfection, never give up the practice of considering each day that you are then beginning, and of conducting yourselves always as you did on the day you began."

Thus also we find that St. Gregory, St. Bernard and St. Charles acted and advised others to act. To render clearer to all the necessity and utility of this method, they made use of two beautiful comparisons, saying that we must act in this like travelers who do not regard the road they have gone over, but, rather, what remains for them to traverse—and this they keep always before their eyes, even to their journey's end; or, like merchants eager for riches who make no account of what they have hitherto acquired, nor of the fatigue they have borne, but put all their thought and care upon new acquisitions, and upon daily multiplying their possessions, as if in the past they had made no profit at all.

2   We must begin with a strong and constant resolution to give ourselves wholly to God, professing to Him, in a tender, loving manner, from the bottom of our hearts, that we intend to be His without any reserve, and then we must often go back and renew this same resolution.

—ST. FRANCIS DE SALES

One of the means for the acquisition of perfection which was chiefly inculcated and much practiced by St. Philip Neri was a frequent renewal of good resolutions.

St. Francis de Sales made from time to time a spiritual renovation, and always conceived in it new desires to serve God better.

St. John Berchmans, at his very entrance into religion, planted in his heart a strong resolution to become a Saint, and then he not only remained constant in all the practices and resolutions which he took up for this end, but he went on daily gaining new vigor to his spiritual advantage.

When a holy religious was giving the Exercises at Torre di Specchi in Rome, a nun called Sr. Marie Bonaventura, who was living a very relaxed life, did not wish to be present. By many entreaties she was finally induced to attend. The first meditation, on the end of man, enkindled such fervor in her heart that the Father had scarcely finished when she called him to her, and said: "Father, I mean to be a Saint, and quickly." She then withdrew to her cell, and, writing the same words on a scrap of paper, fastened them to the foot of her crucifix. From this moment, she applied herself with so much earnestness to the practice of perfection that a memoir of her was written at her death, which occurred eleven months later.

3 The Lord chiefly desires of us that we should be completely perfect, that we may be wholly one with Him. Let us aim, therefore, at whatever we need to reach this
—ST. TERESA

Father Peter Faber, a companion of St. Ignatius and highly esteemed by St. Francis de Sales, often dwelt on the thought that God greatly desires our advancement. And so he endeavored to grow constantly, and not to let a day pass without some progress in virtue, so that he gradually rose to great perfection and a high reputation for sanctity.

St. Pachomius and St. Anthony, by studying the virtues of others, stimulated themselves to attain similar excellence.

The Venerable Sister Mary Villani had the following vision. On the Feast of St. Francis, for whom she had a particular devotion, this Saint appeared to her and led her to a lofty place, more beautiful than any she had ever seen. To reach it, one was obliged to ascend four very high terraces, which signified, as the Saint revealed to her, the four degrees of perfection. With great difficulty she ascended, by his help, the first terrace; and he explained to her that this was the first state of perfection, called purity of conscience, which borders on angelic purity. In it the soul becomes like that of a little child, enjoys a pure and holy tranquility, never thinks evil of others, nor interests itself in what does not belong to its own position. Thence he brought her up to the second terrace, telling her that whoever had arrived at purity of conscience becomes capable of prayer and of true love, which is the inseparable fruit of prayer. Here he enumerated to her the properties of true love, which is pure, simple, unselfish and founded upon the truth of God, who can give Himself only to souls already possessed of purity. Then he raised her to the third terrace, that of the cross and mortification, adding that from purity and love the soul passes on to taking up the cross courageously and to being itself crucified, and that to arrive at this state one must acquire four

cardinal virtues. These are: a true mortification of all vices and of every earthly affection; a perfect poverty of spirit, which tramples underfoot all temporal goods; a living death, by which the soul dies to itself and to all affections of sense, and lives in a total annihilation and transformation into its crucified Lord, so as to be able to say: "I live, now not I; but Christ liveth in me." [*Gal.* 2:20] The soul that has gained this state seems to have conquered the world, and bears sufferings and crosses as if it could no longer feel them. The fourth terrace, he said, typified the state of real and perfect union.

4 I hear nothing talked of but perfection; yet I see it practiced only by few. Everyone forms his own ideal of it. Some place it in simplicity of attire; some in austerity; some in almsgiving; some in frequent reception of the Sacraments; this one, in prayer; that one, in passive contemplation; and another, in the gifts called gratuitous. But, by a general mistake, they take the effects for the cause, and the means for the end. For my part, I know of no other perfection than loving God with all the heart, and our neighbor as ourselves. Whoever imagines any other kind of perfection deceives himself, for the whole accumulation of virtues without this is but a heap of stones. And if we do not immediately and perfectly enjoy this treasure of holy love, the fault is in us. We are too slow and ungenerous with God, and do not give ourselves up entirely to Him, as the Saints did.

—ST. FRANCIS DE SALES

Who does not see that the perfection of this Saint must have been of a true and very sublime character, when his love for God and his neighbor was so great and so pure? The same may be said also of St. Vincent de Paul and many others.

St. Mary Magdalen de' Pazzi was truly admirable in both of these points. As we shall hereafter see, she was so much inflamed with the love of God that she could not bear the excessive ardor of this divine fire, and was obliged to cool her glowing bosom with linen cloths soaked in water; and she carried the love of her neighbor so far as to desire and procure others' good in preference to her own.

5 All perfection is founded upon only two principles, by means of which, with due attention to the daily actions suited to our state, we shall certainly arrive at the summit and fullness of it. The first principle is a very low esteem for all created things, but, above all, for ourselves. This low esteem should show itself, in practice, by renouncing ourselves and all creatures; in our hearts, by a firm resolution; and in our lives, in such ways as may be suitable, especially by manifesting contentment and cheerfulness when the Lord takes from us any good. The second principle is a very high esteem of God, which may be easily acquired by the light of faith, as He is Omnipotent, the Supreme Good and our End; as also because He has loved us so much, and is ever present with us, and guides us in all things, both as to nature and grace, and, in particular, has called us and leads us by a special vocation

to a lofty perfection. From this esteem there must certainly arise in us a great submission of will, and of every power and faculty, to His greater glory, without any mingling of our own interest, though it be ever so holy. At the same time, there will be great conformity with the Divine Will, which will be the actual measure of all our designs, affections, and works. In this manner, the soul arrives at union—not, indeed, at the mystic union of raptures, elevations of the spirit, and vehement affections; but the solid, real, and practical union of a will thoroughly conformed to the Divine Will by the perfect love which works out all things in God and for God without special lights. Of this, all are capable; and all, with certainty, though not without crosses, can arrive at it.

—FR. ACHILLE GAGLIARDI

It was always the principal study of St. Vincent de Paul to establish and perfect himself in these two principles. Therefore, as his profound humility made him believe himself incapable of great things, he thought only of fulfilling faithfully towards God the obligations of a true and perfect Christian. And since he knew, by heavenly illuminations, that all Christian perfection depends upon a good use of these two principles, he aimed at them alone and sought above all to penetrate them well and to fix them in his soul, that they might serve as an unerring rule and guide for all his actions. And the plan succeeded well. For God, who exalts the humble, did not think it enough to guide him by this means to that Christian perfection which he had prescribed

to himself, but willed to exalt him to a sanctity equally solid and eminent, and which may truly be called singular, as, in fact, there are certainly few persons who without the help of extraordinary and mystic lights, under the guidance only of the lights of ordinary grace, have reached so lofty a sanctity as has this servant of God.

6 Perfection consists in one thing alone, which is doing the will of God. For, according to Our Lord's words, it suffices for perfection to deny self, to take up the cross and to follow Him. Now, who denies himself and takes up his cross and follows Christ better than he who seeks not to do his own will, but always that of God? Behold, now, how little is needed to become a Saint! Nothing more than to acquire the habit of willing, on every occasion, what God wills.

—ST. VINCENT DE PAUL

More than in anything else the Saint just quoted showed the purity and solidity of his virtue, in always aiming to follow and obey the will of God. This was the great principle on which all his resolutions were founded, and by which he faithfully and firmly carried them into practice, trampling underfoot his own interest, and preferring the Divine Will and the glory and service of God to anything else, without exception.

The Lord said of David that he was a man after His own heart, and the foundation for such high praise is given in these words: "for in all things he will do My will."

St. Mary Magdalen de' Pazzi was so much attached to this practice that she often said that she would never determine upon anything, however trivial, such as going from one room to another, if she thought it not in conformity with the Divine Will, nor would she omit to do anything she believed in conformity with it. And she added that if it came into her mind while she was in the midst of an action that such an act was contrary to the will of God, she would abandon it on the instant, though to do so might cost her life.

Taulerus relates of a certain holy and learned man that when his friends entreated him, on his deathbed, to leave them some good precept, he said: "The sum and substance of all instruction is to take all that comes as from the hand of God, and to wish for nothing different, but to do in all things His Divine Will."

The Venerable Seraphina of God had so great a love for the Divine Will that she often entreated her director to manifest it to her, saying, "Counsel me, Father, as to what I am to do, and do not let me do anything of myself, that I may please the Divine Majesty. For to see God ever so little displeased would be worse than the loss of a thousand worlds." One day there came to her so great a desire to do nothing according to her own will, but only according to that of God, that with the consent of her director, she made a vow to that effect.

7 A servant of God signifies one who has a great charity towards his neighbor, and an inviolable resolution to follow in everything the Divine Will; who bears with

his own deficiencies, and patiently supports the imperfections of others.

—ST. FRANCIS DE SALES

The whole life of this Saint, as well as of St. Vincent de Paul,
was but a faithful and continual exercise of these virtues, on the
occasions which every day presented themselves. In this way they
both became great servants of God.

In the Lives of the Fathers of the West, it is told of St. Fin-
tan that he was daily visited by an angel, but that once the visit
was omitted for several days. When the Saint had the happiness of seeing him again, he asked the angel why he had been
so long deprived of his most sweet companionship. "Because,"
replied the angel, "I had to be present at the death of Motua,
who was a great servant of God, and better than yourself,
for he did what you have not done. This man never spoke a
harsh word to anyone present, nor an unkind word of anyone
absent. He never complained of heat or cold, nor of anything
else, whatever it might be, or however it might happen; but
always conformed himself to the will of God, in whose hands
are all things."

When St. Gertrude was one day mourning over a little fault
into which she was accustomed to fall at times, she earnestly
entreated the Lord to free her from it. But He said to her, with
great sweetness: "Would you wish that I should be deprived
of a great honor and you yourself of a great reward? Know
that every time one perceives a fault of his own and resolves to
avoid it for the future, he gains a great reward; and as often as
he keeps himself from falling into it again for My sake, he does

Me as much honor as a valiant soldier does his king, when he fights manfully against his enemies and conquers them."

8 To be perfect in one's vocation is nothing else than to perform the duties and offices to which one is obliged, solely for the honor and love of God, referring all to His glory. Whoever works in this manner may be called perfect in his state, a man according to the heart and will of God.

—ST. FRANCIS DE SALES

In the Lives of the Holy Fathers it is narrated of the Abbot Paphnutius, who was highly celebrated for sanctity, that one day he expressed a desire to know from the Lord whether he had any merit in His eyes. He received the reply that he had gained equal merit with a certain nobleman, whose name was given. The Saint immediately visited this gentleman, by whom he was kindly treated and hospitably entertained. When the repast was over, the Abbot begged of his host to tell him what was his manner of life. The Baron excused himself by saying that he did not possess any virtue, but after many entreaties, he said that he was very careful to entertain pilgrims, and provide them with whatever might be necessary for their journey; that he never despised the poor, but helped them in their need as much as he could; that he had justice administered equitably, and always gave honest decisions, never swerving from right through fear or favor; that he never oppressed his subjects; that he allowed anyone to become his tenant, and expected from no one more than what was justly his due; that no one could

complain of ever having received harm or damage from his family or cattle; that he had never offended or slandered anyone, but treated all with respect, helped all as far as he was able and endeavored to keep all in peace and harmony. On hearing this the holy Abbot was greatly edified, and understood that true perfection consisted not in great deeds, but in fulfilling our duties.

In San Cesario in the province of Lecce there lived in the time of St. Joseph da Cupertino a nun who had a great reputation for sanctity. One day, when the Saint happened to visit the house of the Marquis of that place, he was asked his opinion of this report in regard to the nun. He answered, "You have a real saint here among you, who is not known"; and he named a poor widow, of whom not a word had ever been said. The Marquis inquired as to what were her good qualities, and found that she remained always shut up in her poor little home, with some of her daughters, and that they worked constantly to support themselves and were never seen abroad but once a day, which was very early in the morning when they were going to church to hear Mass.

9 Although in entering religion and taking care not to offend God, we may appear to have done everything, ah! how often certain worms remain, which do not allow themselves to be perceived until they have gnawed away our virtues! Such worms are self-love, self-esteem, harsh judgments of others, though in trifles, and a great want of charity towards our neighbor. But if, indeed, by dragging on, we satisfy our obligations,

we do not do it with that perfection which God would expect of us.

—ST. TERESA

To one of these worms, self-esteem, Monseigneur de Palafox attributed his own relaxation after his conversion and his narrow escape from eternal ruin. "For," said he, "though I was humble, had I, therefore, a right to believe that I was truly humble? and though I desired and intended to be good, ought I, therefore, to presume that I was truly good? This hidden pride obliged the Divine Goodness to overwhelm me, in order that I might see that I was not good, but bad, weak, miserable, full of pride, sensuality and unfaithfulness, and a prodigal scorner of the gifts of grace."

It is told in the Lives of the Fathers that two of them had received the gift of beholding mutually the grace which was in the heart of the other. One of them, leaving his cell early one Friday morning, found a monk who was eating at the hour contrary to their custom. He judged him to be in fault, and reproved him. When he returned home, his companion did not see in him the usual sign of grace, and asked him what he had done. But when the other remembered nothing, he added, "Think whether you may not have said some idle word." Then he remembered his rash judgment, and related what had happened. For this fault they both fasted two whole weeks, at the end of which the usual sign appeared in the brother who had been culpable.

10 Observe that perfection is not acquired by sitting with our arms folded, but it is necessary to work in earnest,

in order to conquer ourselves and to bring ourselves to live, not according to our inclinations and passions, but according to reason, our Rule, and obedience. The thing is hard, it cannot be denied, but necessary. With practice, however, it becomes easy and pleasing.

—ST. FRANCIS DE SALES

Plutarch relates of Lycurgus that he once took two puppies of the same litter and trained up one in the kitchen and the other to hunting. When they were grown (one day when he was going to address the people), he took them into the forum, where he threw down some fish bones and at the same time let loose a hare. The first immediately began to gnaw the bones, while the other set off in pursuit of the hare. Then Lycurgus commanded silence, and turning to the people, said: "Do you see this? These two dogs are of the same breed, yet they are not inclined to the same thing, but each to that which he has been accustomed to. So true is it that habit ends in overcoming even the most violent inclinations of nature."

It is written of St. Ignatius Loyola, that through the continual struggle which he had made to mortify himself and to bear contradictions patiently, he had arrived at such a point as to appear to have no longer any inclination. The same thing has also been noticed in many others.

11 All the science of the Saints is included in these two things: To do, and to suffer. And whoever has done these two things best, has made himself most saintly.

—ST. FRANCIS DE SALES

Anyone who reads the Lives of Sts. Ambrose, Basil, Jerome, Chrysostom, Dominic, Vincent de Paul and other great Saints will not be surprised that they became so remarkable for holiness, when he sees the innumerable good works which they wrought and the great sufferings which they endured.

We are told in the Lives of the Fathers that this was the method chiefly employed by St. Dorotheus, to sanctify his disciple Dositheus. This Saint kept the latter constantly occupied, especially in things opposed to his own wishes. If he saw in his possession any article that was convenient and well made, even though it might be necessary for his work, he took it from him; if Dositheus called his master's attention to anything which he had done well, the Saint sent him away without any answer; and thus, in every desire, the Saint sought to mortify his disciple, while the latter, in the meantime, obeyed promptly in everything and bore all without reply. And thus, in the course of only five years, he reached a very high perfection and sanctity.

12 I wish I could persuade spiritual persons that the way of perfection does not consist in many devices, nor in much cogitation, but in denying themselves completely and yielding themselves to suffer everything for love of Christ. And if there is failure in this exercise, all other methods of walking in the spiritual way are merely a beating about the bush, and profitless trifling, although a person should have a very high contemplation and communication with God.

—ST. JOHN OF THE CROSS

Cassian wrote concerning the Abbot Paphnutius that the road by which he arrived at such great sanctity was that of constantly mortifying himself; and that in this manner he extinguished in himself all vices, and perfected in himself all virtues.

Father Balthasar Alvarez practiced continual mortification and self-denial in all that nature desired, not only in great things but also in small; and by this he arrived at high perfection.

The Blessed Angela di Foligno, in ecstasy, saw the Lord bestowing marks of love upon some of His servants, but upon one, more; upon another, less. Desiring to understand the cause of this difference, she advanced to inquire of Our Lord, who answered thus: "I invite all to Me, but all are not willing to come, because the way is interlaced with thorns. To all who come, I offer My bread to eat and My cup to drink. But My food is not pleasing to sense, and My cup is full of bitterness, so that all do not desire to satiate themselves with those labors which were My meat while I was in the world. But those who are most constant in bearing Me company, they certainly are My dearest and most favored ones." When the Saint had heard this, she was filled with so great a desire of suffering and denying herself in all ways that when many difficulties were afterwards placed in her way by her religious and by her own family, she experienced in them as great comfort as a worldling could have found in any plan made for his pleasure and advantage.

13 The greatest fault among those who have a good will is that they wish to be something they cannot be, and do not wish to be what they necessarily must be. They conceive desires to do great things for which, perhaps,

no opportunity may ever come to them, and meantime neglect the small which the Lord puts into their hands. There are a thousand little acts of virtue, such as bearing with the importunities and imperfections of our neighbors, not resenting an unpleasant word or a trifling injury, restraining an emotion of anger, mortifying some little affection, some ill-regulated desire to speak or to listen, excusing an indiscretion, or yielding to another in trifles. These are things to be done by all; why not practice them? The occasions for great gains come but rarely, but of little gains many can be made each day; and by managing these little gains with judgment, there are some who grow rich. Oh, how holy and rich in merits we should make ourselves, if we but knew how to profit by the opportunities which our vocation supplies to us! Yes, yes, let us apply ourselves to follow well the path which is close before us, and to do well on the first opportunity, without occupying ourselves with thoughts of the last, and thus we shall make good progress.

—ST. FRANCIS DE SALES

St. Philip Neri, enkindled with a desire of martyrdom, had resolved to go to preach the Faith in India. But when God informed him, by revelation, that his India must be in Rome, he employed himself there, and by leading a life full of virtuous actions he became a great Saint.

St. John Berchmans, in only five years of religious life, certainly reached a lofty perfection. Now, how did he accomplish it?

By nothing except striving to be faithful to do exactly all those things which he knew to be right and possible for him, in the way of not neglecting any part of perfection, which, with the aid of grace, he might be able to acquire.

St. Gertrude, feeling very weak one day, decided to make an effort to say Matins. When she had finished the First Nocturn, another sick sister came to ask her to say the Office with her; and she immediately went back to the beginning. That same morning she had a vision in which she saw her soul adorned with jewels of great value, and the Lord said to her that by the act of charity which she had performed for His love, she had merited this ornament in which the jewels equalled in number the words she had repeated.

We read of a young Jesuit student that, one morning in vacation, when he was just starting for a walk with some of his companions, he was requested by one of the Fathers to wait half an hour and serve Mass, which he did. When he had become more advanced in knowledge and age, he went to preach the Faith among the infidels, and there was found worthy to obtain the glory of martyrdom. Then it was revealed to him that so great a grace had been given him by God in reward for the little mortification which he accepted in serving Mass.

14 Our greatest fault is that we wish to serve God in our way, not in His way—according to our will, not according to His will. When He wishes us to be sick, we wish to be well; when He desires us to serve Him by sufferings, we desire to serve Him by works; when He wishes us to exercise charity, we

wish to exercise humility; when He seeks from us resignation, we wish for devotion, a spirit of prayer, or some other virtue. And this is not because the things we desire may be more pleasing to Him, but because they are more to our taste. This is certainly the greatest obstacle we can raise to our own perfection, for it is beyond doubt that if we wish to be Saints according to our own will, we shall never be so at all. To be truly a Saint, it is necessary to be one according to the will of God.

—ST. FRANCIS DE SALES

St. Mary Magdalen de' Pazzi knew this most important truth; and, with the guidance of so clear a light, she knew how to submit her will to that of God so perfectly that she was always contented with what came to her day by day, nor did she ever desire anything extraordinary. She was even accustomed to say that she would consider it a marked defect to ask of the Lord any grace for herself or others, with any greater importunity than simple prayers, and that it was her joy and glory to do His will, not that He should do hers. Even as to the sanctity and perfection of her own soul, she wished that it might be not according to her own desire, but to the will of God. And so, we find among her writings this resolution: To offer myself to God, and to seek *all* that perfection and *only* that perfection which He is pleased that I should have, and in the time and way that He shall wish, and not otherwise. In conversation with an intimate friend, she once said: The good which does not come to me by this way of the Divine Will, does not seem to me

good. I would prefer having no gift at all except that of leaving my will and all my desires in God, to having any gift through desire and will. Yes, yes, *in me sint, Deus, vota tua, et non vota mea*—Thy will, not mine, be done. The grace which she asked most frequently and most earnestly of the Lord was this: that He would make her remain till death entirely subject and submissive to His Divine Will and pleasure; thus it is no wonder that she became so holy.

Even among the heathens, there are to be found those who by the light of reason alone clearly understood this truth. Plutarch disapproved of the common prayer of the people: May God give you all that good which you desire. No, he says, we ought rather to say, May God grant that you shall desire what He desires. And what is more, Epictetus practiced it; for he said: "I am always content with whatever happens, it all happens by the disposal of God, and I am certain that what God wills is better than what I can ever will."

15 Two mistakes I find common among spiritual persons. One is that they ordinarily measure their devotion by the consolations and satisfactions which they experience in the way of God, so that if these happen to be wanting, they think they have lost all devotion. No, this is no more than a sensible devotion. True and substantial devotion does not consist in these things, but in having a will resolute, active, ready, and constant not to offend God, and to perform all that belongs to His service. The other mistake is that if it ever happens to them to do anything

with repugnance and weariness, they believe they have no merit in it. On the other hand, there is *then* far greater merit; so that a single ounce of good done thus by a sheer spiritual effort, amidst darkness and dullness and without interest, is worth more than a hundred pounds done with great facility and sweetness, since the former requires a stronger and purer love. And how great soever may be the aridities and repugnance of the sensible part of our soul, we ought never to lose courage, but pursue our way as travelers treat the barking of dogs.

—ST. FRANCIS DE SALES

A pious matron desiring to know what class of souls was most acceptable to the Lord, He gratified her wish by the following vision. One morning she was hearing Mass when, after the Elevation, she saw Jesus in the form of a most lovely Child, who began to walk about the altar. Thence He descended to a place where three devout nuns were kneeling at its foot. He took one of them by the hand and gave her many caresses. Then approaching the second, He raised her veil and gave her a slight blow on the cheek, and left her as if in anger; but soon returning, and finding her in grief and affliction, He devoted Himself to consoling her with a thousand endearments. Finally, He came to the third, and, with an appearance of great wrath, took her by the arm and drove her away from the altar, loading her with blows, and even tearing the hair from her head, while she bore all with great calmness, humbling herself and blessing God. Then Jesus, turning to the matron, said: "You must know that the first one

is weak in virtue, and very changeable; therefore, to confirm her in the good way, I show Myself altogether amiable and kind; otherwise, she would leave it. The second is more perfect, yet she needs to experience, from time to time, some spiritual sweetness. But the third is so firm and constant in My service, that whatever adversity may come to her, she will not allow herself to be withdrawn from it, and she is My best beloved."

St. Philip Neri, in order to save his penitents from the first of these mistakes, used to tell them that in the spiritual life there are three degrees. The first, which is called animal, includes those who follow the sensible devotion which God usually gives to beginners, in order that, drawn by this delight as animals are by sensible objects, they may give themselves to the spiritual life. The second, which is called the life of man, is led by those who without sensible consolation fight for virtue against their own passions, which is the true characteristic of man. The third is called the angelic life. Those have arrived at it who, after long struggles in subduing their own passions, receive from God a life calm and tranquil and, as it were, angelic even in this world. And if anyone perseveres in the second degree, God will not fail, in His own time, to raise him to the third.

16 We are not to regard great favors from God so much as virtues, but consider who serves the Lord with the greatest mortification, humility, and purity of conscience; for the latter without the former will be the more holy.

—ST. TERESA

Were proofs of this truth wanting, the example of St. Vincent de Paul would be sufficient to confirm it. Very few extraordinary favors are recorded of him, yet he has been, and is now, regarded by all as a man of rare sanctity.

Rufinus of Aquilia tells of St. Macarius, that at one time he believed himself to have made much progress in virtue. But one day, when at prayer, he heard a voice which said to him, "Macarius, know that thou hast not attained as much virtue as two women who live at such a place." Macarius went instantly to find them, and perceived, upon examination, that they possessed great merit, for they had lived together for fifteen years in the same house in perfect union and charity, without the slightest disagreement in word or act occurring between them. The Saint was amazed at this, and confessed that they were, in truth, better and more perfect than he, although he had been gifted by the Divine Goodness with many extraordinary favors.

17 Lord, what wilt Thou have me to do? Here is the true token of a soul absolutely perfect: when one has succeeded in leaving behind his own will to such a degree as no longer to seek, to aim, or to desire to do what he would will, but only what God wills.

—ST. BERNARD

These were the first words of the Apostle St. Paul as he recognized the Lord: "Lord, what wilt Thou have me to do?" And they were uttered by him with so much sincerity of affection, and with such submission of will, that from that day forward he had no other desire and no other aim than to fulfill the Divine

Will in all and through all. Nor in all the adversities, labors, sufferings, and torments which he encountered was there ever a thing sufficient to diminish, or even in the least to shake, his constancy and fidelity.

St. Jane Frances de Chantal had so great a desire to know and follow the Divine Will that on merely hearing those words, "Divine Will," she felt all on fire, as if a torch had been applied to her heart, and she remained in a kind of torture until she knew how she was to understand them.

The venerable Mother Seraphina di Dio testifies of herself that the Lord showed her plainly, by an interior illumination, how good a thing it is to live without any will of one's own and to commit one's self entirely to His holy will. "I remained," she says, "fully persuaded that on account of His greatness and perfection it was the most suitable thing for all His creatures to have no other will than that of their most loving God; and that when one has reached this point, he belongs wholly to God and enjoys Paradise upon earth."

18 If you truly wish to make spiritual profit, you must apply yourself closely to that counsel of the Apostle, *Attende tibi*—Take heed to thyself. This implies two things: The first is not to become entangled in others' affairs, or watchful as to their defects; since he has no little to do who wishes to manage his own affairs well and correct his own failures. The second is to take our own perfection to heart and attend to it incessantly, without regarding whether others attend to theirs or not. For perfection is so

purely individual a matter that, though men who belong to the same order, company, family, or country are here said to make one body; yet, in the world above, it is certain that each one will be separate by himself, and carry his profits and losses to his own account.

—ABBOT PASTOR

A rare pattern of this was St. John Berchmans. From his first entrance into religion, it had been his fixed intention to become a Saint; and from the same time, he made it his aim and his only important business to watch over himself; and to this, in fact, he gave his attention as long as he lived. He did this with such application and such unwearied earnestness that he did not even have time to think of others' occupations or to notice their defects. And thus he never stopped to reflect why others said or did so and so, or whether they did well or ill. Nor did he ever enlist in the defense of one with the danger of offending another, but let everyone go his own way and manage his own affairs for himself. As to the faults of others, he thought of them so little that even when they were committed in his presence he did not notice them; and it was said of him that he was not able to tell what errors the others committed. All his care was to correct his own defects and to perform his own actions well; and so, the pains he took to keep his soul clear of every fault were something extraordinary. For besides carefully making the daily examens and a most rigorous retreat of one day in each month, he often and urgently entreated his superiors and companions to keep their eyes upon him, and inform him of anything they might see

amiss. And when counsel of that kind was given him, he received it as a peculiar favor and offered special prayers for whoever gave it. But not content with this, as he had an ardent desire to render himself as pleasing as possible in the eyes of God, he employed every effort to this end. Therefore he devoted himself with admirable diligence to the most exact observance of his Rules; to executing promptly and faithfully whatever was imposed on him by obedience; to performing well and with particular devotion the spiritual exercises as things which immediately concern the honor of God and one's own profit, paying most attention of all to his Communions, to which he always gave two hours; and finally, to practicing all virtues, especially charity towards the sick. Though he had great fondness for study, he never allowed it to stand in the way of his spiritual exercises, nor of charity or obedience; for his heart did not seek for what afforded most delight, but most merit. And he did all these things without noticing at all whether others did the same or failed in them, because that one precept, *attende tibi*, ever remained planted deeply in his heart.

What harm does it cause the other Apostles now that the unhappy Judas remains suffering in Hell? All the loss falls upon Judas alone. And if Berchmans be higher in Heaven than so many others who were his companions in religion, is not all the gain his?

19 Do not let any occasion of gaining merit pass without taking care to draw some spiritual profit from it; as, for example, from a sharp word which someone may say to you; from an act of obedience imposed against your will; from an opportunity which may occur to humble yourself, or to practice

charity, sweetness, and patience. All these occasions are gain for you, and you should seek to procure them; and at the close of that day, when the greatest number of them have come to you, you should go to rest most cheerful and pleased, as the merchant does on the day when he has had most chance for making money; for on that day business has prospered with him.

—ST. IGNATIUS LOYOLA

It was one of the principal maxims which St. John Berchmans kept fixed in his mind, as we read in his Life, to endeavor to gain merit in everything, and not to let any occasion, however small, escape, if it could be profitable to him. For this reason he continually went in search of such occasions, and when they came to him from others he embraced them all with courage and heartfelt joy, without ever remarking the want of discretion and virtue which they betrayed in others, attending only to his own advancement in humility. And so, from whatever he heard or saw, he was always wont to derive some good fruit for himself; and in this way he attained to the condition of a Saint, which was precisely what he desired.

When St. Matilda was visited by the Lord, accompanied by many Saints, one of them said to her: "Oh, how blessed are you who still live upon earth, on account of the great merit you can acquire!" If a man knew how much he could merit in a day, at the moment he arose in the morning his heart would be filled with joy because the day had appeared in which he could live to his Lord, and, by His grace, increase so greatly His honor and glory

27

and his own merit. This would give him great confidence and strength to do and suffer everything with extreme satisfaction.

We read of St. Francis Xavier that he was stung with shame and self-reproach when he found that merchants had gone to Japan with their merchandise sooner than he himself with the treasures of the Gospel, to spread the Faith and extend the Kingdom of Heaven.

20 Give yourself in earnest to the acquisition of virtue; otherwise, you will remain always a dwarf in it. Never believe that you have acquired a virtue, if you have not made proof of it in resisting its contrary vice, and unless you practice it faithfully on suitable occasions which, for this reason, ought never to be avoided, but rather desired, sought, and embraced with eagerness.

—ST. TERESA

St. Vincent de Paul was not contented, as so many are, with knowing and loving virtues, but he applied himself continually to the practice of them. It was his maxim that labor and patience are the best means of acquiring and planting them firmly in our hearts and that virtues acquired without effort or difficulty can be easily lost, while those which have been beaten by the storms of temptation and practiced amid the difficulties and repugnances of nature, sink their roots deep into the heart. And so, on such occasions, instead of being sad he appeared unusually cheerful. When a certain person was lamenting a mischance which had recently occurred as likely to give bad opinion of his community and give

rise to comments injurious to himself, he replied, "This is good, for it will give us a more favorable occasion to practice virtue."

By this same sentiment, St. Philip Neri encouraged his penitents not to grieve when they suffer temptations and trials, telling them that when the Lord intends to confer on anyone some particular virtue, He is accustomed to permit him to be first assailed by the contrary vice.

St. Francis de Sales illustrated the firmness of virtue in this manner: "If," said he, "the world comes to attack me, I will treat it as I would a viper: I will trample it underfoot, and obey none of its suggestions. If Satan arms his powers, I will not fear them at all. I am stronger than he. God is my Father, and He will have compassion on me, and will fight for me." Here is a fine example of virtue, and of the way to exercise it.

21 Humility and charity are the two master-chords: one, the lowest; the other, the highest; all the others are dependent on them. Therefore it is necessary, above all, to maintain ourselves in these two virtues; for observe well that the preservation of the whole edifice depends on the foundation and the roof.

—ST. FRANCIS DE SALES

Although there never was or can be any Saint destitute of these two most necessary virtues, yet there have been some who, in our eyes at least, have seemed to excel in their brightness. One of these was certainly St. Francis di Paula. Through his great humility, he was not contented with considering himself the least of all men, but he also desired that this should be the

mark distinguishing his order from all others; and as to charity, he was so inflamed with love that he sometimes lit candles by touching them with his finger, just as if he had applied to them a burning torch.

22 The two feet upon which one walks to perfection are mortification and the love of God. The latter is the right, the former the left foot.

By the aid of these, St. Francis Assisi climbed to the loftiest perfection. He led a life so austere and rigid that at the point of death he felt that he must ask pardon of his body for having treated it so ill; and his love of God was so remarkable that he gained not only for himself, but for his order as well, the noble title of Seraphic.

When St. Francis de Sales wished to lead anyone to live in a Christian manner and renounce worldliness, he would not speak of the exterior—of the adornment of the hair, of rich dress, and similar things—but he spoke only to the heart and of the heart, for he knew that if this fortress is captured, all else surrenders and that when the true love of God comes to possess a heart, all that is not God seems to it of no account.

St. Philip Neri adopted the same course with his penitents. He was not accustomed to dwell very much upon any vanities in dress, but he would overlook them as much as possible for some time, that he might more easily arrive at his object. When a lady once asked him whether it was a sin to wear very high heels, his only answer was, "Take care not to fall." A man also came frequently to see him, wearing a collar with

long stiff points. One day, he touched him lightly on the neck and said: "I would oftener give you such marks of friendship if your collar did not hurt my hand." And with these reproofs alone both corrected their faults. A clergyman of noble birth, dressed in bright colors and with much display, came to the Saint every day for a fortnight to consult him in regard to the affairs of his soul. During all this time he said not a word to him in regard to his dress, but only took pains to make him feel compunction for his sins. Finally, becoming ashamed of his style of dress, he changed it of his own accord, made a good general confession, and giving himself wholly into St. Philip's hands became afterwards one of his most intimate and familiar friends.

23 When one is going on really well, he feels in himself a continual desire to advance; and the more he grows in perfection, the more this desire grows. Since his light is increasing every day, it always seems to him that he has no virtue and is doing no good; or if, perhaps, he sees that he has and is doing some good, it yet appears to him very imperfect, and he makes little account of it. And so it comes to pass that he always goes on laboring for the acquisition of virtue without ever being weary.

—ST. LAWRENCE JUSTINIAN

St. Fulgentius was so enamored of perfection that whatever he did towards it always seemed to him little, and he was always desiring to do better.

St. Vincent de Paul every day saw more of his own faults, yet he continually applied anew all his zeal to amend and perfect himself.

St. Ignatius constantly compared one day with another, and the gain on one day with the gain on another. Thus he advanced daily and entertained a constant desire of advancing still more, that he might reach the summit of perfection to which God called him.

St. James the Apostle received great praise because he went on advancing daily in the divine service.

24 To be pleased at correction and reproofs shows that one loves the virtues which are contrary to those faults for which he is corrected and reproved. And, therefore, it is a great sign of advancement in perfection.

—ST. FRANCIS DE SALES

When a monk once visited the Abbot Serapion, he suggested that first of all, they should pray together. But the visitor refused, saying that he was a great sinner and unworthy to wear the habit. A little while after, the Abbot addressed him thus: "My brother, if you wish to become perfect, remain at work in your cell and do not talk much, for going about a great deal is not desirable for you." At these words the monk was not a little perturbed. When the Abbot perceived this, he added, "What is the matter, brother? A moment ago you said you were so great a sinner that you were not worthy to live; and now, when I have shown you, in charity, what you need, are you angry? From this, it would

seem that your humility is not genuine. If you wish to be humble in truth, learn to receive admonitions humbly." At this reproof, the monk recollected himself, acknowledged his fault and went away greatly edified.

The Empress Leonora requested her confessor and those ladies of her court with whom she was most intimate that when they observed anything in her that needed amendment or improvement, to inform her of it with all possible freedom, as they would tell her the pleasantest news; and when they did it, she thanked them very cordially.

When St. Peter was reproved by St. Paul he was not angry; neither did he stand upon his dignity as Superior, nor look down upon the other for having been a persecutor of the Church, but received the advice in good part.

We read of St. Ambrose, that when anyone informed him of a fault, he thanked him as for a special favor; and there was a certain Cistercian who was especially pleased at an admonition, and used to say an Our Father for whoever gave it.

St. John Berchmans always entertained a great desire to have his faults told him in public and to be reproved for them, and if this ever happened he was much pleased. With this intention, he used to write them on scraps of paper, which he gave to the Superiors, that they might read them and reprimand him for them. Not content with this, he asked of the Superior that four of his companions might keep their eyes on him and admonish him. One of these testified that having once drawn his attention to a slight omission into which he had fallen, on account of being occupied in another work of charity at the time, he thanked him cordially for the warning and said the beads for

him three times, promising that he would always do the same whenever he would inform him of any defect.

25 The firmest assurance that we can have in this world of being in the grace of God does not consist at all in sentiments of love to Him, but in complete and irrevocable abandonment of our whole being into His hands, and in the firm resolution never to consent to any sin either great or small.

—ST. FRANCIS DE SALES

We read in old chronicles of a young lady who was so severely afflicted that she seemed to be suffering the pains of Hell. After remaining for a long time in this state, she one day turned her whole heart to God in this prayer: "My sweetest Lord, only remember that I am a poor creature of Thine! for the rest, do with me what pleases Thee, now and through eternity! I abandon myself into Thy hands, and am ready to suffer these torments as long as it shall please Thee." This act of resignation, which she made from her heart with all sincerity, was so pleasing to God that it was scarcely finished when He united her to Himself and immersed her blissfully in the immense ocean of His divinity.

St. Catherine of Genoa said: "I am no more my own; whether I live or die, I am my Saviour's; I have no longer any possession or interest of my own. My God is all; my being consists in being wholly His. O world! thou art always the same, and until now, I have been always the same; but, from this time forth, I will be such no longer."

26 Let us learn from Jesus in the manger, to hold the things of the world in such esteem as they deserve.

—ST. FRANCIS DE SALES

The Ven. Beatrice of Nazareth saw, in a vision, the whole system of the universe beneath her feet and God alone above her head, so that she was standing, as it were, between God and the world—the world beneath, God above, and she herself in the middle. By this, she understood that the height of perfection is gained when one has over his head only God, and all else under his feet, making no more account of it than if it did not exist, placing all his love and interest in God, and nothing else, not even himself, except in God.

St. Hedwig, Queen of Poland, after becoming a nun would never mention or listen to any worldly news unless it concerned the honor of God and the salvation of souls.

27 If you wish for a method brief and compendious, one which contains in itself all other methods and is most efficacious in conquering all temptations and difficulties, and acquiring perfection, this is the exercise of the presence of God.

—ST. BASIL

A priest who was an intimate friend of the same St. Basil suffered many severe temptations and many grievous threats from Julian the Apostate, but always held his ground firmly against them. He himself assigned this reason for his victory: "It was

because," he said, "in all that time, so far as I remember, the Divine Presence never escaped my mind."

Joseph, when solicited to evil, replied, "How shall I do this under the eye of God?" And Susanna said, "It is better for me to fall into your hands without fault, than to sin in the sight of God."

St. Ephrem being solicited to sin by a woman of evil life, professed his readiness, provided the scene of their transgression should be the public square. But when the woman objected to this condition on account of the shame it would involve, "Then," replied the Saint, "you fear shame before the eyes of men, and do you not fear it before the angels of God?" By this consideration, he brought about her conversion.

When Tais learned that God beheld her in the commission of sin, she resisted a thousand temptations and became a Saint.

28 To be able to advance much in perfection, it is necessary to apply ourselves to one thing by itself—to a single book of devotion, to a single spiritual exercise, to a single aspiration, to a single virtue, and so on. Not, indeed, that all other things ought to be quite rejected and passed by, but in such a way that this to which one is applying himself may usually be aimed at more in particular and as the special object of the most frequent effort, so that if one chance to turn to others, these may be like accessories. To do otherwise, by passing from one exercise to another, is to imitate those who spoil their appetite at a banquet by tasting a little of every delicacy. It is perpetually seeking, and never attaining, the science of the Saints, and so

it results in losing that tranquillity of spirit in God, which is the "one thing needful" that Mary chose. We must, however, guard ourselves here from one fault, into which many fall. It is that of attaching ourselves too much to our own practices and spiritual exercises. This, naturally, makes us feel dislike for all methods not conformed to our own; for each one thinks that he employs the only suitable one, and considers as imperfect those who do not work in the same way. Whoever has a good spirit draws edification from everything, and condemns nothing.

—ST. FRANCIS DE SALES

Although the Saints profited by everything, yet each of them chose some practice of his own in which he exercised himself particularly. For example, the favorite author of St. Francis de Sales was Scupoli; that of St. Dominic, Cassian; the most frequent ejaculation of St. Francis was, "My God is my all!" that of St. Vincent de Paul, "In the name of the Lord!" that of St. Bruno, "Oh, Goodness!" Some had the presence of God for their spiritual exercise; some, purity of intention; some, resignation to the Divine Will; and others, the renunciation of themselves. The same was the case with regard to the virtues. One had a greater love for one virtue; another, for another. Whence it happens that almost all excelled particularly in some special virtue.

St. Catherine of Siena, in regarding these various preferences of good souls, disapproved of none of them, but rather rejoiced that the Lord should be served in so many and such different ways.

29 If you wish to arrive speedily at the summit of perfection, animate yourself to a true love of shame, insults, and calumny.

—ST. IGNATIUS

As this Saint was meditating one day on the great advantages which spring from shame and insults, he conceived a vehement desire to go through the public squares of Rome loaded with rags and other rubbish; and he was restrained from carrying it into execution only by the fear that he might not afterwards be as well able to promote the glory of the Lord.

We read of St. Catherine of Bologna that when she met with any slight or insult, she rejoiced at it and it only increased her desire for more. By this she advanced so much in the love of God that she would have been willing, as she herself protested, to endure not only all the trials of this world, but even the pains of Hell to obey His will.

St. Gregory relates of the Abbot Stephen that he had conceived so great a love for insults, calumnies, and vexations that when he received any he thought he had made great profit, and returned affectionate thanks to whoever gave them to him; and by this he attained such reputation for sanctity that whoever did him any harm felt sure that he had secured his friendship.

30 Place thyself under the discipline of a stern and austere man, who will treat thee harshly and with rigor; and then strive to drink in all his reproofs and ill treatment as one would drink milk and honey; and I

assure thee that in a little time thou wilt find thyself on the pinnacle of perfection.

—ABBOT MOSES

It is related in the Lives of the Fathers that the Abbot John diligently and affectionately served one of the old Fathers, who was ill, for a period of twelve years. Though this Father saw what severe and long fatigue the Abbot was enduring, he never gave him one gentle or amiable word, but always treated him with harshness. But when he was dying, he called for the Abbot, and, taking him by the hand, said to him three times, "Abide in God!" and then he recommended him to the Fathers, saying, "This is not a man, but an angel."

31 As it is most certain that the teaching of Christ cannot deceive, if we would walk securely, we ought to attach ourselves to it with the greatest confidence and to profess openly that we live according to it, and not to the maxims of the world, which are all deceitful. This is the fundamental maxim of all Christian perfection.

—ST. VINCENT DE PAUL

This was, indeed, the ordinary chosen basis upon which this Saint himself established his own life and in which he found all his confidence and peace. Whenever he felt that he was supported by a holy maxim he went on courageously, passing over his own judgment and all human respect, or fear that his conduct might meet with blame or opposition.

St. Francis de Sales was often blamed by his friends, as they did not approve of his course in not sustaining his dignity and defending himself more vigorously against the attacks of the malevolent. He replied to them that mildness ought to be the characteristic of bishops; and so, although the world and self-love has established maxims of another kind, he did not wish to make use of them, because they were contrary to those of Jesus Christ, in conformity to which he had always gloried.

FEBRUARY

Humility

Whoever humbleth himself,
shall be exalted.—Lk. 14:11

---

1 Humility is the foundation of all the virtues; therefore, in a soul where it does not exist there can be no true virtue, but the mere appearance only. In like manner, it is the most proper disposition for all celestial gifts. And, finally, it is so necessary to perfection, that of all the ways to reach it, the first is humility; the second, humility; the third, humility. And if the question were repeated a hundred times, I should always give the same answer.

—ST. AUGUSTINE

St. Vincent de Paul perceived that all his advancement and almost all the graces he had received were due to this virtue; and

for this reason he inculcated it so much and so greatly desired to introduce it into his congregation.

St. Aloysius Gonzaga, who knew this truth well, took no greater pains in acquiring any other virtue. For this purpose he recited every day a special prayer to the angels that they would aid him to walk in this royal road, which they themselves had first trodden, that he might finally succeed in gaining the position of one of those stars that fell from Heaven through pride.

A certain man named Pascasius said that for twenty years he had never asked anything of God except humility, and yet that he had but little of it. However, when no one was able to expel a devil from a possessed person, Pascasius had scarcely entered the church before the devil cried out, "This man I fear," and immediately departed.

Fra Maffeo, a companion of St. Francis, once heard, in a conference on humility, that a great servant of God was very remarkable for this virtue, and that on account of it God loaded him with spiritual gifts. He was thus inspired with so great a love for it, that he made a vow never to rest until he should perceive that he had acquired it. He remained, then, shut up in his cell, asking of God true humility, with tears, fasting, mourning, and many prayers. One day he went out in the woods, and while he was sighing and asking this grace from God, with ejaculatory prayers, he heard the Lord saying to him, "Fra Maffeo, what would you give for humility?" He answered, "I would give my eyes!" "And I," replied the Lord, "desire that you should have your eyes, and the grace you seek." Suddenly there entered his heart a great joy, and at the same time he had the lowest possible opinion of himself, so that he considered himself the least of all men.

2 Humility is the mother of many virtues. From it spring obedience, holy fear, reverence, patience, modesty, mildness, and peace; for, whoever is humble easily obeys all, fears to offend any, maintains peace with all, shows himself affable to all, is submissive to all, does not offend or displease any, and does not feel the insults which may be inflicted upon him. He lives happy and contented, and in great peace.

—ST. THOMAS OF VILLANOVA

Here we see the reason why St. Francis, St. Dominic, St. Vincent de Paul and so many others became remarkable for all the virtues above mentioned. It is because they were remarkable for humility.

St. Jane Frances de Chantal had conceived so much affection for this virtue, that she watched over herself with the greatest attention, in order that she might not allow even the smallest occasion of practicing it to escape. And she once said to St. Francis de Sales, "My dearest Father, I beg you, for the love of God, help me to humble myself."

3 Whoever is not very humble, can never draw profit from contemplation, in which any little atom of insufficient humility, though it may seem nothing, works the greatest harm.

—ST. TERESA

One day, the Blessed Virgin prayed her most holy Son that He would bestow some spiritual gifts upon St. Bridget. But He

gave her this reply: "Whoever seeks lofty things ought first to be exercised in the lowly, by the paths of humility." Because the blessed Clara of Montefalco experienced a vain pleasure in some things she had done, the Lord withdrew from her, for fifteen years, His lights and celestial consolations, which she could not regain during all that time, though she begged for them earnestly, with tears, prayers, and the use of the discipline.

4 Humility is necessary not only for the acquisition of virtues, but even for salvation. For the gate of Heaven, as Christ Himself testifies, is so narrow that it admits only little ones.

—ST. BERNARD

The Pharisee was separated by his condition in life from the rest of the people, as this sect formed a kind of religious order, in which they prayed, fasted, and performed many other good works; but he was, notwithstanding, reproved by God. Why, then, was this? For no other reason than that he was wanting in humility; for he felt much satisfaction in his good works, and gloried in them as if they were the result of his own virtue.

William, Bishop of Lyons, tells in his Chronicles, of a monk who often violated the prescribed silence, but upon being admonished spiritually by his Abbot he amended, and became so recollected and so devout that he was worthy to receive from God many revelations. Now, it happened that the Father Abbot was sent for by a hermit, who, having reached the close of a virtuous life, desired to receive from him the last Sacraments. The Abbot went, and took with him the silent monk. On the road, a robber,

hearing the little bell, accompanied the Blessed Sacrament as far as the cell of the dying man; but he stopped outside, considering himself unworthy to enter the abode of a saint. After the hermit had confessed and received Communion with humility, the robber kept repeating at the door, "Oh, Father, if I were but like you, oh, how happy should I be!" The hermit hearing this, said in his heart, with presumption and complacency, "You are right to desire this; who can doubt it?" and immediately expired. Then the good Religious began to weep, and withdrew from the Abbot. The robber followed them, with tears and hatred for his sins, and the full purpose of confessing and doing penance for them, as soon as they should arrive at the monastery. But he was not able to reach it, for on the way he fell unexpectedly to the ground and died. At this accident, the Religious became joyous again and laughed; and when the Abbot asked him why he had been sad at the death of the hermit, and joyful at that of the robber, he replied: "Because the former is lost, in punishment for his presumption, and the latter saved, on account of his strong resolution to do fitting penance for his sins; and the sorrow he felt for them was so great that it has cancelled even all their penalty."

5 The most powerful weapon to conquer the devil is humility. For, as he does not know at all how to employ it, neither does he know how to defend himself from it.

—ST. VINCENT DE PAUL

When Macarius was returning one day to his cell, he met the devil, who, with a scythe in his hand, tried to cut him in

45

pieces. But he could not do it, because as soon as he came near, he lost his strength. Then, full of rage, he said, "Great misery do I suffer from thee, O Macarius; for, though I wish so much to hurt thee, I am not able. It is strange! I do all that thou doest, and even more; thou dost fast sometimes, and I never eat; thou sleepest little, and I never close my eyes; thou art chaste, and so am I. In one thing only thou surpassest me." "And what is that one thing?" inquired Macarius. "It is thy great humility," replied the demon. Saying this, he disappeared, and was seen no more.

The devil once appeared to a monk in the form of the Archangel Gabriel, and said that he was sent to him by God. The monk replied, "See that thou be not sent by another!" And the devil immediately disappeared.

When an old priest was exorcising a possessed person, the demon said that he would never come out, if he did not first tell him what the goats and what the lambs were like. The good priest quickly answered: "The goats are all those who are like me. What the lambs may resemble, God knows." At these words, the devil cried out: "Through your humility I can no longer remain here," and immediately departed.

6 Persons who keep themselves low in their own estimation and love to be considered of little account and despised by others please God in the highest degree; and, therefore, He willingly lowers Himself to them, pours upon them the treasures of His graces, reveals to them His secrets, invites and draws them sweetly to Himself. Thus, the more one lowers and abuses himself before men, the more he rises and becomes great in the

sight of God, and the more clearly he will, one day, behold the Divine Essence.

—THOMAS À KEMPIS

St. Gertrude, one day hearing the little bell ring for Communion and not feeling as well prepared as she desired, said to the Lord: "I see that Thou art even now coming to me; but why hast Thou not first adorned my heart with some ornaments of devotion, with which I might be more suitably prepared to come and meet Thee?" But the Lord answered: "Know that sometimes I am more pleased with the virtue of humility than with exterior devotion."

A Religious, not being able to understand a passage of Holy Scripture, fasted for seven weeks, and not understanding it then resolved to go to another monk and inquire about it. But scarcely had he gone out of his cell when there appeared to him an angel sent expressly from God, who said to him: "Thy fast has not rendered thee pleasing to God, but rather this humiliation of thine"; and then he solved for him the doubt.

After Tais was converted, she held herself always so low in her own eyes, on account of her past evil life, that she did not dare to utter the holy name of God even in invoking Him, but only said, "My Creator, have mercy on me!" And by this humility, she arrived at such a sublime degree of perfection that when Paul the Simple saw a most beautiful place in Paradise, which he supposed to be intended for St. Anthony, he was informed that it would be occupied by Tais within a fortnight.

St. Bonaventure said: "I know a thing to do which will please the Lord. I will consider myself as refuse, I will become

intolerable to myself. And when I find myself shamed, degraded, trampled upon and loaded with insults by others, I will rejoice and exult, because of myself I cannot abuse or detest myself as much as I ought. I will call in help from all creatures, desiring to be confounded and punished by them all, because I have despised their Creator. This shall be my dearest treasure—to solicit insults and slights upon myself, to love above all others those who will help me in this, and to abhor all the consolation and honors of the present life. If I do this, I believe it certain that the treasury of Divine Mercy will open above me, miserable and unworthy as I am."

St. Francis of Assisi considered himself not only a mere nothing, the greatest sinner in the world, and deserving of Hell, but unworthy even that God should give him a thought. One day while he was speaking in this manner to one of his companions, the latter saw, in spirit, that there was prepared for him in Heaven a seat among the Seraphim.

7 One day of humble self-knowledge is a greater grace from the Lord, although it may have cost us many afflictions and trials, than many days of prayer.

—ST. TERESA

St. Gertrude, once reflecting upon the benefits she had received from God, blushed for herself and became so odious in her own eyes that she seemed unworthy to remain in the sight of God, and she would gladly have found some nook, where she might conceal from man, if not from God, the odor of corruption with which she felt herself tainted. At this, Christ humbled

Himself to her with so much goodness that the whole celestial court stood amazed.

The venerable Mother Seraphina di Dio received, one day, a spiritual light, by means of which (as she states in her account of it to her director) she perceived clearly that God, being by His nature luminous truth, can behold in Himself only that which He really is—that is, infinite perfection, in which He rejoices and delights. Therefore, when He wishes to unite a soul to Himself, He communicates to it a light of truth, by which it sees, without error or deception, its own nature; that is, that by itself it has never done any good, neither is it able to do any; that in itself it has only inclination to evil, and what good it has is altogether from God. And such a person has no need of much consideration and analysis, because with such a light of truth, all appears so clear that to think otherwise would be mere darkness and deceit. But though the soul, in this clear light, appears ugly, deformed and odious in its own eyes, yet, in the eyes of God, it seems beautiful and very pleasing, because it becomes like His own most true and luminous nature. It happened that this same servant of God, after leading an innocent and most perfect life, came at one time to know her imperfections with such clearness that they seemed to her to become very grave and frightful sins, so that she experienced great bitterness of spirit and could obtain no peace; when she was reproved for any failure, she was not at all disturbed, but said in her heart: "What you see is nothing. Oh, if you saw all, how you would abhor me!" But the Lord consoled her by telling her interiorly that her past imperfections seemed to her so unusually great because her soul was in a state of clear light, but that these deformities were no longer in existence, as He had already cancelled them by His blood.

8 Hold thyself as vile; rejoice to be so held by others; never exalt thyself by reason of the gifts of God, and thou shalt be perfectly humble.

—ST. BONAVENTURE

A soul of precisely this type was St. Mary Magdalen de' Pazzi. It is recorded of her that she was so vile in her own eyes that she constantly looked upon herself as the lowest of creatures and the most disgraceful and abominable thing upon earth. Being one day called to the grate by the Duchess of Bracciano, she said with great feeling, "If my lady Duchess knew that Sister Mary Magdalen is the abomination of this convent, she would not think of naming her, much less of sending for her." In the same light in which she looked upon herself, she desired also to be viewed by others; and when she was treated contemptuously, or in any way humiliated, she rejoiced so much that in reward for the great gladness with which she received humiliations, she was often rapt in ecstasy after them. For this reason she could not bear to see that she was honored and esteemed, and that others had a good opinion of her; and to prevent this, she would often accuse herself in public and in private of her smallest defects, even with exaggeration.

And so, with things which were not really faults, she mentioned them in such a way as to make them seem grave faults. For example, in cutting up a pineapple one day, she ate two morsels that fell from it. Therefore, she accused herself of gluttony, and of eating outside of the refectory, contrary to the Constitution. She took, besides, all possible pains to conceal from others her virtues and holy works, and when she could not do this, she

would try to depreciate them by showing that they were full of defects; in this way she would make the most perfect actions seem worthy of reproof, or, at least, merely natural, and springing from her own inclination. And as she could neither prevent nor conceal the ecstasies which were granted to her, it displeased her exceedingly to be looked at, or listened to, while they lasted, even to such a degree that she once complained to the Lord, saying: "O my Jesus! how is it that Thou hast conferred upon me so much that is known only to Thee and myself, and now Thou wilt have me reveal it? Hast Thou not promised me that as Thou wast hidden, so should I also be?" Once when her confessor ordered her to report to her companions what happened to her in these ecstasies, she wept bitterly, as she did also in making the relation, so that finally she went so far as to entreat the Lord to make her no more communications of the kind. She was so far from drawing any complacency or self-esteem from this source that, as if she had committed a fault, she would humble herself after these favors, even to the last novice or lay-sister, and set herself to perform the daily exercises with them, and converse with them with so much humility and charity that it was an admirable thing to see and hear her, first holding communion with the Divine Majesty with such loftiness of ideas, and then, immediately after, to behold her so humble, dependent, and submissive to her neighbors.

9 Humility, which Christ recommended to us both by word and example, ought to include three conditions. First, we are to consider ourselves, in all sincerity, worthy of the contempt of men; secondly, to be glad that

others should see what is imperfect in us and what might cause them to despise us; thirdly, when the Lord works any good in us or by our means, to conceal it, if possible, at the sight of our baseness, and if this cannot be done, to ascribe it to the Divine Mercy, and to the merits of others. Whoever shall attain to this humility, happy is he! and to him who shall not attain it, griefs will never be wanting.

—ST. VINCENT DE PAUL

The first condition was certainly to be found in the heart of St. Clare, who used to say to her companions: "Oh, Sisters, if you knew me well, you would abhor and avoid me, like one stricken with the plague, because I am not what you believe me, but a wicked woman." The venerable Sister Maria Crucifixa, who considered herself the vilest creature upon earth, often spoke thus of herself to her companions, and with feelings of such sincere and perfect humiliation as excited her to a high degree of compunction. This even led her to ask leave to retire to a convent of Penitents, which she said was a fitting place for her, as she ought to live the life of a penitent. St. Francis Borgia, too, was so deeply grounded in a low opinion of himself, that he wondered how the people could salute, and not rather stone him, as he passed through the streets.

The second condition was also possessed in a high degree by St. Clare. She revealed the greatest faults of her life to all her confessors, intending that they should conceive a bad opinion of her; but when she found this plan failed, she changed her confessors often, in the hope of finding one who would consider

her the wretched creature that she really believed herself to be. St. Catherine of Bologna, likewise, not only told all her sins to her confessors, but even intentionally dropped the paper on which they were written, that she might be despised by all. St. John of the Cross, too, when he went to Granada, where he was sent as Provincial Vicar, happened to meet there a brother of his, who was so poor that he lived by alms. When he saw him with his cloak all torn, he was as much pleased as another would have been to see his brother in a rich dress; and when the Grand Duke came to visit him, he brought him forward, saying that was his brother, who was working in the monastery. The third condition was possessed, in the highest degree, by St. Mary Magdalen de' Pazzi, who when asked or commanded by her Superior to make the Sign of the Cross over the sick, or to offer a prayer for anyone in need, always called another to join her in this action or prayer, so that when the favor came it might be attributed not to her, but to the virtue of the other, as she always attributed it herself. The same may be said of an abbess named Sara, of whom it is related, in the Lives of the Fathers, that she had been assailed by a demon for thirteen years, but was finally liberated by her fervent prayers. Then the demon said to her, "Thou hast conquered me, Sara!" But she replied, "It is not I who have conquered thee, but truly it is my Lord Jesus Christ."

Monseigneur de Palafax showed that he possessed in a singular degree this beautiful quality of attributing to God all the good he did. For he looked upon his good actions not as his own choice, but as pure effects of grace; and so, instead of believing, as people in general do, that he acquired by them merit before God, he believed that his obligations to God were increased by

doing them. And so he thought, so he spoke; for he was accustomed to confess himself to be under the greatest obligations to God, because He had bestowed upon him great peace of mind, constant repentance for his sins, great patience and consolation in vexations and labors, great love and respect for the poor and for his persecutors, and had taken from him all attachments to riches, honors, convenience, and his own judgment, and had also given him the grace to perform with fervor penances, the visitation of the sick, and many practices of devotion, as well as strength and talent to make wise and useful regulations, to build many churches, and to accomplish every one of his actions purely and solely for the honor and service of His Divine Majesty. And what is certainly most to be admired is that he derived only confusion and fear from so many good and holy works, which ordinarily produce, even in excellent persons, a certain good opinion and esteem of themselves and make them believe themselves deserving of praise from men and reward from God. He looked upon them, on the contrary, as special graces granted to him by the Divine Goodness, for which he must one day give a strict account; and he thought that on the last day, in presence of all the world, they would be so many points of accusation against him because he had not corresponded to so many divine favors by a better and more perfect life.

The humility of St. Vincent de Paul was accompanied by all three of these conditions. He had so low an opinion of himself that he considered himself a great sinner, a cause of scandal, and unworthy to remain even in his own Congregation. Wherefore, he often spoke of himself as a hardened sinner, an abominable sinner, unworthy to live, and standing in the utmost need of the mercy of

God on account of the abominations of his life. One day, prostrate before his missionaries, he said with great feeling: "If you could see my miseries, you would drive me from the house, to which I am a loss, a burden, and a scandal. I am surely unworthy to remain in the Congregation, on account of the scandal that I give." Because he truly felt thus, he desired that others, too, should feel so; and, therefore, he was pleased to have his imperfections visible to all, and he even manifested them openly on occasions, to the end that he might be despised and lightly regarded by all. For this reason, he often said that he was the son of a swineherd, a poor grammar student, and no scholar. For the same cause, he acknowledged as his nephew, before all in the house and even before some noble visitors, a poor young man who had come to ask his aid. And as he felt at first some unwillingness to acknowledge him when he heard of his arrival, he often accused himself of this to his companions as a great fault, exaggerating too the pride that caused it. He could not bear to hear himself praised, or see himself held in high esteem; and so when a poor woman told him, in presence of some persons of rank, that she had been a servant of his mother, hoping to induce him to give her alms, the Saint, to whom such flattery was unpleasant, answered quickly: "My poor woman, you are mistaken. My mother never kept a servant, but she was a servant herself, and afterwards, the wife of a poor peasant." For this cause, too, he was never heard to speak of the excellent works which he had carried on, nor of the wonderful circumstances in which he had been placed. A remarkable proof of this is that though innumerable occasions offered themselves to speak of his slavery in Tunis, especially in the exhortations which he addressed to his Congregation and others, to move them to aid the poor slaves in Barbary, he never let fall a

word concerning himself, nor about what he had said or done to convert his master, and escape with him from the hands of the Infidels, nor as to anything else that happened to him in that country.

This is a rare case, on account of the pleasure which everyone naturally feels in narrating the perils, the dangers and difficulties from which he has happily escaped, especially when his success reveals some virtue and gives occasion for praise. But when necessity, or the good of others, sometimes constrained him to tell something which he had done for the glory of God, if anything had gone ill he attributed to himself whatever might cause humiliation, though he had given no occasion for it; but if all went well, he told of it in very humble terms, setting all to the account of the zeal and labor of others, and suppressing so far as he could those circumstances which would bring praise to himself; and he always ascribed even the slightest good that he did to God, as its primary and only cause. For example, he never said, "I did this; I said this; I thought of this"; but rather, "God inspired me with this thought; put into my mouth these words; gave me strength to do this"; and so on. The humility of St. Francis de Sales was, says St. Jane Frances de Chantal, humility of heart. For it was his maxim that the love of our abjection ought to be with us at every step; and, therefore, he strove to conceal the gifts of grace as much as he could, and endeavored to appear of less account than he really was, so that he was often slow and late in giving his opinion upon subjects with which he was well acquainted.

10 We ought always to consider others as our superiors, and to yield to them, even though they be our inferiors, by offering them every kind of respect and service.

> Oh, what a beautiful thing it would be, if it should please God to confirm us well in such a practice.
>
> —ST. VINCENT DE PAUL

This was precisely the practice of this Saint. He made great account of all, and considered all better than himself, more prudent, more perfect, more capable, and more fit for any employment, and therefore he felt no difficulty in yielding his own opinion to anyone. We read of a good nun named Sister Rachel Pastore who had formed such a humble opinion of herself that she regarded all persons, without exceptions, as her superior; and with this sentiment deeply fixed in her heart, she abased and humbled herself in the presence of all.

11 Our Lord says that whoever wishes to become greatest of all must make himself least of all. This is a truth that all Christians believe; how happens it, then, that so few practice it?

> —ST. VINCENT DE PAUL

The same Saint was one of these few. As he had always but a low opinion of himself and had taken so much pains to lower himself beneath all, God continually exalted him by the many great works which He entrusted to him, by the high regard in which he was generally held and by the abundant benedictions which God bestowed on all his actions.

St. Paula, by the testimony of St. Jerome, excelled so much in self-abasement that if a stranger attracted by her fame had come to visit her, he would never have recognized her, but

would rather have supposed her to be one of the least of her own servants. And when she was surrounded by bands of young maidens, in dress, speech and manner, she always seemed the humblest of them all.

12 Do not believe that thou hast made any advance in perfection unless thou considerest thyself the worst of all, and desirest that all should be preferred to thee; for it is the mark of those who are great in the eyes of God to be small in their own eyes; and the more glorious they are in the sight of God, the more vile they appear in their own sight.

—ST. TERESA

One day when St. Anthony was praying, he heard a voice saying, "Anthony, thou hast not reached the perfection of a man named Coriarius, who lives in Alexandria." The Saint went immediately to find him, and inquired about his life. Coriarius answered: "I do not know that I have ever done anything good, and so, when I rise in the morning, I say in my heart that all people in this city will be saved by their good works, and I alone shall be lost for my sins; and I say the same thing in the evening, in all sincerity, before going to rest." "No! no! no!" replied St. Anthony, "thou hast secured Heaven for thyself by thy wise practice; but I have unwisely failed to attain this excellence of thine."

In the Lives of the Fathers, a certain monk is mentioned who, in giving an account of his interior to the Abbot Sisois, said that he kept continually before his mind the thought of God. The

Abbot answered: "That is nothing great. The great thing would be that you should see yourself below every creature."

One of the chief men of Alexandria, having been received into a monastery, the Abbot judged from his appearance and other signs that he was a hard man, haughty, and inflated with worldly pride. Wishing to lead him by the safe road of humility, he placed him in the porter's lodge, with instructions to throw himself at the feet of all who passed in or out and to beg them to pray to God for him, because he was a great sinner. He obeyed with exactness, and persevered in this exercise for seven years, acquiring thereby great humility. The Abbot then thought it time to give him the habit and admit him to the society of the other members of the Order. But when he heard of this, he implored and entreated to be left as he was for the short time which, as he said, remained to him of life. His request was granted, and he proved to be a true prophet—for, after ten days he died, in great peace and confidence in regard to his salvation. This is related by St. John Climacus, who says that he had spoken with this man, and when he inquired how he occupied himself in all that time when he was remaining at the gate, he replied: "My constant exercise was to consider myself unworthy to stay in the monastery, and to enjoy the sight and company of the Fathers, or even to raise my eyes to look at them."

We read of the venerable Maria Seraphina di Dio that she seemed to have no eyes except to see and exaggerate her own defects, and to admire the virtues of others. So, when she saw others performing any good action, she would say, with feeling: "How happy they are! All, except me, attend to the services of God!" When she saw any going to the confessors, she thought

they would only have to hear and speak of God, while she reproached herself that she went solely to tell her errors and sins. If she ever saw anyone commit a fault, she always found means to excuse or palliate it, and thus she was able, in spite of the sins of others, to retain the opinion which she held of herself as being the worst of all.

13 When one is very remarkable for virtue, and truly great before God, and favored and esteemed by Him, yet with all this remains little and vile in his own eyes—here is that humility so grateful to God and so rare among men, which was found most perfect in the Blessed Virgin, who, on hearing herself chosen to be the Mother of God, acknowledged herself to be a servant and handmaiden.

—ST. BERNARD

St. Mary Magdalen de' Pazzi was an admirable example of this. Though she had arrived at high perfection and sanctity and saw herself enriched by God with extraordinary graces and favors, even to the power of working miracles; yet with all this, she had so low an esteem and so poor an opinion of herself as to astonish those who knew her. Nor was this a matter of pure imagination or of mere words, but true and sincere, and was clearly shown by an ecstasy, in which the Lord showed her the strength and virtue He intended to communicate to her against the fierce temptations she had endured from the devil, and she broke forth with these words: "What confusion for me! that upon the lowest and vilest creature upon earth, as I am, Thou

designest to bestow the immensity of the treasures of Thy liberality and mercy!"

It was the same with St. Vincent de Paul. Though his virtues were known to all, in spite of the contrivances that he used to conceal them, yet to him alone they remained unknown; because, by putting his own baseness continually before his eyes, he cut off the view of them; so that, although he was rich and abounding in virtues and celestial gifts, he always esteemed himself poor, needy, and destitute of all spiritual good. Thence came the title that he usually gave himself: "This poor wretch."

When St. Teresa reflected upon the favors she received from God in such great abundance, she humbled herself the more on account of them, saying that the Lord sustained her extreme weakness in this way, and that these supports proved how great was her tendency to fall, as a house is shown to be tottering, by the props set up to hold it.

14 Vain self-complacency and the desire of making a show of being spoken of, of having our conduct praised, and of hearing it said that we succeed well and are doing wonders—this is an evil which makes us forget God, which infects our holiest actions, and is, of all vices, the most injurious to progress in the spiritual life. I do not understand how anyone can believe and hold it as a truth of faith that he who exalts himself shall be abased if he desires to pass for a man of worth, a person of prudence, foresight, and ability.

—ST. VINCENT DE PAUL

The widely known Franciscan, Brother Justin, entered the Order of St. Francis after refusing great favors and most honorable offices which the King of Hungary offered him. He then advanced so far in religion, that he had frequent ecstasies. One day while dining at the table in the monastery, he was raised in the air and carried over the heads of the Religious, to pray before a picture of the Virgin which was painted high on the wall. On account of this wonder, Pope Eugenius IV sent for him and embraced him, not allowing him to kiss his feet; then, seating him by his side, he had a long conversation with him, and gave him many presents and indulgences. This favor made him vain, and St. John Capestran meeting him on his return, said: "Alas! thou didst go forth an angel, and thou art come back a demon!" In fact, increasing every day in insolence, he killed a monk with a knife. After a term of imprisonment, he escaped into the kingdom of Naples, where he committed many crimes, and finally died in prison.

A holy monk once passed a night in a convent of nuns where there was a boy continually tormented by a devil. Through all that night the child remained undisturbed, and so, in the morning, the monk was requested to take him home to his monastery and keep him until the cure was complete. He did this, and then as nothing more happened to the boy he said to the other monks, with some complacency: "The devil made light of those nuns in tormenting this boy; but since he has come into this monastery of God's servants, he has no longer dared to approach him." No sooner had he said this than the boy, in the presence of them all, began to suffer as he had previously, and the monk bewailed his error.

Another monk once boasted, in presence of his abbot St. Pachomius, that he had made two mats in one day, when the Saint reproved him and ordered him to carry the two mats on his shoulders before the other monks and ask the pardon and prayers of all, because he had valued these two mats more than the Kingdom of Heaven. He also commanded him to remain five months in his cell without ever allowing himself to be seen, and to make two mats a day for all that time.

From his earliest years, St. Thomas Aquinas was always opposed to receiving praise, and he never uttered a word which might lead to it. Therefore, he never felt any temptation to vanity or self-complacency, as he himself testified to Brother Reginald, saying he rendered thanks to God that he had never been tempted by pride.

St. Vincent de Paul made this resolution to close the path against self-complacency: "When I am performing some public action, and may complete it with honor, I will perform it indeed, but I will omit those details which might give it luster or attract notice to myself. Of two thoughts which come into my mind, I will manifest the lower, to humble myself, and I will keep back the higher, to make in my heart a sacrifice of it to God; for it is at times expedient to do a thing less well outwardly, rather than to be pleased with ourselves for having done it well, and to be applauded and esteemed for it; and it is a truth of the Gospel that nothing pleases the Lord so much as humility of heart and simplicity of word and deed. It is here that His spirit resides, and it is in vain to seek it elsewhere." This resolution he observed carefully. One day when traveling with three of his priests, he told them, by way of diversion, an adventure

which had once happened to him. But in the midst of his story he stopped short, striking his breast, and saying that he was a wretch, full of pride and always talking of himself. When he reached home, prostrating himself before them, he asked pardon for the scandal he had given them by talking about himself.

15 What is it, O my God, that we expect to gain by appearing well before creatures, and by pleasing them? What does it matter to us if we are blamed by them, and considered worthless, provided we are great and faultless before Thee? Ah, we never come fully to an understanding of this truth, and so we never succeed in standing upon the summit of perfection! The Saints had no greater pleasure than to live unknown and abject in the hearts of all.

—ST. BERNARD

A holy bishop, in order to live unknown, left his diocese, and putting on a poor dress went secretly to Jerusalem, where he worked as a laborer. There a nobleman saw him several times sleeping on the ground, with a column of fire rising from his body even to the heavens. Wondering at this, he asked him privately who he was. He answered he was a poor man who lived by his work, and had no other means of support. The count, not satisfied with this, urged him to reveal the whole truth, and the bishop, after exacting a promise of secrecy during his lifetime, told him who he was, and how he had left his country to escape from renown and esteem, as he held it to be unworthy of a Christian, who ought always to have in mind the insults

and reproaches heaped upon his Lord, to enjoy the honor and reverence of men.

St. Nicholas of Bari twice threw money secretly, by night, into the house of a gentleman of ruined fortune, that he might be able to give dowries to his daughters, without which they could not be married. On a third visit for the same purpose, he was discovered, and hastily fled.

The Abbot Pitirus, a man celebrated for sanctity, desired to know whether there was in the world any soul more perfect than his own, that he might be able to learn from such a one how to serve God better. Then an angel appeared to him, and said: "Go to a certain convent in the Thebaid. Four hundred and ninety nuns dwell there, among them one called Isidora, who wears a diadem upon her head. Know that she is very far more perfect than thyself." Isidora was a good young girl, who had set her heart upon abasing herself for Christ's sake as much as she could. So she wore a rag twisted around her head, went barefoot, remained always alone, except when she was obliged to be present at the common exercises; she did not eat with the others, but collected for her own food the scraps they had left; and for drink she used the water in which the dishes had been washed: so that all the rest looked on her with so much aversion, that no one could have been induced ever to eat with her. She was, in fact, the jest and scorn of all, and by all insulted, ill-treated, and looked upon as a fool. She, however, never spoke ill of any, harmed no one, never murmured nor complained of any ill treatment she received. Pitirus then arrived at the convent, and after requesting the abbess to send all the nuns to the grate, he could discover upon none of them the sign given by

the angel, so that he confidently asserted that they were not all there. "Indeed," they answered, "no one is absent, except a fool, who always stays shut up in the kitchen." "Well, send for her," he replied. But she, who had known interiorly what was to happen, had hidden herself that she might escape all connection with the matter. Being found after a long search, and earnestly entreated by her superior, she at last came. Pitirus recognized her as soon as he beheld her, and instantly falling at her feet, recommended himself to her prayers. Astonished at such an action, the nuns said to him, "Father, you are mistaken; this is a fool." "You are the fools," replied the Abbot. "Know that she is holier than myself or you!" Then they all threw themselves at her feet, confessed their error, and asked pardon for the wrong they had done her. But she could not bear to receive so much honor, so that she fled from the house a few days after, and was never again seen.

The Empress Leonora, having discovered that her confessor, in response to many requests, had written out some of her heroic and virtuous actions that they might be published after her death, went many times to visit him in his last illness. On one of these occasions she came from his room with a bundle of manuscripts, and when she reached the courtyard where a fire was burning, she threw them into it. It was commonly believed that these were the papers relating to herself, which she had obtained from him by many entreaties, for after his death no such record was found among his writings, though it was known to have existed. But in another matter she did not succeed so well, though she made every effort. When very near death, she remembered a certain chest in which she kept the treasure of her instruments of penance. She had not previously been able to take them out herself,

and now she could do nothing, as her speech had failed. And so, in great distress, she made signs to her confessor, pointing to the spot, and urging him to take out and carry away what was there. But the Lord, who exalts the humble, did not permit these signs to be fully understood, until after her death, when this hidden treasure was revealed. All were moved to tears as they drew out garments stained with blood, scourges—some, bloodstained; others, frayed and worn with long use; many little chains with sharp points, and shirts woven of horsehair, all instruments with which she had macerated her innocent flesh.

16 When you see anyone who desires esteem and honors and avoids contempt, and who, when contradicted or neglected, shows resentment and takes it ill, you may be sure that such a one, though he were to perform miracles, is very far from perfection, for all his virtue is without foundation.

—ST. THOMAS AQUINAS

That the Angelic Doctor held this belief truly before God is certain, for his conduct proves it. Not only did he not desire honors and applause, but he abhorred them and avoided them as far as he could. He was offered the Archbishopric of Naples by Clement IV, at a time when his family, being out of favor with the Emperor, had fallen into great poverty. He was, therefore, earnestly entreated by them, as well as by others, to accept it. However, he not only refused it but obtained from the same Pope a promise that no dignity should ever be offered him for the future. Besides, he entreated his superiors not to compel

him to take the degree of Doctor, as he greatly preferred being learned to being called so; and if he finally took it, it was purely from obedience. But instead of avoiding contempt, he always accepted it with a tranquil soul and a serene countenance. When he was a student, he did not disdain to receive as monitor a fellow student who, finding that he talked but little, attributed it to ignorance and want of talent, and called him "the dumb ox." But he was soon undeceived, when he saw that he had so much talent that he could easily serve not only as a monitor but even as a master to himself. One day when the Saint was reading aloud in the refectory at dinner, he was corrected for mispronouncing a word, and though he knew that he had pronounced it properly, he nevertheless repeated it in the way he was told. Being afterwards asked by his companions why he had done so, "Because," he replied, "it matters little whether we pronounce a syllable long or short, but it matters very much to be humble and obedient."

St. Clare once said: "If I should see myself honored by all the world, it would not arouse in me the slightest vanity; and if I should see myself contemned and despised by all the world, I should not feel the least perturbation."

St. Philip Neri never seemed grieved or displeased at any insult or contempt he might receive. This was a trait so visible and so well known among his associates, that they used to say, "Anything can be said to Father Philip, for nothing ever troubles him." When it was one day reported to him that some people had called him an old simpleton, he laughed and was much pleased at it.

St. Anthony, hearing a monk very much praised, treated him contemptuously; and when he saw that he took this ill, he said:

"This man is like a palace, rich and elegant without, but within, plundered by robbers."

17 I am despised and derided, and I resent it; just so do peacocks and apes. I am despised and derided, and I rejoice at it; thus did the Apostle. This is the deepest grade of humility, to be pleased with humiliation and abjection, as vain minds are pleased with great honors; and to find pain in marks of honor and esteem, as they find it in contempt and affronts.

—ST. FRANCIS DE SALES

St. Dominic remained more willingly in the diocese of Carcassone than in that of Toulouse, where he had converted so many heretics. On being asked his reason, he replied that in the latter he received many honors, but in the former only injuries and insults.

St. Felix the Capuchin experienced great affliction in seeing himself honored and esteemed; and he was often heard to say that he would have been glad to be frightfully deformed, that all might abhor him. He repeated many times that it would have been more agreeable to him to have been dragged and scourged through the streets of Rome, than to have been reverenced by the people.

St. Constantius, when he had taken minor orders, served in a church near Ancona, where he lived so much apart from the world that he had a widespread reputation for sanctity, and people came from different countries to see him. Among others came a peasant, and inquired for him. The Saint was standing

upon a ladder, trimming the lamps; but as he was of a small and delicate figure, the peasant, on looking at him, was sorry that he had made the journey, as it seemed to him for nothing, and ridiculing him in his heart, said to himself, but aloud: "I supposed this would be a great man; but for anything that I can see, he has not even the shape of a man." Constantius, hearing this, instantly left the lamp, and coming down with great haste and gladness, ran up to the rustic and embraced him, saying, "You, alone, out of so many, have your eyes open and have been able to recognize me as I am."

The venerable Sister Maria Crucifixa disliked nothing so much as to hear herself praised, so that when she found others had a good opinion of her, she could not refrain from weeping. She was most unwilling that her supernatural favors should come to the knowledge of others. Therefore when she had ecstasies, the nuns all left her at the first sign of returning to herself, to avoid wounding her feelings. Only her own sister remained with her, who gave her to understand that she looked upon these trances only as fainting fits, caused by weakness, for which she pitied her and offered her remedies. But all this was not enough; so great was her abhorrence of self-esteem, that she believed the love of God to be inseparable from the plausible conceit of being considered a saint. She, therefore, went so far as to make this prayer: "O Lord! I wish to obey Thee; I wish, at Thy touch, to spring up towards Heaven; but Thy way harbors a horrible monster, human esteem, which is for me an insufferable danger; for no one can love Thee without gaining high reputation. I would wish to walk always in Thy way, and this alone is bitter to me, nor do I find any obstacles interposed by Hell but this. So I

remain here waiting until Thou shalt either slay this monster, or change my path."

18 I pray you, do not make much account of certain trifles which some call wrongs and grievances; for we seem to manufacture these things out of straws, like children, with our points of honor. A truly humble person never believes that he can be wronged in anything. Truly, we ought to be ashamed to resent whatever is said or done against us; for it is the greatest shame in the world to see that our Creator bears so many insults from His creatures, and that we resent even a little word that is contradictory. Let contemplative souls, in particular, take notice that if they do not find themselves quite resolved to pardon any injury or affront which may be inflicted upon them, they cannot trust much to their prayer. For the soul which God truly unites to Himself by so lofty a method of prayer, feels none of these things, and no longer cares whether she is esteemed or not, or whether she is spoken well of or ill; nay rather honors and repose give her more pain than dishonor and trials.

—ST. TERESA

If St. Francis de Sales saw that his friends showed displeasure at the malignity of those who spoke ill of him, he would say to them: "Have I ever given you authority to show resentment in my place? Let them talk! This is a cross of words, a tribulation

of wind, the memory of which dies out with the blaze! He must be very delicate, that cannot bear the buzzing of a fly. Would it be well for us to pretend to be blameless? Who knows if these people do not see my faults better than I myself do, and if they are not the ones who truly love me? Often we call a thing evilspeaking, because it is not to our taste. What injury is it if one has a bad opinion of us, since we ought to have the same of ourselves?"

The venerable Maria Crucifixa showed extreme pleasure when she saw herself little regarded or esteemed. Therefore the nuns, to accommodate themselves to her disposition, usually treated her with disrespect, and made little account of her, calling her awkward, stupid, and ignorant. So, when they wished to lead her into spiritual conversation, by which their fervor was greatly increased, they said to her: "Come now, Sister Maria Crucifixa, bring out some of your blunders; let us hear your nonsense." Then believing that she was truly to serve as the butt of their jesting, she would readily begin to speak. But it was still necessary that they should appear to disregard what she was saying by seeming inattentive, and whispering together now and then while she was speaking; otherwise, she would stop. And, for the same reason, they could none of them recommend themselves to her prayers, because this seemed to her a proof that they considered her fit to intercede for them with God. So, in order to obtain her prayers, they would tell her that she was known to be such a miserable creature that the others were obliged to recommend her to God, and therefore, not to be ungrateful, she ought to do as much for them.

19 Whoever is humble, on being humiliated, humbles himself the more; on being rejected, rejoices in the

disgrace; on being placed in low and mean occupations, acknowledges himself to be more honored than he deserves, and performs them willingly; and only abhors and avoids exalted and honorable offices.

—ST. JANE FRANCES DE CHANTAL

A young knight, in a transport of boyish rage, once told St. Vincent de Paul that he was an old fool. Thereupon, the Saint instantly threw himself at his feet and asked pardon for the occasion he had perhaps given him to use such words. A Jansenist, who had tried to instill his false doctrines into the same Saint, at last grew angry at his failure and loaded him with abuse, saying, among other things, that he was an ignorant fellow, and he was astonished that his Congregation could endure him as Superior General. To which he replied: "I am still more astonished at it myself, for I am more ignorant than you can possibly imagine."

Some monks who had heard of the great fame of the Abbot Agatho resolved to test his virtue. Accordingly, they went to him and said that many were disedified by him, because he was proud, sensual, given to complaint, and, moreover, covered his own defects by laying them to others. He replied that he indeed had all these vices, and prostrate at their feet, he entreated them to recommend him to God and obtain for him the pardon of so many sins. They departed with great astonishment and edification.

When the Abbot Moses was ordained priest, his bishop ordered the clergy to drive him contemptuously away when he should approach the altar, and to listen to what he would say.

They did so, saying to him, "Go away, wicked heathen!" But he humbly withdrew, saying to himself: "This is suitable for thee, wicked wretch, who, though unworthy to be called a man, hast presumed to dwell among men!"

On account of the singularity of her life, St. Rose of Lima was often reproached and abused by her mother and brothers. But so great was her humility that she always thought she deserved worse treatment, and therefore never even excused herself, but rather amplified and added to what she had done, that they might not seem to be wrong in punishing her; and all this afforded her the greatest happiness.

St. Mary Magdalen de' Pazzi willingly occupied herself in laborious tasks; and the lower and meaner they were, with the more pleasure and readiness did she accomplish them. The same thing was done by St. Aloysius Gonzaga.

What efforts were made by many great men, especially in the ecclesiastical state, to avoid being raised to lofty positions! St. Philip Benizi, hearing that the cardinals, immediately after the death of the Pope, wished to elect him as his successor, concealed himself on a mountain until the election of another had taken place.

St. Gregory the Great, after being elected Supreme Pontiff, escaped by stealth and hid himself in a grotto. After being discovered there, by means of a column of fire which appeared above the cave, he was forced to accept the dignity; but he still entreated the Emperor Maurice, though without success, not to confirm his election. St. Ambrose, being miraculously chosen Bishop of Milan by the mouth of an infant too young to speak, fled from his house by night, and even did many things to make the people believe him a man of evil life.

St. John Chrysostom, to avoid being made a bishop, fled into the solitude of the deserts; and St. Amonius the hermit, to escape being made a priest, went so far as to cut off one of his ears.

20 Missionaries should rejoice to be considered poor in talent, birth and virtue, the dregs and offscouring of the world. They should be glad whenever there arises any opportunity for abjection and contempt, even though it be not for themselves alone, but also extending to the Congregation. And by this test they will be able to know what progress they are making in humility.

—ST. VINCENT DE PAUL

This Saint, who knew well the great value of humiliations, was so fond of them that a worthy ecclesiastic, who knew him thoroughly, said that he had never been acquainted with any man in the world, who was so ambitious to rise and to be esteemed and honored, as this humble servant of God was desirous to lower and abase himself, and to receive humiliation, confusion, and contempt, so that he seemed to have chosen them as his treasure even in this life. For this cause, he used every effort to take advantage of all occasions of the kind that might offer themselves, and from everything he derived motives for humiliation. And with the same earnestness that he sought it for himself, he desired it also for his Congregation, which he was eager to have despised and held in low estimation. And whenever this happened, he rejoiced not a little. St. Jane Frances de Chantal once undertook

an affair of much importance, and then instantly abandoned it, on considering that success would reflect great credit upon herself. To those who wondered how she had been able to wind up and dispose of so important a matter so readily, she answered: "As soon as the splendor of the Sovereign's majesty revealed itself to my eyes, I was so dazzled and blinded that I could no longer see anything. Ah!" she repeated many times, "the splendor of the daughters of the Visitation is to be without splendor, and all their glory lies in humility and abjection."

21 To bear abasement and reproach is the touchstone of humility, and, at the same time, of true virtue. For in this, one becomes conformed to Jesus Christ, who is the true model of all solid virtues.

—ST. FRANCIS DE SALES

The blessed Seraphino, a Capuchin lay-brother, being gate keeper, was accustomed to pass much time in prayer in a little chapel in the garden, opposite to the gate. One day the Father Guardian, passing that way with a visiting Father, said to his companion, "Would you like to see a saint?" Then approaching the chapel, he reproved Seraphino severely, saying: "What are you doing here, hypocrite? The Lord teaches us to pray in a room with closed doors, and do you pray in public to be seen? Get up, rascal, and be ashamed of deceiving poor strangers in such a way!" Delighted with these reproofs, Brother Seraphino kissed the ground, and then went away with a countenance as full of satisfaction as if he had just heard some news which was much to his pleasure or advantage. Another day, he was asked

by a companion for a needle and a little thread. He replied that he had a needle but no thread; when the other said angrily: "It is plain that you are a fool, and were never good for anything! What can the Order do with such an incapable man as you are? Go away, for I cannot bear to look at you!" Then, without any anger or discomposure, he turned away from the monk who had reproached him, and after a little while came back with his usual serenity of countenance, to the great edification of his fellow religious.

In the Lives of the Fathers, we read that St. Amonius had arrived at such great perfection that he was as insensible to insults as a stone; and no matter how many were inflicted upon him, he never considered that any injury had been done him. In the same Lives, it is related that the Abbot John one day told his disciples the story of a youth, who, for having grievously insulted his master, was condemned to remain for three years in menial employment and to receive all the insults that might be inflicted upon him, without ever avenging himself at all. Returning to his master after this time had expired, he was told that for the next three years he must reward whoever did him an injury. Having faithfully done this, he was sent to Athens to study philosophy. He entered the school of an old master who was accustomed to ill-treat all his scholars at their entrance. He did the same in this case; but the newcomer only laughed, and on being asked the reason of his conduct, he answered: "How can I help laughing, when I have so long paid for ill-usage, and now I find it without paying anything?" "My children," added the holy Abbot, when he had finished his story, "submission to injuries is the road by which our Fathers have passed to go to the Lord; and difficult as

it appears at first, you see that by habit it becomes not only easy, but even pleasant."

22 He who is truly humble must desire in truth to be despised, mocked, persecuted, and blamed, although wrongfully. If he wishes to imitate Christ, how can he do it better than in this way? Oh, how wise will he, one day, be seen to be, who rejoiced in being accounted vile and even a fool! for such was Wisdom itself esteemed.

—ST. TERESA

Cassian narrates of the Abbot Paphnutius that, being Superior of a monastery and much revered and esteemed by his monks on account of his venerable age and admirable life, he disliked so much honor, and preferring to see himself humiliated, forgotten and despised, he left the monastery secretly, by night, in the dress of a secular. He then went to the monastery of St. Pachomius, which was at a great distance from his own, and remained many days at the gate, humbly asking for the habit. He prostrated himself before the monks, who scornfully reproached him with having spent his life in the enjoyment of the world and then coming at last to serve God, urged by necessity, because he had no means of living. Finally, moved by his urgent entreaties, they gave him the habit, with the charge of the garden, assigning to him another monk as his superior, to whom he was to look for everything. Now, not content with performing his duties with great exactness and humility, he consequently took pains to do all that the rest avoided—all the lowest and most disagreeable tasks in the

house—and would often rise secretly in the night and do many things that the others were to perform, so that in the morning they would wonder, not knowing how their work came to be done. He continued to live in this manner for three years, much pleased with the good opportunity he had to labor and be despised, which was the thing he had so greatly desired. Meanwhile his monks, feeling grievously the loss of such a Father, had gone out in different bands to seek him; they finally found him as he was manuring the ground, and threw themselves at his feet. The bystanders were amazed, but still more so when they heard that this was Paphnutius, whose name was so celebrated among them; and they immediately asked his pardon. The holy old man wept at his misfortune in having been discovered through the envy of the demon, and at having lost the treasure which he had seemed to find. Even by force he was carried back to his monastery, where he was received with indescribable gladness, and watched and guarded with the utmost diligence, that he might not again escape.

23 If we should well consider all that is human and imperfect in us, we should find but too much cause to humiliate ourselves before God and men, even before our inferiors.

—ST. VINCENT DE PAUL

A holy woman, once having asked light of the Lord that she might know herself well, saw so much ugliness and so many miseries in her own heart that, not being able to bear the sight, she prayed to God to relieve her from such distress; for she said if it had lasted longer she would have sunk under it.

The venerable Mother Seraphina di Dio once had a very clear supernatural illumination which made her see her soul full of so many and such abominable faults that it seemed like a receptacle of all that was foul; and she judged it must be even worse in reality; for she said, "If I had more light, I should see more." "It has often come into my mind," she added, "to retire to some cave, when I think how little I exercise myself in virtue; as to humility, in particular, I seem to myself a Lucifer. Religion is beautiful for those who practice virtue, but not for me, who cultivate only vices." Therefore, when she received insults and contempt, she was never disturbed, nor complained, but said: "They speak well; they do well; that suits me well." Nor was any adversity or trial in her whole life ever sufficient to make her change her sentiments.

24 In my opinion, we shall never acquire true humility unless we raise our eyes to behold God. Looking upon His greatness, the soul sees better her own littleness; beholding His purity, she is the more aware of her own uncleanness; considering His patience, she feels how far she is from being patient; in fine, turning her glance upon the divine perfections, she discovers in herself so many imperfections that she would gladly close her eyes to them.

—ST. TERESA

This was, in truth, one of the principal fountains from which St. Vincent de Paul drew that humble opinion which he had of himself, as well as his great desire for humiliations. That is to say,

he derived them from the profound knowledge which he had of the infinite perfections of God, and of the extreme weakness and misery of creatures; so that he thought it a manifest injustice not to humiliate himself always and in all things. In a conference one day with his priests, he spoke thus: "In truth, if each of us will give his attention to knowing himself well before God, he will find it to be the most just and reasonable thing to despise and humble himself. For, if we seriously consider the natural and continual inclination we have to evil, our natural incapacity for good, and the experience we all have had that even when we think we have succeeded well in something and that our plans are wise, the matter often turns out quite different from our anticipations, and God permits us to be considered wanting in judgment; and that, finally, in all we think, say, or do, both in substance and circumstances, we are always filled and encompassed with motives for humiliation and confusion—how shall we not consider ourselves worthy to be repulsed and despised in reflecting upon such things, and in seeing ourselves so far from the holiness and sublime perfections of God, and from the marvellous operations of His grace, and from the life of Christ our Lord?"

25 One who wishes to become truly holy ought not, except in a few unusual cases, to excuse himself, although that for which he is blamed be not true. Jesus Christ acted thus. He heard Himself charged with evil which He had not done, but said not a word to free Himself from the disgrace.

—ST. PHILIP NERI

The Empress Leonora was treated by her mother always with harshness, and without any appearance of affection. For the smallest things that were observed by no one else, her mother reproved her sharply at every turn, and frequently struck her. The good child remained always in silence, with her eyes cast down, uttering not a word in her defense, still less complaining or weeping. Often when the tempest has passed, she would kneel and kiss her mother's feet, asking her pardon and promising amendment.

St. Vincent de Paul never justified himself against the complaints and calumnies brought against him and his Congregation, whatever trouble or loss they might cause. Once when he had used his influence to prevent a bishopric from being conferred on one of his subjects, whom he considered unworthy of it, the disappointed candidate invented an enormous calumny against him, which came to the ears of the Queen. One day, meeting the Saint, she told him laughingly that he had been accused of such and such a thing. He calmly replied, "Madam, I am a great sinner." When her Majesty said that he ought to assert his innocence, he answered, "Quite as much was said against Christ our Lord, and He never justified Himself." It happened that, one time, in a public hall, a nobleman said that the missionary zeal of St. Vincent's followers had greatly cooled. When the Saint heard this, he would not say a word in defense, though he could easily have proved the contrary of the assertion, for in that year and the preceding more missions had been given than ever before. To one who urged him to take notice of the affair by telling him that this gentleman, though not knowing the truth, was continuing to speak evil of the Congregation, he answered, "We will let him talk. For my part, I will never justify myself

except by my works." It chanced, one day, that a prelate, having summoned the Saint to an assembly where many persons of rank were present, reproved him publicly for a thing for which he was not at all to blame. But he, without a word of complaint or excuse, immediately knelt and asked pardon, to the great admiration of those present, to whom his innocence was known. One of them, a man of much piety and learning, after the assembly was over and the Saint was gone, said that he was a man of extraordinary virtue and of a supernatural and divine spirit.

The venerable Mother Seraphina never excused herself, even to her confessors, though they might blame her wrongfully; nor did she explain how matters really stood, unless obliged by obedience. Once, in particular, when she was sharply reproved by her director, though the thing laid to her charge was not true, she replied only: "You are right." Afterwards, he commanded her to tell him the truth, and on hearing it he was sorry for his wrongful accusations.

26 Sometimes a soul rises more towards perfection by not excusing herself than by ten sermons. Since by this means one begins to acquire freedom, and indifference as to what good or evil may be said. Nay more; by a habit of not replying, one arrives at such a point that when he hears anything said of himself, it does not seem as if it related to him, but rather like an affair belonging to someone else.

—ST. TERESA

Father Alvarez, the confessor of St. Teresa, having been falsely accused of a grave fault in a provincial assembly and seriously

reproved for it in public, said nothing, either in public or private, in his own defense. Afterwards, God rewarded this heroic silence with extraordinary favors.

Among the ancient monks, there was one named Eulogius, very humble and patient. Wherefore, the lax and negligent threw all their faults upon him; and he, being corrected and reproved for them, humbly accepted, without any denial or excuse, the penances which were given for them and performed them with great patience. The older Fathers, seeing him every day under reprehension, were displeased with him, and told the Abbot that he ought to apply some remedy, for they could not bear this state of things any longer. The Abbot took time, and, in prayer, entreated the Lord to enlighten him, and teach him what he ought to do with this brother. Then God revealed to him his innocence and great sanctity. Being extremely astonished at this, he called together all the monks, and said to them: "Believe me, I would prefer the faults of Eulogius with his patience and humility, to all the good works and virtues of many others who murmur against him, and think they are doing well themselves. And that you may see how great is the virtue of our companion, let each of you bring here the mat on which he sleeps." When all the mats were brought, he had a good fire lit and threw them all into it. Every one was instantly burned except that of Brother Eulogius, which remained. Then, prostrate upon the ground, they all asked pardon of God, and conceived the highest opinion of their brother. But he was grieved at being discovered, and the next night fled to the desert, where he would be unknown; for he knew very well that no one can be honored in this world and in the next.

27 Here is one of the best means to acquire humility: fix well in mind this maxim: One is as much as he is in the sight of God, and no more.

—THOMAS À KEMPIS

St. Francis made a beginning of sanctity by trampling underfoot human respect; for he had thoroughly penetrated the truth of this holy maxim which he often revolved in his mind.

In this solid maxim, St. Francis de Sales was equally well-founded and established. Therefore, he had his own reputation very little at heart, and did not care at all how others might feel in regard to him. In conversation, he once said: "Oh that it were God's pleasure that my innocence should never be recognized even in the day of universal judgment, but that it should remain always hidden and eternally concealed in the secret recesses of the eternal wisdom!" And again: "If the grace of God had caused me to perform any work of righteousness, or had wrought any good by my means, I should be content that in the day of judgment, when the secrets of hearts are manifested, God alone should know of my righteousness; and my unrighteousness, on the contrary, should be seen by every creature!"

28 All those who have truly wished to arrive at the possession of humility have applied themselves with all their power to the practice of humiliation, because they know that this is the quickest and shortest road thereto.

—ST. BERNARD

The blessed Alessandro Sauli, Bishop of Aleria, a man of learning and esteemed in his Order, willingly occupied himself, even when he was Superior, in humble employments such as sweeping the house, washing the dishes, drawing water, bringing wood to the kitchen, working in the garden, serving the old and the sick, carrying heavy burdens on his back, taking charge of the door, ringing the bells, or helping the sacristan. When, on account of preaching or other spiritual works, he was at any time prevented from performing these daily exercises, he was accustomed to supply the omission by doing double work on the next day.

St. Camillus de Lelli was also remarkable in this way. When he was Superior General of his Order, he was often seen serving in the refectory, washing dishes in the kitchen, carrying the cross, and sometimes even the coffin, at funerals, and going about Rome with a wallet on his shoulders, begging bread—though he was blamed for it by some great nobles and cardinals who were his friends and happened to meet him in the streets in this guise.

The venerable Mother Seraphina often employed herself in humble tasks; she was also seen many times rubbing her face with an old shoe.

St. Mary Magdalen de' Pazzi, of her own accord, adopted practices that might bring her into contempt, such as having her eyes bandaged, her hands tied behind her back, being trampled upon, struck, or rudely addressed.

We read of St. Policronius that he wore a wretched habit, ate poor and very scanty food, and passed almost all night in prayer with an oak log on his shoulders, so heavy that Theodoret, the author of his life, who had seen the log, found by experiment that he could scarcely lift it from the ground with both hands.

St. Rose of Lima, besides occupying herself as a servant in the lowest offices every day, invented a strange method of lowering herself still more. Having in the house a woman-servant of harsh temper and exceedingly coarse nature, she induced her, by urgent entreaties, to maltreat her both in words and acts. Retiring with her into a lonely part of the house, and throwing herself upon the floor, the Saint would cause this person to spit in her face, trample her underfoot, strike her with her fist, kick and beat her, as teamsters sometimes do a horse; nor would she rise to her feet until she had obtained as much of this treatment as she desired.

St. John Climacus tells of a monk who had a great love for humility, that he devised this plan to overcome the thoughts of pride with which the devil inspired him. He wrote upon the wall of his cell these memorable words: Perfect charity. Loftiest contemplation. Total mortification. Unalterable sweetness. Unconquerable patience. Angelic chastity. Profoundest humility. Filial confidence. Promptest diligence. Utter resignation. So, when the devil began to urge him to pride, he answered within himself, "Let us try the test." Then approaching the wall, he read these headings: *"Perfect charity.* Charity, yes, but how perfect, if I speak evil of others? *Profoundest humility.* This I have not; it is quite enough if I claim the profound. *Angelic chastity.* How can this be mine, when I allow admittance to unchaste thoughts? *Loftiest contemplation.* No, I have many distractions. *Total mortification.* No, for I seek my own gratification. *Unalterable sweetness.* No, for at the least vexation I lose my self-control." And so with all the rest. In this way he banished the temptation to vanity.

29 Humility, to be true, must be always accompanied by charity; that is, loving, seeking, and accepting humiliations to please God, and to become more like Jesus Christ; to do otherwise, would be to practice it in the manner of the heathen.

—ST. FRANCIS DE SALES

It cannot be said that St. Vincent de Paul was wanting in true humility. However much he did to conceal, abase, humiliate, and render himself despicable in the eyes of the world, allowing no opportunity for humbling himself to pass without accepting it with all willingness and joy, he yet did it all because it expressed the sentiments of his own heart in regard to himself and his nothingness, as well as to act out and imitate the humiliations of the Son of God, who, as he said one day in a conference, being the brightness of His Father's glory and the image of His substance, not content with having led a life which might be called a continual humiliation, willed even after His death to remain before our eyes in a state of extreme ignominy, when He hung upon the Cross. Thus the humility of this servant of God was from his heart, and so sincere that it could be read on his brow, in his eyes, and in his whole exterior.

St. Jerome relates of St. Paula that when she heard it said that she had become a fool through too much spiritual fervor and that it would be well if a hole were made in her head to give air to her brain, she answered modestly, in the words of the Apostle, *"Nos stulti propter Christum"*—We are fools for Christ's sake. She added also that the same thing had happened to Jesus Christ, when His relations wished to confine him as a madman.

St. Jerome also says that when she received insults, contempt, or ignominy, she never allowed the slightest word of resentment to escape from her lips, but was accustomed in such cases to repeat to herself the words of the psalm: *Ego autem quasi surdus non audiebam, et quasi mutus, non aperiens os suum*—But I as a deaf man, heard not, and as a dumb man, who opens not his mouth.

MARCH

Mortification

---

*Whoever will come after Me, let
him deny himself.*—Matt. 16:24

---

1 The first step to be taken by one who wishes to follow
Christ is, according to Our Lord's own words, that of
renouncing himself—that is, his own senses, his own
passions, his own will, his own judgment, and all the
movements of nature, making to God a sacrifice of all
these things, and of all their acts, which are surely sac-
rifices very acceptable to the Lord. And we must never
grow weary of this; for if anyone having, so to speak,
one foot already in Heaven, should abandon this exercise, when the time should come for him to put the
other there, he would run much risk of being lost.

—ST. VINCENT DE PAUL

The same Saint made himself such a proficient in this virtue that it might be called the weapon most frequently and constantly handled by him through his whole life until his last breath; and by this he succeeded in gaining absolute dominion over all the movements of his inferior nature. Therefore, he kept his own passions so completely subject to reason, that he could scarcely be known to have any.

St. John Climacus says that the ancient Fathers, even those who were most perfect, exercised themselves in many kinds of mortification and contempt. For they said that if they should give up training themselves because men thought them already consummate in virtue, they would come, in time, to abandon and lose that modesty and patience which they possessed; just as a field, though rich and fertile, if it be no longer cultivated, becomes unsightly and ends in producing only thorns and thistles.

2 The measure of our advancement in the spiritual life should be taken from the progress we make in the virtue of mortification; for it should be held as certain that the greater violence we shall do ourselves in mortification, the greater advance we shall make in perfection.

—ST. JEROME

When St. Francis Borgia heard it said that anyone was a saint, he used to answer, "He is, if he is mortified." In this way he himself became so great a saint; for he exercised himself in mortification to such a degree that only that day seemed to him truly wretched in which he had not undergone some mortification, either bodily or spiritually.

When a young monk once asked an aged saint why, among so many who aim at perfection, so few are found perfect, he replied, "Because in order to be perfect it is necessary to die wholly to one's own inclinations, and there are few who arrive at this."

3 It should be our principal business to conquer ourselves, and, from day to day, to go on increasing in strength and perfection. Above all, however, it is necessary for us to strive to conquer our little temptations, such as fits of anger, suspicions, jealousies, envy, deceitfulness, vanity, attachments, and evil thoughts. For in this way we shall acquire strength to subdue greater ones.

—ST. FRANCIS DE SALES

A certain physiognomist, looking at Socrates, pronounced him to be inclined to dishonesty, gluttony, drunkenness, and many other vices. His disciples, being angry at this, wished to lay violent hands on the man who had spoken so ill of their master. But Socrates said: "Be calm, for he has told the truth. I should have been just such a man as he describes, if I had not given myself to mortification."

When an old monk was asked how he could bear the noise of some shepherd boys near him, he answered: "I was at first inclined to say something to them; but I thought better of it, and said to myself, 'If I cannot endure so little as this, how shall I endure greater trials, when they come to me?'"

St. Francis Xavier acted in the same way on occasion, and said that we must not deceive ourselves; for whoever does not

conquer himself in trifles, will not be able to do so in greater matters.

4 He who allows himself to be ruled or guided by the lower and animal part of his nature, deserves to be called a beast rather than a man.

—ST. VINCENT DE PAUL

Philip, Count of Nemours, after leading a very bad life, experienced on his deathbed wonderful contrition, so that he begged his confessor to have his body carried to the public square and left there, saying, "I have lived like a dog, and like a dog I ought to die."

5 Whoever makes little account of exterior mortifications, alleging that the interior are more perfect, shows clearly that he is not mortified at all, either exteriorly or interiorly.

—ST. VINCENT DE PAUL

This Saint was always an enemy to his body, treating it with much austerity—chastising it with haircloth, iron chains, and leather belts armed with sharp points. Every morning on rising, he took a severe discipline—a practice which he had begun before founding the Congregation, and which he never omitted on account of the hardships of journeys, or in his convalescence from any illness; but, on the contrary, he took additional ones on special occasions. All his life he slept upon a simple straw bed, and always rose at the usual hour for the

Community, though he was generally the last of all to retire to rest, and though he often could not sleep more than two hours out of the night, on account of his infirmities. From this it frequently happened that he was much tormented during the day by drowsiness, which he would drive away by remaining on his feet or in some uncomfortable posture, or by inflicting on himself some annoyance. Besides, he willingly bore great cold in winter, and great heat in summer, with other inconveniences; in a word, he embraced, or rather sought, all the sufferings he could, and was very careful never to allow any opportunity for mortifying himself to escape.

A holy woman, being compelled by her husband to go to a ball, put dry mustard on her shoulders, which, in dancing, caused her such intense pain that she fainted several times, and had to be carried from the ballroom.

St. Edmund, Archbishop of Canterbury, wore for thirty successive years a band of haircloth next to his skin, and always slept on the floor without pillow or coverlet. St. Louis, King of France, constantly chastised his body with fasts and haircloth. St. Casimir, son of the King of Poland, did the same, and also slept on the bare ground. St. Margaret, Queen of Scotland, as well at St. Cajetan, often used the discipline during whole nights.

Finally, there can be found among the Confessors no saint, either man or woman, who did not have great love for exterior mortifications, and who did not practice them as much as possible.

6 Mortification of the appetite is the A, B, C of spiritual life. Whoever cannot control himself in this, will

hardly be able to conquer temptations more difficult to subdue.

—ST. VINCENT DE PAUL

This Saint had, by long habit, so mortified his sense of taste that he never gave a sign of being pleased with anything, but took indifferently all that was given him, however insipid or ill-cooked it might be; and so little did he regard what he was eating, that when a couple of raw eggs were once set before him by mistake, he ate them without taking the least notice. He always seemed to go to the table unwillingly, and only from necessity, eating always with great moderation, and with a view solely to the glory of God; nor did he ever leave the table without having mortified himself in something, either as to quantity or quality. For many years, too, he kept a bitter powder to mix with his food; and he usually ate so little that he frequently fainted from weakness.

The Empress Leonora was remarkable for this virtue. Her usual dinner was of herbs, pulse, and other food of the poor, always the same both in kind and quantity. She had four dishes at dinner, and three at supper, frequently setting aside some of them for no reason except that they pleased her. And if these dishes came to the table covered with pastry or other delicacies used by the rich, they always went back whole and untouched. When she was at the Emperor's table or at formal banquets, she spent the time in cutting into the smallest bits whatever was placed before her; then when another course was brought, she sent away the first without having tasted it, and went on as before. When she ate apples baked in the ashes, she never

peeled them, but ate them with whatever ashes were upon them. On Fridays she lived on bread and water alone, in memory of the Redeemer's Passion. She bore the most parching thirst on the hottest summer days, without permitting even a sip of water to pass her burning lips.

St. Elizabeth, Queen of Portugal, fasted on bread and water about half the year.

St. Francis Xavier waged as constant and lasting war against his appetite, so that he never took food or drink for pleasure, but from pure necessity; nor did he ever take as much as he desired, even of bread.

St. Edmund of Canterbury never ate either meat or fish, but only bread and other common food, and suffered so much from thirst that his lips chapped.

The blessed Henry Suso drank nothing for six successive months; and in order to feel thirst more acutely, he ate salty food, and then going to a stream, he bent his head down close to its surface, yet without allowing his lips to touch it.

The blessed Joanna of St. Damien practiced such great austerities in regard to food, that she was entreated by the other nuns to moderate them. But she answered: "I am sorry that I cannot feed this body of mine on straw. I know how much harm liberty does to it, and I thank God, who has given me this knowledge."

When St. Mary Magdalen de' Pazzi was seriously ill, extremely weak, and suffering from nausea, if she happened to think of any kind of food which would please her, she considered it a fault to ask for it or allude to it, and carefully abstained from doing so.

The blessed Jacopone, having one day a desire for meat, bought a piece. He hung it up in his room and kept it until it

was spoiled; then he had it cooked and ate it with unspeakable disgust.

By a long and constant habit of abstinence and mortification, St. Anselm became unable to perceive the taste of food. It was the same with St. Bernard, who for that reason drank oil one day instead of wine, without perceiving it at all, and he reached such a point that going to the table seemed to him a kind of torture.

St. Teresa said that she experienced a similar difficulty in eating; and St. Isidore suffered from it so excessively that he could not go to the table without tears, and the command of his Superior was needed to force him to take some nourishment.

7 One of the things that keep us at a distance from perfection is, without doubt, our tongue. For when one has gone so far as to commit no faults in speaking, the Holy Spirit Himself assures us that he is perfect. And since the worst way of speaking is to speak too much, speak little and well, little and gently, little and simply, little and charitably, little and amiably.

—ST. FRANCIS DE SALES

St. Ignatius Loyola governed his tongue so well that his speech was simple, grave, considerate, and brief.

St. John Berchmans was a man of few words, and so considerate in his speech that there was never heard from his mouth an idle word, one contrary to rule, one that was neither necessary, useful, nor directed to any good purpose. Being once asked by a brother novice how he managed never to commit a

fault in speaking, he replied thus: "I never say anything without first considering it, and recommending it to God, that I may say nothing which can displease Him." Besides, he was never observed to violate silence and when asked how he could keep this rule so perfectly, he answered: "This is the way I do: I salute humbly all those I meet; if anyone asks any service of me, I show the greatest readiness to render it; if anyone asks me a question, I listen, and answer briefly; and I avoid saying a single superfluous word."

St. Vincent de Paul made himself so completely master of his tongue, that useless or superfluous words were rarely heard from his mouth, and never a single one inconsiderate, contrary to charity, or such as might savor of vanity, flattery, or ostentation. It often happened that after opening his mouth to say something unusual that came into his mind, he closed it suddenly, stifling the words, and apparently reflecting in his own heart, and considering before God whether it was expedient to say them. He then continued to speak, not according to his inclination, for he had none, but as he felt sure would be most pleasing to God. When anything was told him which he already knew, he listened with attention, giving no sign of having heard it before. He did this to mortify self-love, which always makes us desire to prove that we know as much as others. When insult, reproach, or wrong of any kind was inflicted upon him, he never opened his lips to complain, to justify himself, or to repel the injury; but he recollected himself, and placed all his strength in silence and patience, blessing in his heart those who had ill-treated him, and praying for them. When he found himself overwhelmed with excessive work, he did not complain, but his

ordinary words were: "Blessed be God! we must accept willingly all that He deigns to send us."

St. Aloysius Gonzaga, when about to converse with anyone, fervently repeated this prayer: *Pone Domine, custodiam ori meo, &c.*—Set a watch, O Lord, before my lips, &c.

A certain virgin once observed silence from the Festival of the Holy Cross, in September, until Christmas, with such rigor that in all that time she did not speak one word. This mortification was so pleasing to God, that it was revealed to a holy soul, that as a reward for it, she should never pass through Purgatory.

Among the lofty eulogiums that St. Jerome bestows upon his pupil St. Paula is this—that she was as cautious in speaking as she was ready to listen.

8 It is a common doctrine of the Saints that one of the principal means of leading a good and exemplary life is modesty and custody of the eyes. For, as there is nothing so adapted to preserve devotion in a soul, and to cause compunction and edification in others, as this modesty, so there is nothing which so much exposes a person to relaxation and scandals as its opposite.

—ST. ALPHONSUS RODRIGUEZ

In his life of St. Bernard, Surius relates that when Pope Innocent III went with his Cardinals to visit Clairvaux, the Saint, with all his monks, came out to meet him, but with such a modest and composed exterior as moved to compunction the Cardinals and the Pope himself; for they were astonished that on such

a festival, and such an unusual and solemn occasion of rejoicing, they all kept their eyes cast down and fastened upon the ground without turning them in any direction, and that while all were gazing at them, they looked at no one. He also tells of St. Bernard, that he practiced custody of the eyes to such a degree that after a year's novitiate he did not know how the ceiling of his cell was made, whether it was arched or flat; that he always believed there was one window in the church, while there were three; that he walked, one day, with his companions on the short of a lake, without knowing it was there, so that when they were speaking of the lake in the evening, he asked where they had seen it.

It is narrated of St. Bernardine of Siena that his modesty was so great that his mere presence acted as a restraint upon his companions; so that if one only said, "Bernardine is coming," they would check themselves immediately. Surius also tells, in his Life of St. Lucian the Martyr, that the heathens were converted and became Christians by merely looking upon him, on account of his composure and modesty.

The blessed Clara di Montefalco never raised her eyes to the face of anyone with whom she was speaking. When she was asked by a monk the reason of this, she answered: "As we speak only with the tongue, what need is there of looking in the face of the person we are talking with?"

St. John Berchmans was greatly to be admired for mortification of the eyes. He would never turn to look at anything, however new and unexpected it might be, and even a noise behind him would never cause him to turn, natural as it is to do so. Happening to be present one day at a college exhibition, he took a seat on a bench and remained motionless, without ever raising his eyes, and

with so much recollection that a nobleman who occupied the next seat was amazed, and said, "This Father must be a saint."

There are, on the other hand, innumerable instances of those who have become relaxed and a cause of scandal through want of custody of the eyes. It will be enough to cite the example of David, who, by a simple unguarded glance, prompted by curiosity, was suddenly changed from a great saint into a great sinner, the scandal of his whole kingdom.

9 Believe me that the mortification of the senses in seeing, hearing, and speaking, is worth much more than wearing chains or haircloth.

—ST. FRANCIS DE SALES

It is known of St. Catherine of Siena that while her family were celebrating the Carnival in their house, she was not willing to join them, protesting that as she had no other love, so she had no other pleasure, but in her Jesus. He then appeared to her in company with the Blessed Virgin and other Saints, and espoused her with so much clearness and certainty, that the Dominicans, by Apostolic Indulgence, celebrate a festival in commemoration of it on the last day of the Carnival.

A very devout penitent of his once confessed to St. Francis Xavier that she had looked upon a man with more tenderness than was suitable. The Saint closed what he had to say to her with these words: "You are unworthy to have God look upon you, since for the sake of looking upon a man, you do not regard the risk of losing God." This was enough, for, during the rest of her life, she never again turned her eyes toward any man.

The Empress Leonora kept her eyes down, and raised them only when she was welcomed by monks or nuns to their house; she returned their salutations courteously, with a cheerful countenance and a kind smile. When present at the theater, to which she was obliged to go, she rarely glanced at the splendid gathering of the nobility or at the superb scenes which succeeded each other, with views of gardens, forests, and palaces, in perspective. She spent all this time with her mind in Heaven, contemplating the delights of Paradise, and reciting Psalms, which, to avoid notice, she had bound in the same style as the books of the plays, so that she seemed to everyone very attentive to the play, while she was, in reality, enjoying a very different sight.

St. Vincent de Paul practiced continual mortification of the senses, depriving them even of lawful gratifications, and often inflicting on them voluntary sufferings. When he was traveling, instead of allowing his eyes to wander over the country, he usually kept them on his crucifix. When walking in the city, he went with eyes cast down or closed, that he might see God alone. Visiting the palaces of the nobility, he did not look at the tapestry or other beautiful objects, but remained with downcast glance and full of recollection. He practiced the same thing in the churches, never raising his eyes except to behold the Blessed Sacrament, not to look at the decorations, however beautiful they might be. He was never seen to gather flowers in the gardens, or take up anything that was pleasing to the sense of smell; on the contrary, he greatly enjoyed remaining in places where there was an unpleasant odor, such as hospitals and the houses of the sick poor. His tongue he employed only in praise of God and virtue, in opposing vice and in consoling, instructing, and edifying his

neighbor. His ears he opened only to discourse which tended to good, for it gave him pain to hear news and worldly talk, and he made every effort to avoid listening to what would delight the hearing without profit to the soul.

When a penitent who was somewhat reckless in his speech asked his director for a hairshirt to mortify the flesh, "My son," said the priest, laying his finger upon his lips, "the best hairshirt is to watch carefully all that comes out at this door."

St. Aloysius Gonzaga was admirable for mortification of the eyes, for it is narrated in his Life that he never looked any woman in the face. After he had served the Empress as page for two years, a report was spread that she was coming into Italy, where he happened to be, and some congratulated him on the prospect of seeing his mistress again. But he replied: "I shall not recognize her except by her voice, for I do not know her face." His rare mortification was well rewarded by God even in his life, for he was never attacked by temptations of the flesh.

10 There are some so much inclined to mortify themselves that they take care to find in everything some means of mortification. What a beautiful practice is this, and of how much advantage.

—ST. ALPHONSUS RODRIGUEZ

Sister Joanna Maria of the Trinity, a Discalced Carmelite, had this excellent custom of seeking and finding mortification in everything. And so she always selected what was most insipid in food; poorest in clothing and shelter; most laborious in work; most unpleasant in matters of inclination. In a word, she always

chose what was most inconvenient and disagreeable for herself, seeking in all things only the pleasure, honor, and glory of God.

St. Francis Borgia also made much use of the same practice. He wore pebbles in his shoes; slept little at night; when walking in the sun in summer, he remained out as long as possible; he swallowed medicine slowly, and chewed pills, that he might keep them longer in his mouth.

11 Upon interior mortification depends the right adjustment of our whole exterior, its arrangement with most perfection, with most sweetness and peace.

—ST. TERESA

St. Philip Neri, when anyone asked him what he should do to become a saint, used to put his hand to his forehead, saying, "Give me those four fingers, and I will make you a saint"; meaning that all sanctity depends on denying one's own will and one's own judgment. And to a penitent who often asked permission to take the discipline, he once gave this answer: "How are the shoulders to blame, if the head is hard?"

12 Our profit does not depend so much upon mortifying ourselves, as upon knowing how to mortify ourselves; that is, upon knowing how to choose the best mortifications, which are those most repugnant to our natural inclinations. Some are inclined to disciplines and fasts, and though they be difficult things, they embrace them with fervor, and practice them gladly and easily, on account

of this leaning which they have toward them. But then they will be so sensitive in regard to reputation and honor, that the least ridicule, disapproval, or slight is sufficient to throw them into a state of impatience and perturbation and to give rise to such complaints as show an equal want of peace and reason. These are the mortifications which they ought to embrace with the greatest readiness, if they wish to make progress.

—ST. FRANCIS DE SALES

The venerable Monseigneur de Palafox understood this doctrine well, for he said that the reason why he had never advanced in virtue was that he had never taken special pains to avoid all that was most conformed to his inclinations. Whoever, then, perceives in himself any disposition to contradict, for example, or to rely on his own judgment, and is not very attentive to combat, and to keep at a distance from all that can entice or subject him to it, will not only fail to go forward, but will go backward, and perhaps so far backward as to arrive at his own ruin.

A religious who was a priest, having been chosen as assistant to the cook, experienced the greatest repugnance and temptations in regard to this charge. To conquer himself, he made a vow before a crucifix to remain in this office all his life, if the Superiors should be willing. Through this and similar victories he arrived at such perfection as to be able to say that he believed no work could be offered to him, however repugnant to the senses, that he could not do, by the help of God, with perfect ease.

13 The mortifications which come to us from God, or from men by His permission, are always worth more than those which are the children of our own will; for it must be considered a general rule, that the less our taste and choice intervene in our actions, the more they will have of goodness, solidity, devotion, the pleasure of God, and our own profit.

—ST. FRANCIS DE SALES

Aldolphus, Count of Alsace, having entered the Order of St. Francis, was one day collecting alms in the form of milk, when he met his sons and felt ashamed of his occupation. Then instantly recollecting himself, he emptied the can of milk upon his head, saying, "Unhappy one! thou art ashamed of the poverty of Jesus Christ! Let them see now what thou art carrying!" After that, he suffered no more from any similar temptation.

It is narrated in the Lives of the Fathers, that an old solitary, who had heard the virtue of a certain youthful monk greatly praised, resolved to test it. For this purpose he went to the monk's cell, and entering the garden, which he found well cultivated and in excellent order, he began, as if in sport, to break down with his staff all the herbs and plants which were there, not leaving any untouched. Afterwards, according to the custom of the monks, they began to recite Psalms together; and when this was ended the youth, with a cheerful and modest air, asked the old man if he would like to have him prepare such of the herbs as were left for his repast. Astonished at such an invitation, he, for answer, threw his arms around his neck, exclaiming: "Now I see, my son, that you are truly dead to your inclinations, as was told me!"

14 The more one mortifies his natural inclinations, the more he becomes capable of receiving the divine inspirations, and the more he gains in virtue.

—ST. FRANCIS DE SALES

The celebrated Father Laynez, one of the companions of St. Ignatius, by means of this practice arrived at great purity of mind and imperturbable tranquillity of soul.

St. Philip Neri made great use of this practice, both with his penitents and for himself. One example out of many will suffice. A nobleman of high rank had a dog, named Capriccio, of which he was very fond. One morning, an attendant of his brought the dog with him to the lodging of St. Philip, who, on seeing him, caressed him a little. Upon this, the dog took such a fancy to him that he could not in any way be persuaded to leave him. He was again and again sent back to his master, who had him kindly treated and kept tied up for a while; but immediately on being released, he would go back to the Saint's rooms, so that finally they were obliged to let him remain there. St. Philip afterwards made much use of this dog for his own mortification, and that of his spiritual children. Sometimes he made them wash and comb him; sometimes, carry him in their arms, or lead him by a chain through the streets of Rome; and he himself would walk with them. These and similar mortifications lasted for a space of fifteen years.

15 The greater part of Christians usually practice incision instead of circumcision. They will make a cut indeed in a diseased part; but as for employing the

knife of circumcision, to take away whatever is superfluous from the heart, few go so far.

—ST. FRANCIS DE SALES

The example of the venerable Sister Francesca Farnese confirms this truth. Immediately after her profession, she began to yield to relaxation, into which she fell so far that she cared for nothing except vain ornaments in dress, flirting, remaining all day at the grate, and, finally, covering the walls of her cell with hangings and mirrors. She was many times warned, corrected, and sharply reproved by her Superior, her confessor and, above all, by a nun who was her aunt. She felt and understood the force of these admonitions and reproofs and often formed good resolutions; she even put them in practice by taking off her vain ornaments, abandoning the grate, and breaking and throwing from the windows her mirrors and tapestry; but a little while after, she went back again to all these things, and became as she was before. These miserable alternations lasted for a long time, and might have continued for her whole life, as the reforms which she made were nothing more than incisions. But, happily, the Divine Mercy was pleased to stir her heart by a strong inspiration, so that, unable to resist the reproaches of her own conscience, she had courage to make a true circumcision, by leaving not only all vain amusements, but also by forming for herself a rule more rigorous than her own, and so well planned that it made her foundress of a new order, in which she spent the rest of her life in an exemplary manner, and died in the odor of sanctity, as is sufficiently proved by the fact that her body remained unchanged for many years.

Somewhat different was the career of St. Paula, who, as St. Jerome relates, even from her earliest years, undertook to practice a true circumcision of the heart, and with increasing age applied herself to it more and more, cutting off and retrenching on all sides whatever seemed superfluous or beyond what was suited to her state. So, while her husband was living, she led a life so well regulated and dutiful that she was an example to all the matrons of Rome, and no one ever dared to charge her with the slightest error. But when she was freed from the restraints of the world, after God took away her husband, she began a most austere life and never wavered in it until death. She no longer slept upon a mattress, but upon the bare ground, covered only with haircloth. Indeed, she slept but little, for she passed almost the whole night in prayer and tears. She chastised her body with rigorous fasts and very severe disciplines, without stint or mercy. In confessing her slightest faults, she shed so many tears that anyone who did not know her might have supposed her guilty of the gravest offenses; and when she was entreated not to weep so much, that she might preserve her sight for reading; and not to practice so many austerities and penances, that she might not wholly lose her health, "No," she replied, "with all reason should this face be disfigured, which I have so often beautified with washes contrary to the precept of the Lord; this body ought, indeed, to be afflicted, which has enjoyed so many delights; long laughter ought to be compensated for by continual weeping; rich and delicate garments ought to be changed into haircloth: for I, who have taken so much pains to please the world, now desire to please God." Thus she spoke and acted, in reparation for the disorders of her past life, which, nevertheless, had been most circumspect and modest.

16 Whoever wishes to make progress in perfection should use particular diligence in not allowing himself to be led away by his passions, which destroy with one hand the spiritual edifice which is rising by the labors of the other. But to succeed well in this, resistance should be begun while the passions are yet weak; for after they are thoroughly rooted and grown up, there is scarcely any remedy.

—ST. VINCENT DE PAUL

St. Dorotheus tells us of an old monk, who, walking with one of his disciples in a grove of cypresses, commanded him to pull some of them up, pointing out to him first, one which was but just beginning to sprout from the ground; after that, another, which had grown into a sapling; and finally, one that was a full-grown tree. The disciple set himself to the work and tore up the first with one hand and with all possible ease; the second also with one hand, but with some difficulty; to pull up the third he was obliged to try several times, with both hands and all his strength. But when he arrived at the fourth, he encountered the real difficulty; and though he tried again and again, with all his force, and in every way that his ingenuity could suggest, he was not able to stir it in the least from the spot. Then the aged Saint said: "Now, my son, it is the same as this with our passions. While they are still small, with a little vigilance and mortification one can easily repress and disable them; but, if we let them take root in our souls, there is no human force sufficient to conquer them; it requires the omnipotent hand of God. Therefore, my son, if you wish to acquire virtue, watch the first irregular movements

of your soul, and study to repress them promptly, by contrary acts, at their very birth. Upon this, everything depends."

17 The ignorance of some is greatly to be pitied, who load themselves with unwise penances and other unsuitable exercises of their devising, putting all their confidence in them, and expecting to become saints by their means. If they would put half of this labor upon mortifying their appetites and passions, they would gain more in a month than by all their other exercises in many years.

—ST. JOHN OF THE CROSS

We read of St. Ignatius that by means of continual mortification he had arrived at such a point that he seemed to be a man without passions; and if it was sometimes desirable to bring them into action, they appeared like so many modest slaves who dared not move of themselves, nor farther than reason, their absolute mistress, ordered them to go.

A Genoese lady, on account of the desire she had to listen to the contract for her marriage made by her father, left the world and became a nun and a saint.

St. Mary Magdalen de' Pazzi impressed this, above all things, upon the minds of the novices, when she was their mistress. And so, when she saw one too much inclined to pray, she sent her to sleep or to perform some active labor. Upon another who was inclined to exterior works, she imposed prayer or some other interior work. To whoever wished for many penances and mortifications, she gave one *Pater and Ave.* To whoever

felt repugnance for them, she prescribed severe mortifications and humiliations. Among other instances, she made one of the novices throw into the fire a little book of spiritual exercises, which she had written with her own hand, and to which she showed attachment. And thus, the Saint constantly accustomed her novices to subject their inclinations, and, at the same time, their judgment and their will.

18 The principal thing upon which we have to turn our attention, that we may mortify it and eradicate it from our hearts, is the predominant passion— that is, the affection, inclination, vice, or bad habit, which reigns most in us, which makes us its captive, which brings us into greatest danger, and most frequently causes us to fall into grave transgressions. When the king is taken, the battle is won. And until we do this, we shall make no great advance in perfection.

—ST. ALPHONSUS RODRIGUEZ

An event of the kind upon which Rodriguez founds his comparison occurred, as Holy Scripture narrates, in the war between the King of Syria and the King of Israel. The latter commanded all his captains to attack no one in the hostile army except the king himself, wisely judging that if the king should be conquered, the whole army would be overcome. This happened in fact, for when King Achab was struck down, the battle ended.

St. Ignatius once had a novice of a fiery disposition, to whom he often said: "My son, conquer this temperament of yours, and

you will have in Heaven a more resplendent crown than many who are gentle by nature." One day, the Father in charge accused this young man to him as intractable. "Not so," answered the Saint; "for I believe he has made more improvement in a few months, than such a one, who is naturally gentle, in a year." The same Saint was himself of a bilious-sanguine temperament. But he took his predominant passion so steadily in hand, and so conquered and changed himself by the grace of God, that he was considered by all, even by physicians, to be phlegmatic.

St. Francis de Sales confessed that the dominant passions he had most difficulty in subduing were love and anger, and that he had conquered the former by stratagem, the latter by open force; that is, he had conquered love by diverting his mind, and proposing to himself another object of love; for he said that as the human soul cannot exist without some love, the whole secret lies in giving to it only what is good, pure, and holy. Anger, on the other hand, he had subdued by attacking it in front, and never yielding to it at all. Whence it happened that though he was naturally passionate, he was thought to be of a gentle temper.

19 Every time that one sees himself urged on, with vehemence of affection, to any particular work, even though it be holy and important, he ought to put it off to another occasion, and not take it up again until his heart has recovered perfect tranquillity and indifference. This should be done to prevent self-love from sullying the purity of our intention.

—ST. VINCENT DE PAUL

The Saint who gives this advice practiced it faithfully himself. One day a business proposition was made to him that was very important for his Congregation. When he was urged by some of them to give his consent to it immediately, he answered: "I do not think we ought to pay attention to this matter at present, that we may blunt the natural inclination which leads us to pursue promptly what is to our own advantage, and also that we may practice holy indifference, and give time to God to manifest His will to us, while we continue offering our prayers to recommend the affair to Him." Another time, when someone importuned him about a similar matter, his reply was this: "I desire always to keep up the practice of not deciding or undertaking anything while I find myself agitated by the hope and desire of something great." Still another incident is even more admirable. As he saw, by experience, the great utility of missions, he embraced them with much fervor and earnestness. But when he perceived that his thoughts and ardent desires were gradually taking away the peace of heart he had hitherto enjoyed, he began to suspect that nature might have some part in them; therefore, he esteemed it necessary to interrupt this exercise for some time. The better to understand the movements of his heart, he retired for a few days of spiritual retreat, and perceiving in this that his great gladness and excessive solicitude were, in part, caused by self-love, he asked pardon of God with many tears, praying Him to change his heart and purify it from every inordinate affection, to the greater glory of His Divine Majesty. Afterwards, he found himself quite free from all anxiety and superfluous care, nor had he any other object than the Divine love; so that he was able to thank God that for thirty years he was not conscious of having done anything deliberately that was not directed to His greater glory.

St. Francis de Sales once stopped in the course of a journey to visit St. Jane Frances de Chantal, who had been eagerly expecting him, that she might confer with him about her own spiritual interests. She was the more desirous of doing this, because she had enjoyed no such opportunity for three years and a half, on account of the numerous occupations in which he was engaged. When they met, the holy prelate said: "We have a few hours free, Mother; which of us two shall be the first to speak?" "Myself," she answered, with some haste, "for certainly my soul greatly needs to pass under your eye." At this, the Saint, wishing to correct the anxiety she showed about speaking to him, with serious but gentle gravity rejoined: "Do you then still nourish desires, Mother? Have you yet a choice? I expected to find everything angelic. We will then put off speaking of you until we meet next, and for the present talk about the affairs of our Congregation." The good and holy Mother, without a word of objection, laid aside all that related to herself, though she was holding in her hands a list of things she had wished to speak of; and for four successive hours they discussed the interests of the Institute, and then parted.

St. Dorotheus, being sick and hearing raw eggs recommended as a remedy, after some time told his master of it, but, at the same time he asked him not to give them to him, because the thought of them was a distraction to him.

20 Do not weary thyself in vain; for thou wilt never succeed in possessing true spiritual sweetness and satisfaction, unless thou first deny all thy desires.

—ST. JOHN OF THE CROSS

The Abbot Ellem, as we read in the Lives of the Fathers, saw a honeycomb hanging from a rock and some fruit that had fallen from a tree, but he abstained from them. He then fell into a sleep, from which he was wakened by an angel, when he found himself by the side of a fountain surrounded by the freshest herbs, some of which he ate, and declared that he had never before tasted so great a delicacy.

Eriberto Rosveido relates of St. Macarius of Alexandria that, to overcome drowsiness, which annoyed him greatly, he never entered his cell for twenty consecutive days and nights; and when he was compelled by necessity to take some sleep, he took it with his head resting against a wall. He also says that being grievously assailed by sensual temptations, he remained for six months in a swamp, with his naked body exposed to the stings of the gnats, which in that region are as large as wasps; and when he came out he was so covered with swellings and sores that he looked like a leper. The Saint also once said of himself that he never took what he desired either of bread or water, but always took bread by weight, and water by measure; and that by mortifying his appetites in this manner, he merited so many graces from God, and advanced so much in the love and knowledge of Him, that he was wont to pass whole days and nights uninterruptedly in the sweetest contemplation.

21 Some pursue their own taste and satisfaction in spiritual things in preference to the way of perfection, which consists in denying their own wishes and tastes for the love of God. If such persons perform

some exercise through obedience, even though it suit their inclination, they soon lose the wish for it, and all devotion in it, because their only pleasure is in doing what their own will directs, which ordinarily would be better left undone. The Saints did not act thus.

—ST. JOHN OF THE CROSS

The blessed Seraphino, a Capuchin lay-brother, said to a friend that he would be glad to be in the house of Loretto or at Rome, that he might serve as many Masses as possible. When it was suggested that he might ask this favor of the Superiors, who would have readily granted it, he replied: "Oh, not that! Any holy desire would be profaned by one's own will, and every good intention ought to be subject to obedience, the only true directress of all holy thoughts."

St. Felix the Capuchin never did anything without the consent and express wish of his Superiors, though his employment of seeking alms would give occasion for some liberty. And when these Superiors, being well acquainted with his integrity and virtue, were accustomed to leave everything at his free disposal, he—instead of being pleased at this—found it rather a cause of sorrow and bitterness, as he saw that it hindered that entire subjection and dependence which he desired so much, and constrained him to do his own will, which he abhorred extremely.

22 If we do not pay great attention to mortifying our own will, there are many things that can take from us that holy liberty of spirit, which we seek in order

to be able to mount freely towards our Creator, without being always weighed down with earth and lead. Besides, in a soul that belongs to itself, and is attached to its own will, there can never be solid virtue.

—ST. TERESA

St. Mary Magdalen de' Pazzi said one day that she asked nothing of the Lord except that He would take her own will from her; for she knew that through the vivacity of her disposition, she did not advance so much as she desired in those virtues which render a soul most pleasing to the Lord. After saying this, she raised her eyes to Heaven and fell into an ecstasy, in which she was shown by God how much harm is done to souls, especially those of religious, when they are guided by their own will—which they once consecrated to God by vow. In the course of the ecstasy, she took her Superior by the hand and led her to the oratory, where she knelt and prayed the Virgin to enlighten her Superior also, that she might take pains to despoil her of her will; and after prostrating herself three times upon the ground, she recovered from her trance. She was so much in earnest in this matter that she once said she did not remember ever to have tried, either secretly or openly, to incline the will of her Superior to her own.

23 Make it your constant effort to mortify and trample underfoot your own will, to such a degree as not to satisfy it in anything, if it be possible. Be careful, therefore, to desire and rejoice that it may be often

crossed; and when you see anyone oppose it either in temporal or spiritual things, follow his will rather than your own, if only his be good, even though your own be better. For, contending with another, by lessening your humility, tranquillity, and peace, will always inflict upon you a loss greater than the advantage brought by any exercise of virtue performed through your own will, in opposition to another's.

—ST. VINCENT FERRER

St. Catherine of Genoa practiced this. She loved to submit her preference to that of others, in all things; and if a wish to pursue any course arose in her own mind, it was sufficient to make her avoid it.

When Father Thomas Sanchez would to go his Superiors to make a request, he used first to ask God, if it might be according to His pleasure, to move their hearts to refuse it.

24 Thou oughtest not to let a day pass in which thou hast not trampled upon thy will; and if such a thing should happen, consider that on that day thou hast not been a religious.

—ST. JOHN CLIMACUS

St. Mary Magdalen de' Pazzi was extremely fond of not doing her own will, and made a study of it, so that she regarded that day as utterly lost in which she had not in some manner broken and denied it.

25 Do you know what is the highest degree of abnegation of one's own will? It consists in allowing ourselves to be employed in such things as others choose, without ever making any resistance.

—ST. FRANCIS DE SALES

When St. Basil was visiting the monasteries of his diocese, he asked an abbot if he had no monk who showed more than the rest that he belonged to the number of the predestinate. The Abbot presented to him one who was very simple. The Saint ordered him to bring some water, and when he had quickly brought it, told him to sit down and wash his feet, which he did immediately, without showing the slightest reluctance. The following day, as he was going into the sacristy, he bade him approach the altar, as he wished to ordain him priest; and he received the priesthood without any resistance. From these things, the Saint considered him dead to his own will and his own judgment, and therefore worthy to be held as one of the predestinate. A little while after, some strangers entered his cell by night, took him, and led him unresistingly into their country, and there shut him up in a wretched hut, where he remained quietly, without a word to anyone. But a few days after, some men from another region took him out, still without a word on his part, and carried him away to the place from which they came, and there he stayed contentedly, as one dead to the world.

26 The greatest gift one can receive from God in this world is wisdom, power and will to conquer himself, by denying self-will.

—ST. FRANCIS OF ASSISI

121

The Abbot Pastor had the highest opinion of this exercise, and used to say that our own will is an iron wall that disunites and separates us from God.

St. Colette, of the Order of St. Francis, often said that she thought it a greater mortification to deny one's own judgment and will than to abandon all the riches in the world, and therefore she practiced it to the utmost of her ability.

St. Bernard also entertained the same sentiments, and said that all evils spring from a single root, which is self-will.

27 Take heed not to foster thy own judgment, for, without doubt, it will inebriate thee; as there is no difference between an intoxicated man and one full of his own opinion, and one is no more capable of reasoning than the other.

—ST. FRANCIS DE SALES

The blessed Alexander Sauli, a Corsican bishop, always asked others' advice in the affairs of his diocese, not trusting to his own opinion. He considered himself ignorant and totally unfit for the duties of his office, though he had been a famous professor of theology and director of St. Charles, and had even been called the ideal of bishops.

St. Francis de Paula, though endowed with the gift of prophecy, in doubtful cases always took counsel, even in the smallest matters, and with his own subjects.

28 Everyone has opinions of his own, nor is this opposed to virtue. It is only the love and attachment we have

to our own opinions, and the high value we set on them, which is infinitely contrary to our perfection. This is the last thing to be abandoned, and the cause why so few are perfect.

—ST. FRANCIS DE SALES

This Saint succeeded in abandoning this last thing, so that he was once able to write to a friend that he had no such attachment to his own opinion as to wish anyone ill who did not follow it, and that he did not claim that his sentiments should serve as a rule to anyone.

The venerable Father John Leonardi, founder of the Regular Clerics of the Mother of God, although he was gifted with the highest degree of prudence and had brought to a successful issue many affairs of great note, nevertheless depended so much upon the advice of his subjects, nay even of the young and inexperienced among them, that he never decided on anything of importance without first hearing their opinion and gaining their approval. Often he even followed their judgment in preference to his own.

Father Suarez, though he possessed much talent and learning, often gave his books even to his pupils to be revised; and if one of them disapproved of anything, he altered it with great readiness. St. Vincent Ferrer also had so little regard for his own opinion that he gave his writings to his companions to be reviewed, even though they were inferior to him in learning; and he did this not only when he was a student, but afterwards when a lecturer.

29 The true and only remedy for this evil is to make little account of what suggests itself to our mind. When asked

for our opinion, let us give it frankly, but with indifference as to whether or not it be accepted or approved, and let us be careful to follow the judgment of others rather than our own, whenever it can be lawfully done.

—ST. FRANCIS DE SALES

It is narrated in the Lives of the Fathers that when the Abbot John, who was very celebrated for holiness, was about to die, his disciples begged him to leave them some good advice for acquiring perfection. He replied to them: "This is all is I can tell you: I have labored not according to my own judgment, but according to the judgment of others; nor have I ever commanded another to do anything, without having first done it myself."

St. Jane Frances de Chantal had a mind at once lofty, and quick to reach the point at which it aimed. But for all this, when she was asked for advice in important affairs, she never trusted wholly to the knowledge she had acquired by long experience; but besides having recourse to God in prayer, she wished to consult with her spiritual fathers and with persons acquainted with those affairs. She would then express her own sentiments in this way: "This is my opinion, but take in addition the advice of someone wiser and more judicious."

St. Vincent Ferrer, in matters relating to the direction and government of that Order of which he was the head, as a general thing, followed the wishes and opinions of his companions rather than his own.

30 As to be holy is nothing else than to will what God wills, so to be wise is nothing else than to judge of

things as God judges of them. Now, who knows whether thy sentiments be always in conformity with those of God? How many times hast thou discovered thyself to be deceived in thy judgments and decisions?

—ST. VINCENT DE PAUL

St. Vincent de Paul excelled in this mortification of his own judgment. He was gifted with so much foresight that he was considered one of the most prudent men of his time; yet he always distrusted himself, and in all his affairs had recourse not only to God, but also to men. He would ask their opinion and follow it rather than his own, as far as justice and charity permitted, even though they had but little talent, or were his inferiors. When he was asked for advice, after raising his mind for a moment to God, he gave it, not setting things arbitrarily, but explaining his views with modesty, and leaving the person to decide for himself. His way of speaking was: "It seems that it might be done so." "There would be this reason, which seems to lead to such a conclusion," and if he was urged to decide absolutely, he would say: "It seems to me that it would be well or expedient to do such a thing, to act in such a way." Besides, he always preferred, and himself suggested, that the opinion of others also should be asked, and was pleased to have it followed rather than his own—not because he did not usually know best, on account of his long experience and the great light he received from God, but purely from love of submission and mortification, and because of his great love of humility, which made him esteem everyone better than himself. At a meeting of the Ladies of Charity, an

institution established by him to promote several pious objects, a matron present observed this trait. She informed the servant of God of it very gracefully, at the end of the conference, expressing to him her surprise that he would not support his views, which deserved to be preferred to all the others. "May it never be," he answered, "that my poor, weak judgment should prevail over that of others! I shall always rejoice to have God work what He will without me, a wretched sinner." He was so fully persuaded that resolutions taken with mature consideration and the advice of others were pleasing to the Lord, that he rejected as a temptation anything opposed to them which came into his mind. He was accustomed to say that when an affair had been recommended to God and consulted upon with others, we ought to be firm in what we undertake, and believe that God will not impute it to us for a fault, as we can offer this legitimate excuse: "O Lord, I recommended the affair to Thee, and took the advice of others, which was all that could be done to know Thy will."

31 The life of our flesh is the delight of sensuality; its death is to take from it all sensible delight. The life of our judgment and our will is to dispose of ourselves and what is ours, according to our own views and wishes; their death, then, is to submit ourselves in all things to the judgment and will of others. The life of the desire for esteem and respect is to be well thought of by everyone; its death, therefore, is to hide ourselves so as not to be known, by means of continual acts of humility and self-abasement. Until one succeeds in dying in this manner, he will never

be a servant of God, nor will God ever perfectly live
in him.

—ST. MARY MAGDALEN DE' PAZZI

With great frankness this beautiful soul expressed to others so lofty a sentiment, because she knew that it was precisely
in this way that, to her infinite profit, she had attained to the
death of her own flesh, her own judgment and will, and her own
human respect; of her own flesh, which she never ceased to treat
with the greatest harshness and rigor; of her own judgment and
will, which she always strove to keep subject to, and dependent
upon, others; of her human respect, by abhorring and avoiding
constantly every occasion of being honored and esteemed.

Another great example of this was the glorious St. Philip
Neri, who chastised his body severely with haircloth and the discipline. While quite young, he lived for years almost entirely
upon bread and water. When he became a priest, he added to
this spare diet only a little wine, some herbs or fruit, or perhaps an egg. He rarely took any other dairy products, or fish, or
meat, or soup, except on account of illness, or when at table with
strangers. As to his own judgment and will, he showed all possible earnestness in banishing all that could feed either, and in
trampling upon both to the extent of his power. But he rendered
himself especially admirable in combating and annihilating that
regard for human esteem, which is so dangerous an enemy to
corrupt humanity, and from which even the holiest souls are
not exempt. To subdue this common adversary, he made it his
object to be considered by all a vile and abject creature, and took
care, on every occasion, to give cause for such an idea of him.

With this intention, he would do things that, both at home and abroad, appeared like folly.

Many examples of this are recorded, of which we will mention a few. Once he began to jump and dance in front of a church, where there was a great concourse of people on account of a festival held there, and one in the crowd was heard to say: "Look at that old fool!" Again, meeting a water carrier in a busy street, he asked leave to drink from one of his casks; and when it was granted, he put his mouth to the opening and drank with much apparent satisfaction, while the carrier wondered that a man of his position should drink in that way in the presence of so many people. Another time, he drank in the same manner from the flask of St. Felix the Capuchin, in view of many. Being invited one day to dinner by Cardinal Alexandrino, he took with him one of his penitents, whom he told to bring him a handful of beans ready cooked, concealed under his mantle. When all were seated at the table, he had them brought out, for the sake of appearing ill-bred. But the Cardinal, who knew his virtues, instead of taking the matter ill and despising him, asked for some himself, and so did all the guests. Cardinal Gesualdo, who loved him tenderly, thought a coat of martin fur would be useful to him, on account of his advanced age and constant attendance in the confessional. He gave him one, exacting, at the same time, a promise that he would wear it. The Saint kept the promise, but made use of the occasion to cause himself to be laughed at, by wearing it all the time in public for a month, walking with a dignified air, and stopping now and then to look at it. For the same purpose, he went many times through Rome, accompanied by his penitents, carrying an immense bunch of

flowers. Once when he had had his beard shaved only on one side, he came out in public, leaping and rejoicing, as if it were a great victory.

At home he was continually doing such things. He often wore a pair of white slippers, with a little cap on his head, and a red vest, which came down to his knees, over his long cassock. In this costume he received whoever came to visit him, even if they were men of rank or great nobles. He kept in his room books of stories, jest books, and others of a similar sort, and when gentlemen came to see him, especially if they were of high rank, he would have one of them read, and listen to it with a great show of attention and pleasure. He did this in a marked manner when Pope Clement VIII sent him some Polish nobles, that they might gain fervor and edification from his discourse. When he was informed that they were coming, he immediately told one of his household to take one of these books and read it to him, not stopping till he should tell him. When the noblemen arrived, he said to them, without disturbing himself at all: "Please wait till we come to the end of this interesting story." While the reading went on, he showed great attention and pleasure, like a person who is listening to something important and profitable. Finally he stopped it and said to the visitors: "Have I not still some fine books? Was not that one worth listening to?" And so he went on, without uttering a word on spiritual subjects. The strangers remained for a time, exchanging glances with one another, and then went away astonished and annoyed. After they were gone, he had the book put away, saying, "We have done what was necessary." For it was precisely what he desired—that these distinguished strangers should have a low opinion of him.

APRIL

Patience

Whoever taketh not up his cross and followeth Me, is not worthy of Me.—MATT. 10:38

---

1   The Cross is the true gate through which to enter into the temple of holiness; and by any other way it is not possible to come into it. Therefore, we ought more than once to immolate our hearts to the love of Jesus, upon that same altar of the Cross on which He sacrificed His love for us.

Father Alvarez made this resolution: "I will consider all aridity, disquiet, and every trial which shall come to me in prayer as a martyrdom, and as such I will bear them with constancy." He pursued this course faithfully for sixteen years, after which he had so many consolations and celestial lights as were an abundant recompense for all the sufferings he had previously endured.

St. Teresa bore the greatest aridity for eighteen years, and then to what heights was she not exalted!

St. Bernard said of himself: "All those things that the world loves, such as pleasure, honors, praise, and riches, are to me crosses; and all things which the world counts as crosses, I seek and embrace with the greatest affection."

2   If you see that you have not yet suffered tribulations, consider it certain that you have not begun to be a true servant of God; for the Apostle says plainly that all who choose to live piously in Christ, shall suffer persecutions.

—ST. AUGUSTINE

St. Athanasius, St. Basil, St. John Chrysostom, St. Jerome, and St. Cyril were all charged with a thousand crimes, and in that way were greatly afflicted.

St. Romualdo was slanderously accused by one of his monks of the commission of a shameful crime, was condemned in a public assembly to be burnt at the stake as a punishment, and in the meantime was suspended from his function as a priest. But, though he was then a centenarian, he bore all with the greatest tranquillity.

St. Francis Xavier was grieved when he saw everything going on successfully with him in Lisbon; and if such favorable circumstances had continued to exist, he would have thought that he was not serving God well.

3   By working out our salvation through sufferings, the Son of God has wished to teach us that there is

nothing in us so fitted to glorify God and to sanctify our souls as suffering. Yes, yes, to suffer for love of the Lord is the way of truth! Therefore, the more one can suffer, the more let him suffer, for he will be the most fortunate of all; and whoever does not resolve upon this, will never make much progress.

—ST. TERESA

St. Mary Magdalen de' Pazzi was so much enamored of suffering that she said: "I do not desire to die soon, because in Heaven there is nothing to suffer; but I desire to live a long time, because I wish to suffer long for love of my Spouse. Nor would I have a brief martyrdom only, but an accumulation of pains, calumnies, misfortunes, and all adversities that can possibly happen to me." And when she went through a long and painful illness this not only failed to extinguish in her this great thirst for suffering, but after tasting it in such a way, she longed for it the more, so that while the Superior endeavored to lessen her hardships for the preservation of her health, she was at the same time seeking in every way to invent new kinds of sufferings that no one would perceive. It happened one day, in the course of her last illness, that having received a marked affront, she not only bore it patiently, but showed signs of particular friendship for the offender. When one of the Sisters manifested astonishment, she told her that she was glad she had not died before it occurred, that she might not lose such an excellent opportunity for suffering.

4 The way is narrow. Whoever expects to walk in it with ease must go detached from all things, leaning on the

staff of the Cross; that is firmly resolving to be willing
to suffer in all things for love of God.

—ST. JOHN OF THE CROSS

Taulerus relates that he knew a great servant of God who had
many visions and revelations, and was acquainted with the inter-
pretations of Scripture and the secrets of hearts. But becoming
afraid that gifts of one sort might prove a hindrance to favors of
another kind, and so prevent him from being loved by God, he
earnestly besought the Lord to be pleased to take away from him
every consolation; and he was heard. For five years in succession,
he never had the slightest spiritual joy nor any celestial inspiration
or illumination, but always led a life full of afflictions, temptations
and spiritual aridity. Finally, the Lord was moved with pity at so
much suffering, and one day sent two angels to console him a little. But he, contented in his sorrows, refused this consolation, and
turning his heart to God said: "O Lord, I do not desire any pleasure in this world, nor do I wish that anyone should enter my heart
save Thyself, O my Beloved! for it is enough consolation for me
if Thy holy will be done in me." This beautiful act of detachment
pleased God so much that the Eternal Father proclaimed him His
beloved child, in these words: *Tu es filius Meus in quo Mihi bene
complacui*—Thou art My son, in whom I am well pleased.

5 If anyone, O Lord does Thee a service, Thou repayest
him by some trial. Oh, what an inestimable reward is
this for those who truly love Thee, if it might be given
them to know its value!

—ST. TERESA

When the venerable Marco di Palfox saw that after he had done a good work, some tribulation, reproach, or calumny came upon him, he considered this as a special favor from the Lord; "For," he said, "as I receive no reward in this world, it is a sign that God means to reward me fully in Heaven."

The Lord once appeared to the blessed Clara di Montefalco and offered her for a gift a cross which hung from His neck. The saint received the present with the greatest consolation; and there was then impressed upon her heart an image of the crucifix, of the size of a finger. She preserved this so well that, in her last agony, when one of the nuns was looking for a cross upon the bed, she said to her, "Take my heart, for you will find the crucifix there." In fact, it was found there after her death.

6 O ye souls who wish to go on with so much safety and consolation, if you knew how pleasing to God is suffering, and how much it helps in acquiring other good things, you would never seek consolation in anything; but you would rather look upon it as a great happiness to bear the Cross after the Lord.

—ST. JOHN OF THE CROSS

Blessed William the Abbot saw, one night in a dream, some angels who were weaving a crown of marvellous richness and beauty; and when he asked them for whom they were making it, they said that it was for him, and would be finished when he had suffered enough.

St. Gertrude once prayed the Lord, at the time of the Carnival, to show her some special service pleasing to Him that she

might perform on those three days, on which He had to suffer so many insults from the world. The Lord made her this reply: "My daughter, you will never be able to do Me a greater service at any time than bearing patiently, in honor of My Passion, whatever tribulation may come to you, whether it be interior or exterior, always forcing yourself to do all those things that are most contrary to your desires."

The Lord appeared one day to St. Teresa and addressed her thus: "Know that those souls are most pleasing to My Heavenly Father, that are tried by the very greatest afflictions and sufferings!" From that time, the Saint conceived such a love for suffering that she found no consolation but in bearing it; and when she was without any trouble, she was disquieted, and even said that she would not have exchanged her trials for all the treasures in the world; and she often had upon her lips those beautiful words, "To suffer, or to die." After her death, she appeared to one of the Sisters, and revealed to her that she was rewarded in Heaven for nothing so much as for the contradiction she had suffered in life, and that if she could wish to return to earth for any reason, the only one would be that she might suffer something.

7 One ounce of the Cross is worth more than a million pounds of prayer. One day of crucifixion is worth more than a hundred years of all other exercises. It is worth more to remain a moment upon the Cross, than to taste the delights of Paradise.

—VEN. SISTER MARIA VITTORIA ANGELINI

St. Bridget once received and bore patiently a succession of trials from various persons. One of them made an insulting remark to her; another praised her in her presence, but complained of her in her absence; another calumniated her; another spoke ill of a servant of God, in her presence, to her great displeasure; one did her a grievous wrong, and she blessed her; one caused her a loss, and she prayed for her; and a seventh gave her false information of the death of her son, which she received with tranquillity and resignation. After all this, St. Agnes the Martyr appeared to her, bringing in her hand a most beautiful crown adorned with seven precious stones, telling her that they had been placed there by these seven persons. Then she put it upon her head and disappeared. How could so much have been gained by any other exercise?

The Blessed Angela di Foligno, when asked how she was able to receive and endure sufferings with so much cheerfulness, replied: "Believe me, the grandeur and value of sufferings are not known to us. For, if we knew the worth of our trials, they would become for us objects of plunder, and we should go about trying to snatch from one another opportunities to suffer."

8 One "Thanks be to God," or one "Blessed be God," in adversity, is worth more than a thousand thanksgivings in prosperity.

—FATHER M. D'AVILA

When St. Francis was suffering much bodily pain in illness, one of his monks told him that he would pray to God to grant

him some relief. The Saint reproved him, and bowing his head to the ground, said: "O Lord, I give Thee thanks for this pain which I am suffering, and I pray Thee to be pleased to increase it. What can or should be more acceptable to me than this, that Thou shouldst afflict me without mercy, for this is the very thing that I desire above all."

9 If the Lord should give you power to raise the dead, He would give much less than He does when He bestows suffering. By miracles you would make yourself debtor to Him, while by suffering He may become debtor to you. And even if sufferings had no other reward than being able to bear something for that God who loves you, is not this a great reward and a sufficient remuneration? Whoever loves, understands what I say.

—ST. JOHN CHRYSOSTOM

This Saint set so high a value on suffering, that he even said: "I venerate St. Paul not so much for having been raised to the third heaven, as for the imprisonment he suffered. And so, if I were asked whether I would be placed in Heaven among the angels, or in prison with Paul, I would prefer the latter. And if it were left to my choice whether I should be Peter in chains, or the angels that released him, I would certainly rather be the first than the second."

St. Louis the King, when conversing with the King of England about the slavery he endured in Turkey, in which he suffered many trials, expressed himself in this manner: "I thank God for the ill success of that war, and I rejoice more at the

patience which the Lord granted me at that time, than if I had subjugated the country."

The Lord once appeared to the Blessed Baptista Verrani, and said to her: "Believe, My daughter, that I have shown you greater love in sending you afflictions, than in lavishing upon you every mark of tenderness. In what could I show My love more than in seeking for you what I chose for Myself? Know that to keep from sin is a great good, to perform good works a greater, but the greatest of all is to suffer."

10 It ought to be considered a great misfortune, not only for individuals, but also for Houses and Congregations, to have everything in conformity with their wishes; to go on quietly, and to suffer nothing for the love of God. Yes, consider it certain that a person or a Congregation that does not suffer and is applauded by all the world is near a fall.

—ST. VINCENT DE PAUL

How fully St. Vincent was persuaded of this truth, he showed by the manner in which he informed his disciples of a considerable loss which had befallen the house. "As I had been considering," he said, "for a long time how happily the affairs of the Congregation were going on, and how well everything succeeded, I began to be much afraid of this calm, for I knew that God is accustomed to try His servants. But blessed be the Divine Goodness, which has designed to visit us with a very considerable loss."

A holy old man who was very often sick was much grieved at passing a whole year without an illness, saying that God must have abandoned him, as He had ceased to visit him.

Sts. Francis and Andrew Avellino entertained the same sentiments. They thought on any day when they suffered nothing for the love of God, that He had forgotten and abandoned them.

One night when Father Avila was sick, his pain increased excessively after the candle went out and the attendants had gone to sleep. He was unwilling to awake them, but after a while, overcome by the sharpness of the pain, he prayed the Lord to be pleased to deliver him from such agony. He then fell asleep, and on awaking, found himself free from pain. Whereupon, he said to one of his disciples, "What a severe blow the Lord has dealt me this night!" By this he meant that in hearing his prayer, God had taken from him the occasion of suffering and of meriting.

11 We have never so much cause for consolation, as when we find ourselves oppressed by sufferings and trials; for these make us like Christ our Lord, and this resemblance is the true mark of our predestination.
—ST. VINCENT DE PAUL

No one has understood this great truth so well as St. Andrew the Apostle. At first sight of the cross on which he was to be crucified, he was filled with joy, and broke forth into this exclamation: "O cross so much desired, so much loved, and so much sought by me! behold how I come to thee full of security and joy! Do thou separate me from men, and restore me to my

Master, so that by thy means He may receive me, who by thy means redeemed me."

The Lord once said to St. Gertrude: "The more you are tried, and the more your way of life is disapproved without any fault of your own, the dearer you will be to Me, on account of the increased resemblance to Me which you will thus attain; for anyone who greatly resembles a king, is usually very dear to him; and I lived in constant suffering, and was opposed in all I did."

When St. Matilda was suffering from a severe illness, Jesus Christ came to her and told her that when He beheld persons grievously afflicted and tormented, He embraced them with His left arm, to draw them very near His heart.

12 There is no more evident sign that anyone is a saint and of the number of the elect, than to see him leading a good life and at the same time a prey to desolation, suffering, and trials.

—ST. ALOYSIUS GONZAGA

Because St. Ignatius Loyola was perfect and dear to God, persecutions came upon him to such an extent that it would often happen that while he was at a distance, his companions lived in great tranquillity, and immediately upon his return, some trial would fall upon the house.

St. Teresa once received some money from a merchant who recommended himself to her prayers. A little while after, she said to him: "I have prayed for you, and it has been revealed to me that your name is written in the Book of Life; and as a token of this, nothing in future will go on prosperously with

you." And this came to pass exactly; for, within a short time, all his ships were lost, and he became bankrupt. When his friends heard of these disasters, they provided him with another ship, which was also soon wrecked. Then, of his own accord, he entered the debtors' prison. But his creditors, knowing how good he was, would not harm him, and set him free. Having thus become poor, he ended his life like a saint, content with God alone.

13 If God causes you to suffer much, it is a sign that He has great designs for you, and that He certainly intends to make you a saint. And if you wish to become a great saint, entreat Him yourself to give you much opportunity for suffering; for there is no wood better to kindle the fire of holy love than the wood of the cross, which Christ used for His own great sacrifice of boundless charity.

—ST. IGNATIUS LOYOLA

Joseph suffered great afflictions and trials from his brethren, and these formed precisely the way by which the Lord led him to his great exaltation.

St. Teresa, who was formed for so lofty a destiny, suffered incredible trials from all sorts of people, even from the good and spiritual. Many considered her deluded by the devil. Many ridiculed her prayers and revelations. Some wished to exorcise her as possessed. Others accused her to the Holy Office; and she suffered, besides, much opposition and trouble from her Superiors, in regard to the monasteries which she founded.

14 There is no better test to distinguish the chaff from the grain, in the Church of God, than the manner in which sufferings, contradiction, and contempt are borne. Whoever remains unmoved under these, is grain. Whoever rises against them is chaff; and the lighter and more worthless he is, the higher he rises—that is, the more he is agitated, and the more proudly he replies.

—ST. AUGUSTINE

A person of high rank presented himself to St. Francis de Sales to ask a benefice for an ecclesiastic who enjoyed his patronage. The Saint replied that as to conferring benefices he had tied his own hands, for he had decided that they should be given only after a competitive examination; but that he would not forget his recommendation, if this priest would offer himself to be examined with the others. The gentleman, who was quick-tempered, believing this to be only a pretext for refusal, accused him of duplicity and hypocrisy, and even threatened him. When the Saint perceived that gentle words did no good, he entreated him not to object at least to a private examination; and, as he was still dissatisfied, "Then," said St. Francis, "you wish that I should entrust to him a portion of my charge with my eyes closed? Consider whether that is just!" At this, the gentleman began to raise his voice angrily, and to make all kinds of insulting remarks to the holy bishop, who bore all in unbroken silence.

An acquaintance of his, who was present, asked him after the scene was over how he had been able to endure such insults without showing the least resentment. "Do not be astonished

at this," said the Saint, "for it was not he that spoke, but his anger. Outside of this he is one of my dearest friends, and you will see after a while that my silence will increase his attachment for me." "But did you not feel any resentment at all?" pursued the other. "I turned my thoughts in another direction," was the answer, "setting myself to consider the good qualities of this person, whose friendship I had previously so much enjoyed." The gentleman afterwards came and asked pardon, even with tears, and they became firmer friends than ever before.

One day, as St. Felix the Capuchin was going through the street in Rome with a flask of wine on his back, he met a gentleman on a spirited horse, which he spurred so furiously that it trampled upon one foot of the servant of God, who fell to the ground. The flask was broken, and the wine ran out upon the pavement, mingled with the blood which flowed freely from the wound. All the bystanders, affrighted at the accident, expressed their pity for the Saint. He alone retained his usual serenity of countenance, and looking at the gentleman with a mild glance, asked his pardon for his imprudence and rudeness in obstructing his path. The rider, however, instead of appreciating so much virtue, was angry, and with a haughty look and without a word of answer, spurred his horse and rode proudly away. Brother Felix, being assisted to rise by those who had gathered around, went back to his monastery as best he might. As he was not able to walk quickly for some time, on account of the injury to his foot, he used to say to himself: "Get on, you beast of an ass! what are you loitering for? You are so slow and spiritless that you will deserve the stick!" Then turning his heart to God, he would break forth into devout thanksgivings for His infinite

goodness. But after the gentleman had recollected himself a little and reflected upon the wrong he had done by his scornful treatment of an innocent and holy religious, he went the next day to the monastery and falling on his knees before the Saint, begged pardon for the proud and cruel treatment he had given him. The servant of God forgave him with so much cordiality and courtesy, that he resolved to change his habits and his whole life.

This beautiful truth was known even to pagan philosophers. St. Basil relates of Socrates, that when he was one day struck in the face, in the public square, by one of the rabble, he not only showed no anger at such an insult but, with tranquil mind and serene countenance, stood quite still until his face was livid with blows. Still more remarkable is this anecdote of Epictetus. One day his master, who had a violent temper, gave him a blow on one leg. He said to him coolly, that he had better take care not to break it; and when, by repeated blows, his master actually broke the bone, Epictetus added, without any emotion: "Did I not tell you that you were running a risk of breaking it?"

15 It is certain that the true spirit is inclined rather to afflictions, aridity, disgust, and trials, than to sweet and pleasing communications; for it knows that the former is that following of Christ and that denial of self so much inculcated by the Lord.

—ST. JOHN OF THE CROSS

The Lord appeared to St. Catherine with two crowns in His hand, one of gold, the other of thorns, and told her to choose whichever she preferred. She chose the second. From

that time she conceived so great a love for afflictions and trials, that she said: "There is nothing that consoles me so much, and gives me so much comfort, as afflictions and crosses, and it seems to me that if I had not this support from time to time I should live the most wretched life in the world; and if God should give me my choice whether to go now into Paradise or to remain a little longer here to suffer, I should choose the latter rather than the former, for I know how much glory is increased by sufferings."

The blessed Maria d'Ognes used to sleep with the ground for her bed, a stone for her pillow, and haircloth for a blanket. Being one day tried beyond measure by the pains of paralysis, she uttered such mournful sighs that a holy man prayed to God for her, and she was relieved from her illness. But when she was sensible of the cure, she sent to ask the saint not to pray for her any more, saying that she valued sickness much more than health.

16 Those who have arrived at perfection, and especially true contemplatives, do not ask the Lord to free them from trials and temptations. They rather desire and value them as worldlings value gold and jewels, for they know that these are to make them rich.

—ST. TERESA

St. Catherine of Genoa once said in the midst of extreme pain and severe torture: "O Lord! it is thirty-six years since Thou first gavest me spiritual light, and ever since, I have desired nothing but sufferings, interior and exterior."

The Venerable Anna Maria of St. Joseph, a Discalced Carmelite and a person of no ordinary piety, exercised herself continually in the sharpest penances and austerities. When the others tried to turn her away from these practices, she replied: "No, I will never cease until the Lord satiates me with His griefs and reproaches." She often said, too, that she wished for neither relics, nor rosary, nor a cell, nor anything but a cross upon which to crucify herself.

St. Francis Xavier, when he had a cross, used to make this prayer: "O Lord, do not take it away from me, unless to give me a greater."

17 Kiss frequently the crosses which the Lord sends you, and with all your heart, without regarding of what sort they may be; for the more vile and mean they are, the more they deserve their name. The merit of crosses does not consist in their weight, but in the manner in which they are borne. It may show much greater virtue to bear a cross of straw than a very hard and heavy one, because the light ones are also the most hidden and contemned, and therefore least comfortable to our inclination, which always seeks what is showy.

—ST. FRANCIS DE SALES

In the many long and painful journeys made by this Saint, he was never heard to complain of cold, or wind, or the heat of the sun or the quality of his food; but he took all things peacefully from the hand of God, and was particularly pleased with

the worst and most inconvenient articles—and when he could, he always chose them for himself.

Mention is made in the Chronicles of St. Dominic of a novice of that Order who died in the monastery of Argentina and who opened his eyes unexpectedly, while the religious were saying the last prayers for his soul, and said: "Listen, dearest Brothers: I am like one who goes to a fair, and buys a great deal for a little money. Behold, I am receiving the Kingdom of Heaven for a few trials, and I do not see how I deserve it." Having spoken thus, he reposed in the Lord.

St. John Climacus says that he found in a monastery a young monk who received little penances from the Superior for trifling faults, and haughty and discourteous treatment from almost all the rest. The Saint showed sympathy for him, and wished to console him; but the good youth said: "Father, do not give yourself any trouble. They treat me in this way, not because they have bad dispositions and little charity, but the Lord permits it to exercise me in patience, which is necessary to show whether I am serving God truly. Certainly I have no cause to complain, for even gold is not made perfect without being tried." Two years after, added the holy Abbot, this youth passed to a better life, saying to his Brothers before he expired: "I render thanks to Jesus Christ and to you, Fathers, and I testify that through having been tried by you to my profit and advancement, I have lived free from the snares of the devil, and now depart in peace."

In the Lives of the Fathers, a story is told of a holy monk who every night gave his disciple an instruction, and afterwards sent him to rest. Now, one evening while giving it, the old man fell asleep, and the good novice, while waiting for him to awake,

was much tempted to impatience and to go away to sleep. He conquered himself, however, seven times, with great earnestness and fervor. At midnight, the old man awoke and dismissed him. While saying his final prayers, the old Father had a vision of an angel, who showed him a most beautiful throne with seven crowns above it. In answer to his questions, the angel said that they were for his disciple, who had gained them that night by his victory over seven temptations. When his disciples told him all in the morning, he was struck with wonder to see how bountifully God recompenses all our good actions.

18 If we could but know what a precious treasure lies concealed in infirmities, we would receive them with as much joy as we would the greatest benefits, and we would bear them without complaint or any sign of annoyance.

—ST. VINCENT DE PAUL

This Saint was tried by many long and most painful infirmities, which often deprived him of the use of his limbs, and left him no rest by day or night. He bore them all with unalterable tranquillity, and conversed with the same affability and serenity of countenance that he had when he was well. A word of complaint never escaped from his lips, but he praised and thanked God constantly for sending to him these sufferings, and looked on them as special favors. The most he did when the pain was at its worst, was to turn to the crucifix and animate himself to patience by devout interior aspirations. If he ever happened to speak of his sufferings, he mentioned them as a thing of no

account, saying that he suffered little in comparison with what he deserved, or with what Christ suffered for love of us. One of his household was one day applying a dressing to his limbs, which were diseased for forty years, when moved with compassion at seeing them so swollen and ulcerated, he exclaimed, "Alas, how grievous are your sufferings!" But the saint quickly replied: "How can you apply the word *grievous* to the work of God, and His divine arrangement in causing a miserable sinner to suffer? May God pardon you for what you have just said! This is not the way to speak in the school of Christ! Is it not right that the guilty should suffer and be chastised? And cannot the Lord do with us whatever pleases Him?"

Once writing of his sufferings to an intimate friend, he said: "I did not wish to let you know of my sickness, fearing it would make you sad. But God is good! How long shall we be so weak that we shall not have courage to reveal to one another the graces and favors God bestows on us in visiting us with sickness? May it please His divine goodness to give us a little more spirit, that we may find our satisfaction in His!" Through all his illnesses he never ceased to take an interest in the affairs of the house and of the whole Congregation. He received persons of all sorts, whether belonging to his Order or not, if they came to him on business or for other reasons, and always with such a smiling face and with so much amiability and serenity that if they had not known his state of health from others, they would have considered him well. Neither did such great infirmities cause him to change his usual mode of life. Up to his death he continued to sleep on straw, and to take the common food. When the physicians and some persons of rank tried to persuade him to take

delicacies, he did so once or twice to please them, but immediately returned to what he generally ate, under the pretext that his stomach would not bear other food.

When St. Felix the Capuchin was suffering severely from colic, he was asked, by the doctor, how he felt, and answered: "The wicked ass of a body would be glad to escape the stick, but it must stand and receive the blow." When he was urged to have recourse to the divine aid, by invoking the most holy name of Jesus, from whom he might expect relief—"What do you say?" cried the Saint; "to what do you advise me? Never! These are not pains, but celestial flowers which Paradise produces, and the Lord shares among His children." Then he began to praise and bless the Divine Goodness which dealt thus with him.

19 There are some sick persons who grieve and lament not so much for their own troubles, as for what they cause to those around them, and because they cannot occupy themselves in good works, and especially in prayer, as they did when they were well. In this they deceive themselves greatly, for as to the trouble given to others, whoever is truly patient wishes for all that God wishes, and in the manner and with the inconveniences that He wishes; as to works, one day of suffering borne with resignation is worth more than a month of great labors; and as to prayer, which is better: to remain upon the Cross with Christ, or to stay at the foot of it and contemplate His sufferings? Besides, to offer to the Lord His own weakness, to remember for whom it was suffered, and

to conform ourselves to His holy will, is certainly a
very excellent prayer.

—ST. FRANCIS DE SALES

This Saint bore well not only the afflictions and trials which
came to him, but also their consequences, such as the inconvenience which his illnesses caused those who waited on him or
lived with him. And in all other things it was the same.

Father Alvarez saw, in a trance, the great glory which God
had prepared for a nun who was tried by a most grievous illness,
which she bore with all possible patience. He said that she had
merited more in eight months of sickness than some healthy
and devout persons in many years.

St. Aldegonda, having been forewarned of the day of her
death, prayed the Lord to send her first some painful disease,
that purified by it, she might fly the more lightly to Heaven. She
was heard, for there came to her an acute fever with very sharp
pain. In this state she rejoiced, considering the fever a refresh-
ing coolness; the pain, consolation; and the sweats, a soothing
bath by which she should be thoroughly purified for her flight
to Heaven.

While St. Francis was suffering very acute pain in his eyes,
he gave thanks constantly to God, and prayed to Him for perseverance in His service. One day the Lord said to him: "Rejoice,
Francis, for the treasure of eternal life is in store for you, and
these pains are a pledge of it."

When St. Vincent de Paul was seriously ill, he used to practice a method of prayer which was easily and pleasant, and at the
same time profitable. It was to remain quietly in the presence

of God, without forcibly applying his intellect to any consider-ations, only exciting his soul to frequent acts of resignation to the will of God, confidence, love, or thanksgiving.

20 Observe that we gain more in a single day by trials which come to us from God and our neighbor, than we would in ten years by penances and other exer-cises, which we take up of ourselves.

—ST. TERESA

St. Lionina, after suffering for thirty-eight years from a cruel disease, longed to endure yet greater pains, and to finish her course as a martyr. While she was burning with this desire, she was uplifted in an ecstasy, and saw a most beautiful crown, still unfinished, which she was told was in preparation for her. Eager to have it completed, she prayed the Lord to increase her tor-ments, and He sent two soldiers, who tortured her with blows and insults. After this, an angel appeared to her with a crown in his hand, quite finished, and told her that these last trials had placed in it the jewels that were previously wanting.

An angel appeared one day to the blessed Henry Suso, and offered him a shield, a lance, and spurs, saying: "Hitherto you have fought among the infantry, and now you will join the cavalry; hitherto you have practiced mortifications of your own choice, now you shall be mortified by the scourge of evil tongues; hitherto you have enjoyed milk from the breast of Christ, now you shall be inebriated with His gall; hitherto you have been pleasing to men, now they will rise against you." The following day, as the servant of God was meditating upon this vision, he

felt impelled to go to the window, and on looking out, he saw a goat in the courtyard with a rag in its mouth, which it was pulling and tearing. Then he heard a voice which said: "Thus are you to be torn by the mouths of others." He, thereupon, went downstairs and picked up the rag, which he preserved as a precious pledge of his cross.

21 He has not true patience who is willing to suffer only what he pleases, and from whom he pleases. The truly patient man does not regard the length nor the kind of his sufferings, not yet the person who makes him suffer—whether he be a superior, an equal, or an inferior; whether he be a holy man or ill-disposed and dishonorable. His only aim is to suffer.

—THOMAS À KEMPIS

We are told, in the Lives of the Fathers, of a young monk who dwelt with an aged monk who went every morning to the city to sell the articles which they had both made on the preceding day, and who spent all they brought upon wine for himself, bringing home only a bit of bread for the youth. The young man bore this way of life for three years; but at last, finding himself in rags and dying of hunger, he began to consider whether it would not be well to leave such a companion and go elsewhere. Then an angel appeared to him and said: "Have patience a little longer, for tomorrow you shall be with me in Paradise." He told this vision to the old man, who did not believe it. But the following day, as they were discussing the matter, the holy youth peacefully

expired, and the old man was converted and mourned for his previous life.

22 The Lord sends us tribulation and infirmities to give us the means of paying the immense debts we have contracted with Him. Therefore, those who have good sense receive them joyfully, for they think more of the good which they may derive from them than of the pain which they experience on account of them.

—ST. VINCENT FERRER

This Saint unfolded this same sentiment more fully in a sermon which contained this pleasing parable: There was a king who had in prison two men who both owed him large sums of money. Seeing that they were unable to pay because they possessed nothing, he threw down a purse full of money upon each of them with so much force that they both felt the pain. One, angry at the blow, showed his impatience without making any account of the purse; but the other, not regarding the pain, recognized the favor done him, and taking the purse, gave thanks to the king and paid his debt with the money. "Now, precisely the same thing happens with us," added the Saint. "We all owe heavy debts to God for the many benefits we have received from Him, and for the many sins we have committed against Him, nor have we anything of our own to pay them. Therefore, moved by pity for us, He sends us the gold of patience in the purse of tribulations, that we may use it to pay our debts. Whoever will not do this only increases his debts and renders himself, at the same time, more displeasing to God."

The example of the two thieves crucified with Christ confirms this truth. By his patience, one paid his debts and gained Paradise; while the other, by his impatience, made himself more than ever a debtor, and obtained for himself eternal pains.

Cesairus tells of a Cistercian monk who appeared to his Abbot in great glory the night after his death, and said to him: "Know, my Father, that the sharp pains and tortures of my illness supplied for me the place of Purgatory by anticipation; and therefore I rose directly from earth to Heaven."

23 Do not be vexed at the contradictions you meet in ordinary intercourse, for they give an opportunity to practice the most precious and amiable virtues, which Our Lord has recommended to us. Believe me that true virtue is no more reared in outward repose, than good fish in the stagnant water of a swamp. How shall we prove our love for God, who has suffered so much for us, if not among contradictions and repugnances?

—ST. FRANCIS DE SALES

The blessed Seraphino the Capuchin was once in company with his Superiors and a young secular, who, seeing him so simple, humble, and imperturbable, took a fancy to tyrannize over him and to go so far as to slight, insult, and even strike him. Brother Seraphino, unmoved by all these insults, only said, with perfect amiability: "Ah, my little saint! my little saint!" (It was by this name that he would call those who insulted him.) "Let us do good in the service of God."

One of the Fathers of the Desert used to imagine Jesus Christ standing by his side in his tribulations, and saying to him: "You are My brother, and are you not ashamed to make any difficulty about suffering this, when you know how much I have suffered for you?"

24 If any house should be found where there was no monk who was troublesome and of a bad disposition, it would be well to look for one, and to pay him at a high rate for the great good that results from this evil when judiciously managed.

—ST. BERNARD

When St. Philip Neri was living at San Girolamo, he had a great concourse of penitents. The sacristans of the church, annoyed by this, took a dislike to him, and did him all the ill-turns they could. Sometimes when he was going to say Mass, they locked the door in his face; or they would not give him the sacred vestments, or only cheap and torn ones, with many rude and insulting remarks. Sometimes they took from his hands the missal and chalice, or hid them, or compelled him to take off his vestments when he already had them on. Again, they would make him leave one altar and go to another, or perhaps back to the sacristy—and all to irritate him and induce him to leave the place. But the holy man, without ever complaining of the bad treatment he received, or giving any sign of annoyance, went on concealing his feelings and praying for these men, treating them also with charity and respect, and doing them any services that he could. Though

he was often urged by his friends to go and live elsewhere, he would not do it, "because," said he, "I do not wish to fly from the cross which God sends me." This lasted for some years. Finally, seeing that he accomplished nothing by his charity and humility and that his enemies, instead of being softened, rather increased in pertinacity, he had recourse to God for some relief; and one day in particular, fixing his eyes upon a crucifix, he said: "O my good Jesus! why dost Thou not hear me? For so long a time, and with so much earnestness, I have asked for patience; why hast Thou not listened to me?" Then he heard a voice in his heart, which said: "Dost thou not ask Me for patience? I will give it to thee, but it is by this means that I wish thee to gain it." Thence forward, he bore all with greater cheerfulness, and with the most perfect content, to such a degree that he no longer felt any of their injuries, but greatly desired them; and when he was ill-treated by these men or by others, he made no account of it and did not speak of it, nor allow it to be spoken of. If he ever heard any evil said of those who had offended him, he promptly excused them, praised them, and, if it was suitable, visited and protected them. On this account, he acquired such a liking for the place that for thirty years he would never leave it. He could not be induced to abandon his beloved place of suffering, even when he had built the new Oratory of the new church, and many of his sons had gone to live there. Though they tried to prove to him the suitableness and the obligation of living with them as he was their founder and head, all their entreaties and prayers were of no avail until, finally, the authority of the Pope was interposed to give them success.

25 In this life there is no Purgatory, but either Paradise or Hell. He who bears tribulations with patience, has Paradise; he who does not, Hell.

—ST. PHILIP NERI

A prisoner at the bar once called for a Jesuit Father, and said to him: "Father, I wish you to know that I, too, was once of your Order. For some time, I was exact in the observance of the Rules; I lived content, and did everything with ease and pleasure. Then I began, little by little, to relax, till after a time I found so much difficulty and trouble in every trifle, that it seemed best to leave the Order. Finally, you see where my sins have brought me. I have told you this that my example might be of use to others."

When St. Francis de Sales was ill, it was a matter of great edification to notice how simply he told his symptoms, without exaggeration or complaint, how patiently and uncomplainingly he bore them and how he received all remedies without opposition. Though he sometimes suffered most cruel pains in his inferior nature, he always preserved an unalterable serenity of brow and eye, as if he were not suffering at all. Thus he came to enjoy Paradise even while suffering, unlike so many others, who, at every trifling pain, seem impatient and inconsolable.

26 Learn, my Sisters, to suffer something for the love of God, without letting everyone know it.

—ST. TERESA

On a Good Friday, the venerable Father Daponte asked Our Lord the favor of giving him a share in His sufferings. He

answered by sending him fearful pains for the rest of his life, which he received with the greatest possible joy. Once being asked how he felt, he replied: "Oh, how well God chastises this sinner! I tell you that except my head, no part of my body is without its own particular pain." A little while after, he repented of having said so much, and made a vow never to reveal his sufferings to anyone, when he could conceal them without displeasing God.

St. Philip Neri, in his illnesses, which were long, severe, and frequent, was seen always with a cheerful countenance and a serene brow; he never gave any sign of pain, however great it might be, nor talked about his sickness, except to the physicians.

For twenty-eight years St. Clare suffered grievous infirmities, and in all that time was never heard to complain of her sufferings, but instead, she thanked God for them.

It is related in the Lives of the Fathers that when the Abbot Stephen was sick, his companions made for him a fried cake but used, by mistake, a kind of oil which was very bitter. The holy Abbot perceived this on tasting it, but ate a little, without saying anything. When another was made in the same way, the Abbot tasted that also, and left it without a word. This would have continued longer, if his companion, wishing to tempt him to eat by example, had not taken a piece himself. When he perceived how bitter it was, he was very much grieved; but the Abbot said: "Do not trouble yourself about it, my son, for if God had not willed that you should mistake one kind of oil for another, you would not have done it."

St. Mary Magdalen de' Pazzi invented a great and secret mortification, which she afterwards practiced for the rest of

her life. When she noticed that her Superiors, through regard for her health, tried to give her such food as she liked best, she showed a preference for what was disagreeable and unpleasant to her taste, and made it appear that those things which she really desired were objects of aversion, and would make her ill. And so it happened that what she disliked was often given her, and what would have suited her taste was forbidden. In reward for this, she enjoyed imperturbable peace of soul and the constant presence of God.

27 Whoever aspires to perfection must beware of saying, "I was right. They did that to me without reason." If you are not willing to bear any cross which is not given you according to reason, perfection is not for you.

—ST. TERESA

When Brother Egidius of Tarentum, a Franciscan lay-brother, was roughly treated by his Superiors or companions or called a useless and unprofitable servant, he never excused himself, but said with a smile, "Give it to Brother Ass, for he deserves much worse!" On account of the miracles he performed in Tarentum, crowds of people gathered about him, to the no small inconvenience of the other Brothers, so that he was sent away to the monastery in Bari. But scarcely had he arrived when multitudes came to the monastery to see him and receive aid from him; and the monks there, blaming him for the disorder, were as much displeased as the others had been. The Father Guardian reproved him severely in Chapter, saying that he was a drunkard, a fool,

an idle, restless man, full of hypocrisy and ambition, who sought the credit of performing miracles, that he might be regarded as a saint. Finally, they gave him the discipline in public. He did not resent any of these things at all, but, without perturbation, said to himself: "Yes, I am just such a wicked and unworthy man; you say truly, Father Guardian, that it is not I who work the miracles, but the Blessed Virgin."

A prelate once ordered St. Vincent de Paul to receive into his house a certain Religious who was engaged in promoting some special work. He did so, and gave him useful advice. But some persons who were not in favor of the work he was advocating complained of the Saint to the same prelate. He, not remembering that it was in pursuance of his own order, called for St. Vincent, and in presence of these persons gave him a sharp reproof, which he received calmly and without a word of self-justification. God, however, brought back to the mind of the prelate the command he had given, and meeting the Saint one day, he made him a suitable apology, and formed a high opinion of him.

St. Peter Martyr was visited, one day, by three holy virgins, and from this accused of admitting women into his room, condemned in public chapter, and sent to a remote monastery; but he bore all this disgrace without a word.

28 If we should regard tribulations with the eye of a Christian, and wholly clear from our minds those mists of worldly wisdom, which oppose the rays of Faith, and do not allow them to penetrate to the depths of our souls; how fortunate should we consider ourselves in

being calumniated, and regarded not only as idle and incapable, but even as bad and vicious! Is it not, indeed, a great happiness to be persecuted in doing well, when Christ has called those blessed who suffer for justice?

—ST. VINCENT DE PAUL

For this reason the Apostles went away cheerful and contented when they found themselves assailed and persecuted by the chief men of the synagogues. St. Paul, too, says of himself that in such troubles, his heart was filled with consolation and joy because he knew, by the light of faith, how great were the value and advantages of tribulations and trials.

When Brother Juniper was one day insulted by some rude remarks, he took up the folds of his dress, and extending it with both hands, said: "Come now, throw them in, and without any fear fill up this lapful of joys."

Father Alvarez, being informed of a grave calumny that had been spread against him, gave signs of great gladness, and said to the one who had given him the information, and who was gazing at him in wonder: "Now I see that God wishes me well, for He is leading me by the way of those dearest to Him."

A director of the Venerable Maria Seraphina, to whom she revealed her whole life, testifies of her that in all the insults and ridicule which she had suffered, in the bad interpretation which others had put on her good works, and in all her other trials, she never gave way to impatience, nor showed any signs of vexation, but bore everything with the greatest peace and tranquillity both internal and external, always praising and blessing God for the occasion He was giving her to exercise patience. Once when she

had received at the grate many reproaches and menaces, which she bore with the most perfect tranquillity of heart and serenity of countenance, one of her nuns, who had heard and seen all with great astonishment, asked her how she felt, and she replied gaily: "Blessed be God! I am all flowers and joys! blessed be God!" Her way of feeling in such cases became so well known to all in the convent that when they saw her coming back from the grate with a bright face, praising and blessing God, they used to say, "Our Mother must have caught something good today"—meaning that she received some cross; and when they inquired afterwards what had happened, they found this to be the case. The servants, too, had noticed this trait even before she left her father's house, and so, when any illness or trouble came to her, they would say, "Now your day has come—this is your jubilee!"

29 If you look at the rod of Moses lying on the ground, it is a frightful serpent; if you look at it in the hand of Moses, it is a wand of power. It is thus with tribulations. Consider them in themselves, and they are horrors; consider them in the will of God, and they are joys and delights.

—ST. FRANCIS DE SALES

St. Mary Magdalen de' Pazzi used to say she did not think there could be found in the world suffering so bitter, adversity so severe, or trials so painful, that she could not bear them cheerfully, by simply persuading herself that it was the will of God. And in fact, in the great sufferings of an illness that lasted five years, and at the time of her death, whenever anyone reminded

her that it was the will of God that she should suffer those agonies, it would take away all their bitterness and quiet her at once.

It is told in the Life of St. Lupus that when he heard that the terrible Attila was coming to plunder his episcopal city of Troy, he was first much affrighted. But afterwards, nerved to courage by the spirit of God, he went out to meet him, in his pontifical vestments, in the hope of checking his audacity. When he came into Attila's presence, he asked him who he was. "The scourge of God," was Attila's reply. At these words, the Saint exclaimed: "And I, who am the spoiler of God's kingdom, well deserve to be scourged by Him!" Then he ordered the gates to be opened without delay. But when the enemy came in, he passed directly through the city, without doing any harm, as if he had seen no one. By this, God willed to show how much He was pleased with the submission and humility of the holy man, in bowing so readily beneath the scourge He had sent him, and in believing that he deserved it.

30 When it is our lot to suffer pain, trials, or ill-treatment, let us turn our eyes upon what Our Lord suffered, which will instantly render our sufferings sweet and supportable. However sharp our griefs may be they will seem but flowers in comparison with His thorns.

—ST. FRANCIS DE SALES

Count Elzearius received many insults even from his own subjects, and bore them all with great tranquillity. Being asked by his wife how he was able to do this, he answered: "When

I receive insults from anyone, I turn my thoughts to the great affronts which the Son of God suffered from His creatures, and say to myself, 'Even if they were to pull your beard and strike you, what would this be in comparison with what your Lord suffered with so much patience?' But I can tell you, besides, that I sometimes feel in such cases no slight emotions of anger. Then I quickly turn my mind to some similar injury suffered by Our Lord, and keep it fixed upon that, until the emotion has subsided."

A good woman being once confined to her bed and suffering from many ailments, a friend of hers put a crucifix into her hand, inviting her to pray for relief from such great trials. But she said: "Would you have me seek to descend from the cross, when I hold in my hands a crucifix? God keeps me from it! I will rather suffer for Him, who most willingly underwent for me pains incomparably greater than mine."

When St. Teresa was in great suffering, the Lord appeared to her, showing her His wounds and saying: "Behold, My daughter, the sharpness of My torments, and consider whether thine can be compared to Mine." The Saint was so greatly moved by this that she no longer felt the pain, and would often say afterwards: "When I think in how many ways the Lord suffered, and that for no fault of His own, I do not know of what I was thinking when I complained of my sufferings and tried to escape from them."

A servant of God, being much afflicted by the grievous persecutions, calumny and contempt that he experienced, turned to the Lord and said: "How long, O Lord! must I be so tried, without any fault of mine, as Thou knowest?" Then the Lord appeared to him, showing His wounds, and answering: "And for what fault

had I to be treated thus?" At this sight he was so much moved, and filled with such great joy, that he did not feel his afflictions at all, and said that he would not have exchanged his condition for that of any monarch on earth.

For thirty-eight years St. Lidwina suffered constantly all kinds of infirmities—gout in her feet and hands, toothache, fevers, and whatever is most painful—and yet she always remained cheerful and happy, because she kept the sufferings of Christ continually in view.

Dionysius the Carthusian tells of a certain novice who became tepid in the divine service. While in the beginning all went easily with him, he afterwards found great difficulty in performing humble offices and in all the exercises of mortification, and, among other things, he felt especial disgust for a miserable habit such as novices were expected to wear. Now, one night Jesus Christ appeared to him in his sleep, with a long and heavy cross on His shoulders, which with His utmost efforts He was dragging up a staircase. Moved with compassion, he offered to help Him. But the Lord, turning upon him a severe look, said: "How do you presume to carry so heavy a cross—you, who cannot bear for love of Me a habit that weighs so little?" The novice, awakened by this reproach, was at once humiliated and aroused, so that, henceforward he wore the habit with great joy and content; and whenever any trial came in his way, at the mere thought of the great sufferings which Christ bore, everything seemed to him easy and pleasant.

MAY

Meekness

Blessed are the meek, for they shall possess the earth.—MATT. 5:4

---

1 Meekness and mildness of heart is a virtue rarer than chastity, and yet it is more excellent than that and all other virtues, for it is the end of charity, which, as St. Bernard says, is in its perfection when we are not only patient, but also kind. It is necessary, however, to have a great esteem for this virtue, and to use every effort to acquire it.

—ST. FRANCIS DE SALES

St. Francis de Sales himself had the very highest regard for this virtue. He spoke of it so frequently and with so much love, as to show clearly it was his chosen one among all. So, though he excelled in all the virtues, he was singular and remarkable

in this. He always wore a serene countenance, and there was a special grace upon his lips, so that he generally appeared to be smiling, and his face breathed a sweetness which charmed everyone. Though he usually showed great recollection, he sometimes thought it desirable to give proof of amiability, and then he consoled all who met him, and won the love and regard of whoever looked upon him. His words, gestures and actions were never without great suavity and gentleness, so that it seemed that this virtue had taken in him the form of man, and that he was rather meekness itself than a man endowed with that quality. He, too, justly merited the praise bestowed by the Holy Spirit upon Moses, "that he was the meekest man of his time upon earth." And so St. Jane Frances de Chantal was able to say that there was never known a heart so sweet, so gentle, so kind, so gracious and affable, as his. St. Vincent de Paul expressed the same sentiment, saying that he was the kindest man he had ever known, and the first time he saw him, he noticed in the serenity of his countenance and in his manner of conversing such a close resemblance to the meekness of Christ our Lord as instantly won his heart.

The same may be said of St. Vincent de Paul. He was of a bilious-sanguine temperament and, consequently, much inclined to anger, as he himself admitted to a friend, saying that when he was in the house of Condé, he allowed himself to be conquered more than once by his disposition to melancholy and to fits of passion. But having seen that God called him to live in community, and that in such a state he would have to deal with people of every variety of nature and disposition, he had recourse to God, and earnestly prayed Him to change his harsh and unyielding temper into gentleness and benignity; and then he began with

a firm purpose to repress those ebullitions of nature. By prayer and effort combined, he succeeded in making such a change that he seemed no longer to feel any temptations to anger, and his nature was so altered that it became a source of benignity, serenity of countenance and sweetness of manner, which won for him the affection of all who shared his acquaintance. As a rule, he received all those who went to his house with pleasant words, full of respect and esteem, by which he showed his regard for them and his pleasure in seeing them. This he did with all, with the poor as well as those of high rank, adapting himself always to the position of each.

2 Meekness is a virtue which implies loftiness of soul. For this reason worldlings usually are wanting in meekness, for this loftiness is found in them but rarely and imperfectly. If they are not the first to use harsh and discourteous expressions, yet when they are addressed to them by others, they resent and return them promptly, showing by their revenge that they have a rude and ignoble heart. And so the servants of God, remaining always quiet and peaceable, though provoked by words or acts, manifest a perfect loftiness of soul superior to all rudeness.

—ST. THOMAS AQUINAS

This holy Doctor confirmed this noble sentiment by his actions, for in whatever trying position he was placed, he never gave the least sign of resentment, but at all times and on all occasions showed a calm and spiritual insensibility to everything.

The Emperor Constantine illustrated the same thing by his actions, especially on one occasion when he had received a marked affront from his subjects, but was so sustained by his habitual meekness as not to be at all perturbed by it. When some of the court urged him to take a signal vengeance, telling him that it was not right for him to bear such a stain on his face, he replied with a smile, passing his hand gently over his face, "I do not find any stain there."

The same is recorded of the glorious St. Vincent Ferrer, who was never seen angry, whatever insult or injury he received.

3 There is nothing which edifies others so much as charity and kindness, by which, as by the oil in the lamp, the flame of good example is kept alive.

—ST. FRANCIS DE SALES

We read of St. Francis Xavier that his brother Jesuits often visited him, only to enjoy his admirable mildness.

When St. Ignatius was passing one day with a companion, near some reapers, they began to jeer and mock at him. The Saint, not to deprive them of this amusement, stood still, with a tranquil countenance, until they had finished; then he blessed them, and went away. But they, amazed at such conduct, proclaimed him to be a saint.

4 We ought to deal kindly with all, and to manifest those qualities which spring naturally from a heart tender and full of Christian charity; such as affability, love, and humility. These virtues serve wonderfully to gain the

hearts of men, and to encourage them to embrace things that are more repugnant to nature.

—ST. VINCENT DE PAUL

St. Francis de Sales dealt with everyone with so much meekness that without any rough measures he arranged everything according to his own will, and always did what he wished. He did this in a manner so gentle, and at the same time so full of authority, that no one could resist his persuasions. He treated all with respect, welcomed all amiably, and granted requests with great suavity and cordiality. This gave him such influence and power over hearts, that all yielded to him. And as he sought to adapt himself to all, and to be everything to everybody, all willingly fulfilled his desires, which had no other object than to see them occupied in the divine service, and walking in the way of salvation.

St. Francis Xavier treated everyone with great mildness and kindness, which drew to him all—both small and great, won the hearts of all and induced all to do what he wished.

The Abbot Servius being one day treated with great rudeness by a countryman, not only bore it with extreme patience, but replied with much sweetness. At this the man, struck with admiration and compunction, at once threw himself at his feet to ask his pardon, and afterwards became one of his monks.

5 At times a single word is sufficient to cool a person who is burning with anger; and, on the other hand, a single word may be capable of desolating a soul, and infusing into it a bitterness which may be most hurtful.

—ST. VINCENT DE PAUL

One day when St. Macarius was traveling with a disciple in Nitria, the disciple went a little in advance of him, and then met an idol-priest who was hurrying along with a heavy stick on his shoulders. "Where are you going, demon?" he called out. Upon this, the priest laid down his wood, ran upon him, and gave him so many blows that he left him for dead. Then he picked the wood up again, and went on his way in haste. Soon after, Macarius met him and saluted him with the words, "God save you, toiler!" "You have done well," he replied, "to salute me civilly." "I saw you were fatigued," continued the Saint, "and that you were running without regard to your health, and I saluted you, that by stopping, you might get a little rest." "By this I know that you are a true servant of God," replied the idolator, and throwing himself at the Saint's feet, he said that he would never leave him, until he had invested him with the habit of a monk.

Three monks, being on a journey, lost their road, and so were obliged to pass through a field of grain, which they consequently injured. A peasant, seeing this, began to reproach them and call them false monks. Then the oldest told his companions not to reply, and when he came near the man, he said to him, "My son, you have said well." And as he continued to insult them, he added: "You tell the truth, my son; for if we were true monks, we should not have done you this harm. Now, pardon us for the love of God, for we know that we have done wrong." At these words, the rustic, amazed at such great meekness, threw himself at their feet, asked for pardon, and then for the habit, and went away with them.

St. Francis de Sales always spoke with so much sweetness and mildness, that with two or three words he often restored the most troubled hearts to tranquillity.

6 As it is not possible, in this pilgrimage of ours, not to meet and become entangled with each other, if we would preserve interior peace we must possess a great fund of meekness to oppose to the unexpected assaults of anger.

—ST. FRANCIS DE SALES

Philip II, King of Spain, had spent many hours of the night in writing a long letter to the Pope, and when it was finished he gave it to his secretary to be folded and sealed. But he being half-asleep, poured ink over it instead of sand, and nearly died of fright when he saw what he had done. But the king, without any excitement, only said, "Here is another sheet of paper," and went back calmly to his writing. Another day, when he was going to hunt, he took a seat to have his boots put on. When one was on, the other was not to be found, and he waited for it a long time, without giving any sign of impatience, or saying a single word. At the time of his coronation, a soldier, in trying to keep back the crowd with a pole, broke thereby three crystal lamps that were over the throne, so that the oil fell on the rich dresses of the king and queen. "Well," said the king, "this is a sign that in my reign there will be the unction of peace and abundance."

St. Remigius, foreseeing a great famine, had collected a large quantity of grain, and being informed one day that some ill-disposed person had set it on fire, he quickly mounted his horse and hurried to the spot. He found the fire so advanced that there was no hope of extinguishing it; but he was chilled by his ride, as the weather was very cold, so he dismounted, and with

perfect tranquillity both of mind and countenance, he began to warm himself, remarking, "Fire is always good!"

As the venerable Cardinal d'Arezzo was about to give ordination one morning, one of the candidates was not present. He sent for him, and remained waiting in the meantime with perfect composure. At his arrival, without any resentment, he quietly proceeded with the ceremony.

7 There are some characters which appear very gentle as long as everything goes well with them; but at the touch of any adversity or contradiction, they are immediately enkindled, and begin to throw forth smoke like a volcano. Such as these may be called burning coals hidden under ashes. This is not the meekness which Our Lord aimed to teach, that He might make us like Himself. We ought to be like lilies among thorns, which, though they come from amid such sharp points, do not cease to be smooth and pliable.

—ST. BERNARD

This test shows how true was the meekness of St. Francis de Sales, for it is recorded of him that the more he was ill-treated, the more tranquil he appeared. It may be said that he found peace in war, roses among thorns and sweetness amidst the greatest bitterness. He once even said himself: "Of late, the open contradiction and secret opposition which I meet bring me a peace so sweet and soothing that it has no equal, and presages the approaching rest of the soul in its God, which most truly is the single ambition and the single desire of my heart and soul."

In nothing does this admirable peace and tranquillity shine forth more than in the persecutions he suffered on account of the Order of the Visitation—the work of his hands and of his mind, which had cost him prayers, journeys and labors without number, and was certainly dear to him as the apple of his eye. Such great opposition was raised against this most worthy Institute, that several times it was on the point of extinction; yet he never lost his imperturbable peace for that. On the other hand, he wrote that he praised God that his little Congregation had been calumniated, as that was one of the most evident marks of the approbation of Heaven. One day when the Saint was preaching, two lawyers sent up to him a note full of insulting remarks, in the hope of breaking up the sermon. He took the paper, thinking it contained some notice to be given to the people, had the patience to read it through to himself, and then, undisturbed, went on with his sermon. When it was over and he had rested a little, he inquired of the cleric from whom he had received the note and went to visit the two lawyers, one after the other. Without speaking of the letter, he begged them to say in what he had given them offense. When he heard the occasion, he assured them that he had never had the intention of doing so, and asked their pardon on his knees. This caused them much confusion, and they asked his pardon in turn. Thenceforth, they lived on the best terms with him, venerating, as they did, a virtue so heroic and Christian.

This virtue also shone forth in St. Jane Frances de Chantal. When she was, on various occasions, ill-treated by many, she never showed the least sign of resentment or displeasure, but in return gave presents to one, bestowed favors obtained from God

or from persons of rank, upon another. Nor was her love for any of them diminished.

A certain youth who was very angry because a young lady whom he wished to marry had embraced the religious state went to see her, and said many insulting things to her. She listened to them all with great serenity of countenance and so much joy of heart that on leaving the parlor she said to her companion, who had been present at the interview, "I never heard a eulogium more agreeable to me than the one this good youth has just made." Then, moved with compassion at his sinful state, she added, "Let us pray the Lord to give him light." Her prayers were indeed heard, for he repented of his error, came again to ask her pardon, then himself entered religion and finally became a great preacher and a good servant of God.

8 When you have to make arrangements, settle quarrels, or win others to your views, take care to be as mild as possible. You will accomplish more, and conquer more readily, by yielding and humbling yourself, than by harshness and disputation. Who does not know that more flies are caught with an ounce of honey than with a hundred barrels of vinegar?

—ST. FRANCIS DE SALES

The venerable Cardinal d'Arezzo excelled in this. He not only knew how to keep his own household in peace and banish all differences from among them when he was bishop and cardinal; but when he was a simple religious, he was considered to be a man very well adapted to settle lawsuits, to quiet discord and to

calm the most inflamed spirits. He succeeded in this not only by his prudence and dexterity in management, but also by his great affability and mildness, which won the affection of all, and so gave him great power to soften the most obstinate hearts.

St. John Berchmans, even when a child, had great success in settling the little disputes that arise among children, and the reason was that prayers and gentleness were the means he employed.

9 If you wish to labor with fruit in the conversion of souls, you must pour the balsam of sweetness upon the wine of your zeal, that it may not be too fiery, but mild, soothing, patient, and full of compassion. For the human soul is so constituted that by rigor it becomes harder, but mildness completely softens it. Besides, we ought to remember that Jesus Christ came to bless good intentions, and if we leave them to His control, little by little He will make them fruitful.

—ST. FRANCIS DE SALES

This holy Bishop proceeded in this way himself with the most perverse sinners, striving to bring them to repentance in the gentlest ways possible, guiding himself by the great maxim that the spirit of meekness is the spirit of God, as the spirit of mortification is that of the Crucified. A man who had been guilty of enormous crimes once came to his confessional, and went on accusing himself of them with indifference and without any spirit of penitence. After bearing this for some time, the Saint began to weep, and when his penitent asked if anything had happened to him, he merely answered, "Go on." As he went

on with the same ease as before, telling even greater sins, he wept again and again. On being urged to tell the cause, he at last said, in a voice full of compassion, "I weep because you do not weep." These words struck the heart of the sinner with compunction, and he became a true penitent. His gentleness manifested itself especially in his manner of giving advice, encouraging souls at the same time to advance to perfection. When he found them lost in sin and in dangerous occasions of it, he would indeed cry out: "Cut, break, rend, for there are certain bonds which we must not treat with ceremony, or stop to disentangle, but we must dissever and sunder them at once." But on other occasions, where there was no danger, he would lead his penitents step by step to retrench superfluities and banish worldliness from their lives. "Do you not see," he wrote to a lady, "that vines are not pruned with the rough strokes of an axe, but with a fine-edged hook, one shoot after another? I have seen some statues which the sculptor worked on for ten years before they were perfect, cutting with chisels a little here and a little there, until he had removed all that was contrary to accuracy of proportion. No, certainly it is not possible to arrive in a day at the point you aspire to reach. It is necessary to gain one step today, another tomorrow, and to strive to become masters of ourselves by degrees; for this is no small conquest."

St. Vincent de Paul also was accustomed, even in preaching, to speak with the greatest suavity and gentleness, so that he infused into the minds of his hearers, especially the poor, such confidence in himself and such readiness to follow his directions, that after a sermon they would often run after him and entreat him with tears, in the midst of the crowd, to hear their

confessions, in which they revealed to him with great frankness the most hidden wounds of their souls, that they might receive from him a remedy. He once committed a great sinner to the care of one of his priests, that he might do what he could to bring him to repentance. The priest soon found that whatever he said had no effect upon that obstinate heart, and he therefore entreated the Saint to say something himself. He did so, and with such efficacy that he converted him; and in order that the conversion might be lasting, he induced him to make the Spiritual Exercises. The sinner afterwards acknowledged that it was the singular sweetness and charity of the Saint which had gained his heart, and that he had never heard any person speak of God as he did. For this reason the Saint would not permit his missionaries to treat penitents with austerity and harshness; he told them that it was necessary to encourage repentant sinners, and that the infernal spirit ordinarily makes use of rigor and bitterness on the part of priests to lead souls more astray than ever. He used the same method in the conversion of heretics, and succeeded by it in converting many, who afterwards confessed that they had been gained to God by his great patience and cordiality. The Saint explained this when he said: "You see, when one begins to argue with another, the latter easily persuades himself that he wishes to conquer him, and therefore is more prepared to resist than to embrace the truth; so that the contest, instead of disposing his mind to conversion, rather closes his heart, which, on the contrary, remains open to sweetness and affability. We have," he added, "a fine example of this in Monsignor de Sales, who, though very well versed in controversy, converted heretics rather by mildness than by learning, so that Cardinal di Péron

used to say that intellect was enough to convince heretics, but it needed Monsignor de Sales to convert them."

When St. Francis Xavier was preaching in Macao to a great multitude of people, some of the mob threw stones at him. He went on without the least sign of resentment, and he made more conversions in this way than by his preaching.

St. Ludwina, by her great sweetness, converted a sinner whom no preacher or confessor had ever been able to bring to repentance.

St. Philip Neri labored much in the conversion of souls. He drew them to the Lord with so much dexterity that the penitents themselves wondered, for he seemed to charm them in such a way that whoever came to him once appeared unable to refrain from coming again. He was very careful to accommodate himself to the nature of each one. If great sinners and men of evil life came to him, he commanded them in the beginning to abstain from mortal sin, and then led them, by degrees, with admirable skill, to the point he aimed at. There once came to his feet a penitent so addicted to a certain sin that he fell into it almost every day. The only penance he gave him was to come to confession immediately after he committed the sin, without waiting to fall a second time. The penitent obeyed, and the Saint always absolved him, without giving him any other penance. By this method he succeeded in a few months in freeing him not only from this sin, but from all others, and in leading him to a high degree of perfection. He advised a very dissolute young man to say the "Hail, holy Queen," seven times a day, and then to kiss the ground with the words "Tomorrow I may be dead." By doing this the youth soon reformed his life, and

fourteen years after died a holy death. In the same manner, the Saint brought back to the way of God a great number of sinners, many of whom said on their deathbeds, "Blessed be the day and the hour when I first knew Father Philip." And they all remained so attached to him that there was nothing they would not willingly have done for him.

10 Whoever has direction of souls should deal with them as God and the angels do, with admonitions, suggestions, entreaties and "with all patience and doctrine." He must knock at the door of the heart like the Spouse, and try gently to open it: if he succeeds, he must introduce salvation with gladness; but if a refusal comes, he should bear it patiently. It is thus that Our Lord acts. Though He is Master of all hearts, He bears with our long resistance to His lights and our many rebellions against His inspirations; and even if He be forced to withdraw from those who will not walk in His way, He does not cease to renew His inspirations and invitations. Our guardian angels, too, exactly imitate His conduct in this; for they guide, rule, and help as far as they can, those whom God has committed to their charge, and when they see them remaining obstinate, they do not therefore abandon them, nor experience either grief or vexation, nor lose their blessedness in any degree. Now, what better models than these can we desire for our own conduct?

—ST. FRANCIS DE SALES

These surely were the models that this Saint proposed to himself. With weak souls in particular, such as beginners or those who have made but little progress in the spiritual life, he said we ought to copy Jacob, who suited his steps to those of his little sons, and even to the tender lambs.

St. Vincent de Paul also behaved with great suavity and patience to all whom he directed, and especially to scrupulous persons, bearing with their weaknesses and listening to them with unalterable sweetness. He treated in the same way those that were fastidious and hard to please, saying that they ought to be guided with the greatest kindness, as their infirmities of spirit were worthy of even more compassion than bodily ones.

St. Jane Frances de Chantal pursued the same course. Writing to a Superioress of her Order, she says: "The older I grow, the more I feel the necessity of meekness to win and retain hearts, to the end that they may be faithful to the duty they owe to God. Whatever I have tried to do for the benefit of those who have had recourse to me to guide their souls has been done by means of a mild and humble charity, and without any authority but that of a heartfelt entreaty."

11 As without faith it is impossible to please God, so without mildness it is impossible to please men and to govern them well.

—ST. BERNARD

The same Saint proved this by his example. When he was made Abbot, he proceeded at first with much austerity and severity; and though his monks had a high opinion of him, they

could not adapt themselves to each other. Therefore, he was warned by God to show more suavity and sweetness; and when he did so, he gained for himself the affection of all, and a most exact obedience.

Cassiodorus relates of Theobald that after being made king he used to say: "In changing our office we have changed our methods; and if we previously acted with rigor, we now employ clemency altogether."

Nicetus, in his Annals, tells of a certain emperor who at his death called together the chief men of the empire, and said to them: "My two sons, as you see, are both good; but I consider the younger better fitted to govern than the elder, for, besides his other virtues, he is inclined to clemency and docility, and when he has made any mistake, he follows the counsels of others, and obeys the voice of reason. The other is easily made angry, and in his fits of passion he cannot control himself. This trait is most opposed to good counsel, and brings ruin on the wise."

12 I have turned forward and backward and on every side, and what conclusion have I reached? I have considered all methods of governing, and even tried them, and I have finally seen that the best is that which is amiable, sincere, humble, and patient.

—ST. JANE FRANCES DE CHANTAL

It was indeed thus that this Saint lived among her subjects, in a gentle and humble manner, and thus she gained from them whatever she desired. When she asked for anything unimportant, she proceeded with so much submission that they were

overcome by her humility; and when she required what was necessary, she did it with so much sweetness that no one who had a heart could fail to obey her orders promptly.

St. Vincent de Paul wrote thus to a Superior who had complained to him of one of his subjects: "The priest of whom you write to me is a worthy and virtuous man, and before he came to us he was much esteemed in the world. If he is now a little restless, engages in temporal affairs, thinks too much of his relatives and even looks down upon his companions, you must bear with him mildly. If he had not these faults, he would have others; and if you had nothing to bear with, your charity would not have much opportunity for exercise, nor would your conduct and government bear much resemblance to those of Christ our Lord, who chose to have rude disciples, subject to various defects, that He might teach us by practicing amiability and patience with them, how those should behave who hold the office of Superior. I entreat you to form yourself upon this holy model, by which you will learn not only to bear with your brethren, but also to help them in freeing themselves from their imperfections." Writing to another on one of the Missions, who was very unwilling to part with one of his assistants, he said: "I do not doubt that the separation from this dear companion and faithful friend must necessarily be painful to you; but remember that Our Lord separated Himself from His own Mother, and that His disciples, whom the Holy Ghost had so perfectly united, separated themselves from one another for their Master's service."

Plutarch relates of Pericles that whenever he put on his officer's dress, he used to say to himself, as a reminder to be affable

and respectful to all, "Attention, Pericles! you are going to command your brothers, Greeks, citizens of Athens!"

13 Whoever has the charge of others ought not hesitate to resist and correct the vices of those who depend on him, or even to oppose their sentiments when need requires it—always, however, with mildness and peace, especially when he has to enunciate any truths difficult to receive. Such truths must first be heated by a burning fire of charity, which will take away all their sharpness; otherwise, they will be sour fruit, better calculated to cause disease than to give nourishment. Nothing is more bitter than walnut-bark when it is green; but when made into a preserve, it is very sweet and exceedingly wholesome. So reproof, which is very bitter in its nature, heated at the fire of charity and sweetened by amiability, becomes itself pleasing and delicious. And when truth uttered by the tongue is destitute of sweetness, it is a sign that the heart is wanting in true charity.

—ST. FRANCIS DE SALES

When Father Lambert of the Congregation of the Mission was obliged to administer correction to his inferiors, he accompanied it with great sweetness, and never exaggerated their faults. He even overlooked them as far as he could, sometimes when committed in his presence. The venerable Cardinal Bellarmine used to act in the same way.

St. Francis Borgia never let any faults of his subjects pass without correction. When they were slight faults, he never spoke harshly, but would say, "Ah! may God pardon you! May He make you a saint! Oh, brother, how could you say or do this?" If the fault was grave, he summoned the culprit, corrected him kindly, and when he saw any amendment, dismissed the whole matter.

St. Vincent de Paul, when he was obliged to give correction, did it with so much moderation and in a manner at once so sweet and so effective that even the hardest hearts were softened and could not resist the power of his gentleness. He said, on one occasion, that in the whole course of his life he had given correction with harsh words only three times, in which he thought it necessary to do so; but every time he had been afterwards sorry, for the result proved to be bad; and on the contrary, by mildness he had always obtained what he desired. The precautions which he used to render correction fruitful, and to sweeten its bitterness, were the following: In the first place, unless it was absolutely necessary, he never gave correction at the moment the fault was committed, but took some time to consider before God the best way of treating it, especially if the fault was grave and the person little disposed to receive reproof; and when a suitable time came, he would ask him, with much confidence and cordiality, if he would like a little advice, adding that he knew he was himself more imperfect and culpable than any other. In the second place, he would show him marks of affection, and praise him if he could find anything to praise in him. He thus opened the way to reveal to him his fault with tact, and to make him see its gravity and bad effects. He excused it too, and made the least

he could of it, and then suggested a remedy, and as an encouragement to make use of it, added humbly that he, too, needed it. Thirdly, he ended the correction with encouragement, saying that God had permitted that failing as a humiliation, and to give opportunity to attend with greater fervor to the acquisition of virtue. Often he would apparently pass over faults, making it appear that he had scarcely noticed them. It was his opinion that those who had fallen into some faults should be admonished, the first time, at some fitting opportunity, with great kindness and gentleness; the second time, with a little severity and gravity, accompanied, however, with graciousness and the suggestion of easy and charitable remedies; but the third time, with zeal and firmness, and with a warning of the final remedy which would have to be applied.

St. Mary Magdalen de' Pazzi was never known to assail or oppress anyone. On the contrary, when she was mistress of novices, if any one of those whom she reproved answered her with pride and stubbornness, she said nothing, but merely regarded her with an amiable look and waited until some other time to correct her.

When St. Jane Frances de Chantal had to give any correction or penance, she spoke always with great care that there might not escape from her lips any word of reproof or disapproval, which would show the slightest sign of anger, but that all might be accompanied by a cordial compassion and tenderness, which would serve at once to blame the fault and to comfort the offender. Her sole effort was to make the delinquent perceive her error and recollect herself, and she did this in ways so gentle and terms so insinuating that it was almost impossible not to be moved to repentance, and not to receive the admonition

with profit. If an unruly spirit showed itself in anyone, what entreaties, what caresses, what loving stratagems her charitable prudence suggested, to lead her back into the right path!

The venerable Cardinal d'Arezzo, a man most zealous for the glory of God and the salvation of souls, was peculiarly anxious that the ecclesiastical functions should be performed with all possible propriety and perfection. Yet when he saw any of his subjects fail in this, though his heart was deeply moved, all were surprised at the mildness of his correction. But when he heard that any of his flock, and especially any ecclesiastic, was living in some habitual sin or had fallen into a grave transgression, it caused him such pain and affliction that he often wept; and after supplicating God, with fervent and loving prayer, to have compassion on human miseries and frailty, he would turn all his thoughts and efforts towards providing some remedy. First of all, in such cases, he would promulgate anew the decrees and orders of synods, with their penalties annexed, to the end that the guilty parties might be reminded of the danger in which they stood, and might do at least from fear what they would not do from virtue. Afterwards, if necessary he would give an admonition in private—but with admirable tact and with especial tokens of confidence and familiarity. At first sight this course appears strange and contrary to all rules of good government, but one can scarcely believe how much good it did in the hands of this holy pastor. He sometimes sent for priests and even for seculars who were known to be leading evil lives, and invited them to dine with him. After dinner, he took them to his own room and began to admonish them, dilating upon the heinousness of their sin and its enormity before God, with such zeal and affection

that he wept copiously himself, and moved them also to tears and conversion. In this way he gained the greatest results, and admirable changes of life were witnessed, to the extraordinary edification of the people.

14 The only consideration of Superiors ought to be the love of God, and the sanctification of the souls committed to their care. This cannot be better attained than by humility, combined with a peaceable disposition and good example.

—ST. VINCENT DE PAUL

To this end St. Vincent recommended Superiors to take pains that the yoke of obedience should be easy to their subjects, and therefore to cultivate a civil and amiable manner, rather than a harsh and imperious one. To one whom he was sending to a certain house as Superior, he gave this direction: "Do not be domineering in order to appear like a Superior and master. I am not of the opinion of a person who said to me, a few days ago, that to govern well and maintain authority, it was necessary to be known as a Superior. Jesus Christ did not speak thus; He taught us the contrary, both by example and in words, when He said that He came into the world not to be served, but to serve; and that whoever wishes to be Superior, ought to make himself the servant of all. Conform yourself, then, to this holy maxim, behaving towards those for whom you are sent to care, *quasi unus ex illis*—as one of themselves—and telling them, as soon as you arrive, that you have come not to rule, but to serve. If you practice upon this suggestion both at home and abroad, all will be well."

To another whom he was sending as Superior to another house, he spoke thus: "What you ought to do is to trust in God, that you may be a burden to no one, and to treat all with affability and courtesy, always using peaceable and gentle words, never sharp and imperious ones. For, as there is nothing better fitted to gain hearts than this humble and courteous demeanor, so also there is nothing better adapted to attain our object, which is that God may be served and souls sanctified." Writing to the head of a Mission, who had with him a somewhat faulty companion, he said, "If you wish to be accompanied by the blessing of God, make every effort to bear with your assistant meekly. Banishing every thought of superiority from your heart, accommodate yourself to him in a spirit of charity. This is the means by which Jesus Christ won and perfected His disciples, and it is in the same way only that this good priest will be won. Granting this to be true, give a little time to gratifying his humor, never contradict him at the moment when he seems to you to give occasion for it, but, when it is absolutely necessary, admonish him later, and with humility and good feeling."

Such was his own patience, for though he was most rigorous to himself and very exact even in the smallest things, to others he was full of charity and mildness, taking care to please all in everything that he reasonably could. In giving orders, his manner was always so unpretending, and his words so courteous, that he seemed rather to entreat than to command. When he intended to assign to anyone some hard task or difficult business, he prepared him for it by degrees, and with much dexterity smoothed away the difficulties which might have discouraged

him. And in everything he showed so much affability and cordiality that he gained all hearts, and was exactly obeyed even in the most difficult things. Many, too, have confessed that after God, they owed their perseverance to his charity, gentleness and mildness towards them.

St. Francis Borgia was very strict with himself, but most compassionate and kind to his subjects; so that although he would not excuse himself for the slightest defect, he would never speak sharply, but would say with great sweetness: "I entreat you to do this for the love of God. Would you have any difficulty in going to such a place? Would it be convenient for you to do such a thing? I had thought of giving you such a charge, but I would like to know whether it would be agreeable to you."

St. John, a Canon Regular, was once assailed with a volley of abuse by one of the Religious over whom he was appointed Prior. When he did not reply, another who was present said: "You might stop all this insolence by a word, by ordering him to go to his cell."

"No!" replied the Saint, "when fire is consuming a house, would it be well to throw on more wood? This good brother is now burning with anger; if I should reprove him, his anger would be increased; but when this great fire has died out, then it will be time to apply a remedy."

St. Francis de Sales having been obliged to imprison one of his ecclesiastics who was leading a scandalous life, the offender, after a few days, showed great signs of repentance and begged for an interview with the Saint, who had pardoned him on previous occasions. Those who had charge of him did not wish to permit this, for they knew what great compassion the man of God

would feel for him if he saw him; but they finally yielded to his entreaties. When he came into the Saint's presence, he begged for mercy, with fervent promises of amendment. Then the holy Bishop said, with much emotion and many tears: "I conjure you, by the love and mercy of God, in which we all hope, to have pity on me, on the diocese, on the Church, and on the whole Order so much dishonored by the scandalous life you have hitherto led, which gives matter to our adversaries to blaspheme our holy Faith. I pray you to have pity on yourself, on your own soul, which you are sending to perdition for eternity; I exhort you in the name of Jesus Christ, on which you trample; by the goodness of the Saviour, whom you crucify anew; and by that spirit of grace, whom you outrage!" This mild earnestness was so efficacious that he not only did not fall again into his former sins, but became a model of virtue. St. Francis de Sales was once asked by St. Jane Frances de Chantal what she had better do in regard to a novice who had begged importunately to be admitted to profession—which in that Order is regarded as a fault, as profession is granted at a proper time, without any request to those who have been exact in observance. He answered gently that charity should abound on one side, when humility is wanting on the other.

St. Jerome relates of St. Paula that when she was governing a convent built by herself, she failed in none of her obligations and never asked anything of her daughters which she had not first practiced herself; and she showed her authority only by her care in providing for all their wants, by serving them in all their needs, and by leading them to the practice of virtue. She was never absent from choir, but always among the first to

arrive; in the work of the house, she was the most attentive and the most laborious. In regard to others' faults, if any failed in exercises of piety, if anyone was slothful in corporeal exercises, if anyone was careless about her employment—she brought all back to their duty, managing them in different ways, according to their disposition: if passionate, with caresses; if patient, with correction. If discord arose between two, she reunited them with gentle words. If she noticed anyone who was fastidious in dress or behavior who was loquacious, passionate, or quarrelsome, she admonished her with tact more than once; but if she did not amend, she gave her the lowest rank among her Sisters, set her to kneel at the door of the refectory, or to eat by herself, in the hope that shame might succeed where reproof had failed. With the sick she was all cordiality, charity, and liberality, thinking no labor or expense too great for them. But if she was all kindness to others, to herself when sick she was all austerity and hardness, permitting no exceptions in her own favor, even in the matter of food. Once when she was recovering from a burning fever in the month of July, she could not be induced to partake of a little honey, which the physicians had recommended to strengthen her weak digestion.

15 In religious orders, union and peace ought to be preferred above every other good. These depend upon bearing with one another, yielding to one another, and treating one another with that mildness which is a source of peace and a bond of perfection that unites hearts.

—ST. VINCENT DE PAUL

When this Saint was obliged to reprehend anyone for a fault, he took every precaution that the person who had informed him of it should not be known. And if he feared to give occasion for suspicion or aversion, he would omit the correction altogether, rather than disturb the general harmony.

When St. John Berchmans had the office of monitor in the novitiate, he never reported anything to the Superior without first consulting God before the Blessed Sacrament, that he might not disturb the peace of others and also that he might not be deceived by his own judgment or feeling.

16 It is a matter of great importance to make our conversation agreeable. To do so it is necessary to appear humble, patient, respectful, cordial, yielding in all lawful things and to all. Above all, we must avoid contradicting the opinion of anyone, unless there should be an evident necessity for it. In that case, it should be done with all possible mildness, and with the greatest tact, without outraging the feelings of the other party. In this way contests will be avoided which produce only bitterness, and which ordinarily spring rather from attachment to our own opinion, than from love for truth. Believe me, that as there are no dispositions more inimical to human society than those which are given to contradiction—so there is not a person more generally loved than he who contradicts no one.

—ST. FRANCIS DE SALES

Father Lambert Cousteaux of the Congregation of the Mission showed to all great civility and respect, which were always accompanied with remarkable sweetness and cordiality, though by nature he was inclined to rigor. His countenance was always cheerful, and his words courteous and such as could give no one offense. By these pleasant manners he soon won hearts, so that all who talked with him went away content and happy, and greatly pleased with his affability to all and with the Christian condescension with which he yielded to their sentiments and opinions.

St. Vincent de Paul was never heard to contend or dispute about indifferent things, but took the word of others with all facility and adapted himself to their views.

We read of St. John Berchmans that he never quarreled with anyone. For this reason, all his companions not only loved him tenderly, but allowed themselves to be admonished and ruled by him, as if he had authority over them.

17 Let us strive to be amiable, sweet, and humble with all, but especially with those whom God has placed near us, such as our servants. And let us not be of those who seem angels abroad, but demons at home.
—ST. FRANCIS DE SALES

This blessed Saint treated everyone in his house with great kindness, even the servants, whom he never used roughly either in word or deed. His orders to them were given in the form of requests; he always courteously returned their salutations; he never complained of their mistakes in preparing his apartments

or his food; he was most thoughtful in giving directions, sparing them inconvenience as much as he could. When he could not avoid blaming them, he did it with so much kindness and consideration that they were ashamed, and were sure to amend; for mildness has such a charm that everyone surrenders to it. An incident that occurred one evening may serve as an example. A marquis who had visited him on some important business remained until it had grown quite dark. The Bishop's servants in the meantime, trusting their work to one another, not only left their master without attendance but even without a light, so that when the marquis was ready to go, the Bishop was obliged to lead him by the hand through the corridor and across the hall. When they reached the door, they found the servants amusing themselves with those the marquis had brought. After the guest had departed, the Saint said very quietly to his valet: "My friend, two farthings' worth of candle would have done us much credit tonight." Such were the corrections given by this mild prelate, of whom Monsignor di Bellei testifies that there was never a master kinder to his servants, or more beloved by them.

St. Vincent de Paul always showed an admirable gentleness to all the members of his Congregation. He met them with a kind and cheerful countenance, giving them frequent marks of fatherly love and cordiality, especially when he was sending them to a mission or on a long journey. When they returned, he spoke to them with so much affability, and embraced them with so much cordiality, that he completely won their hearts; so that one of them said: "When I am going on a journey, or returning from one, I feel perfumed with the embrace and the welcome which he truly bestows on me." His words were so full of spiritual

unction and efficacy that he could have everything done that he wished, without an effort on his part. His manner was the same when they went to him on their own personal concerns. He listened with courtesy and cordiality, and never gave the least sign of impatience—even if he was engaged in important and urgent business. This courtesy was shown in a special manner towards the lay-brothers. One of them went to him on a certain occasion to complain of harsh treatment he had received from an official in the house. He was welcomed with the greatest cordiality, and invited to come again in any similar case, so that all bitterness was banished from his heart, and he went away consoled and edified to find that he had so good a Father. One of his priests came to him one day, full of trouble, resolved to abandon his vocation and return to his own country. The Saint listened to him and then said, "Well, Father, when do you go? Do you wish to travel on foot, or on horseback?" But the priest, surprised and edified by such meekness, was immediately freed from the temptation, and proclaimed that his Superior was a saint.

The conduct of the Empress Leonora was the same. Her manner of giving orders was so kind and so humble that her household could not ask for a mistress with less air of control and dominion. Her commands almost always took the form of requests, which caused the women in her service so much confusion that they often entreated her to speak to them like a mistress, as she had a right to do. But she replied: "I approve and praise your sentiments; but I know myself to be far different from what I seem to you, and I think myself more worthy to serve than to command." If anything happened to fall when she was working with them, she was always the first to stoop and

pick it up. However great were the faults and errors committed by those in her service, she always had reasons and excuses ready to screen them. She took all possible pains not to displease anyone, and not to cause any jealousies or suspicions to arise among them. Once she entrusted a thing, by mistake, to the chief tiring-woman, instead of the principal lady in waiting. A distraction which she had in prayer brought this error to her recollection, and rising from her knees she went on the instant to apologize to the lady, that she might not consider herself overlooked and feel the slight.

We read of St. Jane Frances de Chantal that while she was still in the world she showed the greatest affability and charity towards all who served her. She did not scold them, as many do, nor reprove them for every little fault, but bore with them with great patience and humility, without ever being weary of helping them to reform, until God gave her the consolation of seeing their amendment. As a proof of this, she never dismissed from her house more than two servants. These were quite incorrigible; but all the rest remained as long as they chose, and were always well sheltered, clothed, and taken care of. Once when the Baron, her husband, was very angry with a servant and she was trying to pacify him, he said to her: "It is true that I am too impulsive, but you are too good."

18 Resist your impatience faithfully, practicing, not only with reason, but even against reason, holy courtesy and sweetness to all, but especially to those who weary you most.

—ST. FRANCIS DE SALES

St. Francis himself excelled in this. We read in his Life that a poor lawyer often visited him in regard to trifling matters of business, and that the Saint always listened to him with great courtesy and without any sign of weariness; so that many wondered how a prelate who had so many important occupations, could listen quietly to stupid trifles which might weary even an idle man.

St. Vincent de Paul furnishes another example. It often happened that he was obliged to repeat the same thing many times, either because people did not understand him, or forgot what they had heard. But he was always calm and showed neither anger nor weariness, nor did he send them away. He welcomed them with a cheerful countenance and with great affability, that they might not feel discouraged or slighted; and when he was in company with anyone of high rank, if he saw them coming, he rose and went to speak to them in private, repeating the same thing always with civility. One of them testified that he made him repeat the same thing five times in succession, when he was engaged, too, with persons of high rank; yet he never gave the least sign of impatience, repeating it the last time with the same quiet and calmness as he did at first, and showing in his face pleasure rather than dissatisfaction.

19 The highest degree of meekness consists in seeing, serving, honoring, and treating amiably, on occasion, those who are not to our taste, and who show themselves unfriendly, ungrateful, and troublesome to us.

—ST. FRANCIS DE SALES

This holy Bishop was at one time laboring for the conversion of a heretical woman, quite advanced in years, who for a long time came to him every day with new doubts. He listened to her with great amiability and without ever showing any weariness, though he could see that he gained nothing. But the woman did not grow tired of knocking at his door three or four times a day, so much was she attracted by his gentle demeanor. Finally, she said that she had no other difficulty except in regard to the celibacy of the clergy. The Saint replied to this that it was necessary for them in order that, being free from the care of a family, they might serve the people, and that indeed it would have been difficult for him to talk with her so often, if he had a wife and children to take care of. This reason was more convincing to her than all the arguments of theologians, and she was converted.

When St. Jane Frances de Chantal was living in the house of her father-in-law, she endeavored by the most obliging and gentle manners to win over an insolent servant who was there, and who behaved as if she herself were the mistress of the house. She tried to please her in all she thought most to her taste, and even went so far as to wash and dress, instruct and take care of, her children like her own. She reproved the servants also if they showed any contempt for her. This went on for seven years, the servant growing all the time more haughty and presumptuous. When anyone told the Saint that she was losing her time in trying to gain over such a woman by civil and gentle methods, she answered: "That would be true, if I had not others besides her in view. Did not Our Lord say that all we do for the poor, whom He commends so specially to us, He will consider as done to Himself? With God, nothing is lost, and the less gratitude we receive from men,

the more account will God make of what we do to them for His sake." To another who said that at her father-in-law's death this servant ought to be thrown into a ditch, she answered: "No, I would take up her defense myself. If God makes use of her that I may have a cross to bear, why should I wish her ill?" Another tried to show her how unsuitable it was that the control of the household should be in the hands of a servant. But she replied: "God ordains it thus for my advantage, that I may have all my time for works of charity." To the father-in-law, who permitted this, she showed every mark of deference and special respect; and when she left the world, she recommended him warmly to a priest, requesting him to be present at his death.

Father John Leonardi was also remarkable for this trait. For the space of forty years he bore persecutions and trials from all kinds of people, yet he never let slip a word of aversion, anger, resentment or ill-feeling towards them, but always tried to do them good, and to help them by word and act. He constantly prayed for them, excused them, defended them, and treated each of them as he would one of his dearest friends. Though he knew that some monks of a certain Order, to which he had been sent as inspector by commission of the Apostolic See, being impatient of the regular discipline he had restored were plotting and writing to the Sacred Congregation against him, he yet showed no resentment and took no steps to defend himself. He behaved to these abbots, on the contrary, with charity and courtesy, as if they were his intimate friends; and when some of them rudely assailed him by word and act, he passed the matter over lightly and gently, correcting them mildly, or giving them some moderate penance when it was necessary, as

he said, to satisfy his own conscience. But he never mentioned what had been done against himself personally, either in writing to the Sacred Congregation, in the general chapters, nor on any other occasion that offered itself. When he was walking one day in Lucca, he met one of these monks who, after loading him with harsh and abusive epithets, without any resistance on his part struck him a heavy blow on one cheek. The servant of God, without any anger, turned the other cheek, as if to receive a second blow; but the assailant, abashed at this, turned his back and went away. Then Father John, glad to see himself reckoned worthy to suffer something for the love of his God, went home, and for many days prayed for this misguided man as a special benefactor.

20 Beware of becoming vexed or impatient at the faults of others; for it would be folly when you see a man falling into a ditch, to throw yourself into another to no purpose.

—ST. BONAVENTURE

Cardinal Cesarini, a man of most gentle disposition, having been told that the mule he usually rode was lost through the neglect of a servant sent for him; but when he asked him about the matter, the man replied very rudely. The Cardinal was silent at first, but when the servant continued his impertinence, he turned to the bystanders and said: "Do not wonder at my silence, for I thought it best to suppress my anger and give reason time to gain control over passion, lest I should fall myself into a fault, by trying to correct the fault of another."

A reckless youth was once brought to St. Francis de Sales, that the Saint might give him a private correction; but instead of rigor, he showed extreme gentleness with him. Seeing his obstinacy, he shed bitter tears, saying that this young man would come to a bad end, as indeed happened, for he was killed in a duel. When St. Francis was afterwards blamed for being too mild on this occasion, he answered: "What would you have me do? I tried as well as I could, to arm myself with an anger that should not be sinful, and therefore I took my heart in both my hands, but I had not strength to fling it in his face. And then, to tell the truth, I feared to lose that little stock of mildness, which I have labored for twenty-two years to collect, like dew, in the vase of my heart. The bees have been many years in gathering the honey, which a man swallows at a draught. Besides, what is the use of speaking to one who does not listen? That foolish youth was not capable of correction, for he was not master of his own judgment. So I could not have helped him, and might have injured myself, like those who are drowned with shipwrecked sailors, whom they are trying to rescue. Charity ought to be judicious and prudent."

21 You should never be displeased at the sight of your own imperfections, except with a displeasure humble, tranquil, and peaceful, not excited and angry; for this latter kind does more harm than good.

—ST. FRANCIS DE SALES

St. Francis practiced this in his own case. He said one day: "For myself, if I had, for example, a great desire not to fall into the vice of vanity, and yet fell very deeply into it, I should not

wish to reproach myself in this manner: 'Are you not a wretch, an abomination, for having allowed yourself to be conquered by this vice, after so many resolutions? Die of shame! do not raise your eyes to Heaven, bold, disloyal traitor to God!' or with similar words. But I would prefer to correct it quietly, and in a compassionate way, saying: 'Come now, my poor heart, here we are fallen again into the ditch, which we have so many times resolved to avoid. Ah, let us rise up, and leave it once for all! Let us have recourse to the mercy of God, and hope in it, for it will aid us to be more constant in future; and in the meantime let us return to the road of humility. Courage! let us rise above ourselves, for God will help us, and we shall advance.' Upon this reproach I would found a firm and solid resolution not to fall again into the error, and to apply suitable remedies."

St. Vincent de Paul never felt anger or bitterness against himself on account of his defects, and often said that vice should be hated and virtue loved, not because the former displeases us, and the latter pleases us, but only for love of God, who hates vices and loves virtue; and thus the pain felt for a defect will have something in it sweet and tranquil.

St. Aloysius Gonzaga was not discouraged when he committed faults, but only turned his glance upon his own heart and said, "*Terra dedit fructum suum*"—The earth has yielded its fruit.

22 If one wishes to acquire liberty of spirit, and not always walk in darkness, he should feel no trouble in regard to aridities, disquiets, distractions, or involuntary thoughts.

—ST. TERESA

The Saint just mentioned practiced this herself. What vexations and trials, internal and external, from her Religious and from others, and from Satan himself, had she not to suffer in her life! Yet, in so many and various adversities, she maintained herself always firm and immovable, like a rock beaten by the waves of the sea, without taking any of these things to heart. In this way she enjoyed a freedom of spirit little less than angelic.

We read the same of St. Francis de Sales, who was never disquieted by whatever happened to him, however adverse it might be. To a lady who had asked his advice upon this subject, he wrote thus: "You would prefer to see yourself without defects and without temptations, rather than in the midst of imperfections and afflictions. I would like it too, and we shall be so in Paradise. But the disquiet which you feel at not being able to arrive at this state of perfection in this life makes you doubt whether your hatred of sin be good. No, it is not pure, for it disquiets you. Hate your imperfections, then, because they are imperfections, but love them because they make you know your nothingness and give to you an opportunity to exercise yourself in virtue, and to God to show His mercy towards you."

23 Be very mild and very gracious in the midst of your exterior occupations, for everyone expects this good example from you.

—ST. FRANCIS DE SALES

It is said of this Saint that amid all his activity he preserved a countenance mild, tranquil, and peaceful, and that he was never

known to lose the least jot of his cheerfulness and serenity, in whatever business he was engaged.

The same is said of St. Vincent de Paul. He never lost his tranquillity of mind in the midst of affairs, however numerous or troublesome they might be. And it was wonderful to see how he received all persons with the same serenity of countenance and satisfied their demands, whatever their rank might be, with great courtesy and without ever giving a sign of weariness or vexation at their importunity.

It is related of the Abbot David that for a period of forty-five years, which he passed in the monastery, he was never seen in a passion nor showing any sign of perturbation; but in whatever he was engaged, his countenance bore a look of imperturbable serenity and tranquillity, as if he were an angel among men. He must, notwithstanding, have been often placed in trying positions, as he was Superior over 150 monks, some of whom could not have failed to be troublesome and unmanageable, and he must also have had many difficult business affairs to conduct. This trait of his character is reported by Theodoret, who says that he not only heard of it from others, but observed it himself in the course of a week's visit.

The process of canonization of St. Thomas Aquinas states that he was never seen angry or even disturbed, but that at all times and in all occupations he retained serenity and cheerfulness of countenance to such a degree that those connected with him experienced consolation and a certain spiritual joy by merely looking at him.

St. Athanasius writes of St. Anthony that he always appeared so joyful that every day seemed like Easter with him, and that a stranger coming to see him could pick him out from a multitude

of monks by the gladness and benignity which shone upon his countenance. And the same writer adds that this joy was occasioned by the great hope which he had of Paradise; for he had his mind always fixed on the eternal things above, of which he could not think without rejoicing.

24 Know and be assured that all those thoughts which give disquiet and agitation of mind are not in any wise from God, who is the Prince of Peace; but they always proceed either from the devil, or from self-love, or from the esteem which we have of ourselves. These are the three fountains from which all our perturbation springs. Therefore, when thoughts of such a nature come to us, we ought to reject them at once and make no account of them.

—ST. FRANCIS DE SALES

Here is the reason why this Saint was never seen perturbed or disquieted. It was because he scorned the temptations of the devil, and was humble in heart, and a sworn enemy of self-love.

When the Abbot Isaac was asked by another monk why the devils feared him so much, he replied: "At the time I entered religion, I made a resolution never to let an impatient act or angry word escape me, and by the grace of God, I have never broken it." Yet God knows how many temptations and trying circumstances he had met!

25 Humble mildness is the virtue of virtues which Our Lord has recommended to us, and therefore we

ought to practice it everywhere and always. Evil is to be shunned, but peaceably. Good is to be done, but with suavity. Take this for your rule: Do what you see can be done with charity, and what cannot be done without disturbance, leave undone. In short, peace and tranquillity of heart ought to be uppermost in all our actions, as olive oil floats above all liquors.

—ST. FRANCIS DE SALES

We read of this Saint that he enjoyed an imperturbable peace of heart. He said himself, one day: "What is there that can possibly disturb our peace? If all the world were in confusion, I should not be troubled; for what is all the world worth in comparison with peace of heart?" His acts, too, corresponded to his words. Though he had the reform of the monasteries much at heart, he never used his authority to carry it out, knowing well that what is done by force is not lasting. So he preferred to fail in his plans rather than to execute them by violence and waited until time, or rather until God, should work those changes in hearts, that are above the power of any creature.

It was St. Vincent de Paul's maxim that though one ought to hold firmly to the end proposed in good undertakings, it was equally suitable to employ all possible amiability and sweetness in the means ordained to that end. For this is an imitation of the Divine Wisdom, which, though it reaches its ends strongly, yet disposes sweetly the means that lead to them.

26 If it be possible, never yield to anger nor admit any pretext for opening to it the door of your heart; for

should it once enter there, it will not be in your power to expel it when you please, or ever to control it. If you see that through your weakness it has gained a foothold in your spirit, instantly gather all your forces to re-establish peace and tranquillity. But this must be done quietly and never violently; for it is a matter of much importance not to irritate the wound.

—ST. FRANCIS DE SALES

The same Saint employed in his own conduct this principle of applying self-control where it could be useful, without concerning himself with what was involuntary, as he says in these words: "Have I made, for example, a resolution to acquire mildness? Very well, now let anger make a chaos of my poor heart, let my brain be all on fire, let my blood boil like a seething caldron—I make no account of all this. Meanwhile, I do not cease to be mild in all such ways as are possible, and I silence and choke all the reasons that nature would offer in justification of this passion."

It once happened that one of his relatives, aggrieved by something which he thought this holy man had done, went to his house and loaded him with insults and threats. The Saint, who was entirely innocent, sought to undeceive him and tried to pacify him with great mildness and courtesy. But the gentleman, overcome by anger, would listen to nothing and went on abusing and insulting him, until he finally went away still storming and full of ill-will. Then the Saint, turning to a Religious who was present and was much astonished at his patience, said to him: "Father, it was not desirable to exasperate this good man still

211

more by showing him his rashness. He will know it well some day, and will repent of it." And so he did; for, a few days after, he came to ask pardon. It is said that the patience of St. Francis was never known to waver, nor was his heart ever known to cherish resentment against anyone. From this it clearly appears that this holy virtue which shone so remarkably in him did not result, as many believe, from a disposition all sweetness by nature, but from the great and continual violence he had done to himself. On the contrary, he was of a bilious temperament and confessed of himself that he had taken the greatest pains to conquer it, and that he had labored at this for 22 years with great constancy and courage. This was clearly shown after his death, for when his body was opened there was nothing found in the gallbladder but 300 grains of sand, which was a manifest proof of his innumerable struggles to repress the emotions of anger.

Such was the case of many other Saints, in whose Lives we read that they were never seen to give way to anger, but that even on the most exciting occasions they always showed the same tranquillity of countenance and serenity of soul. Among these were St. Anthony, St. Ephrem, St. Thomas Aquinas, St. Vincent de Paul, and others—especially the glorious St. Philip Neri, who would sometimes put on an appearance of severity to exercise his novices in humility. Then, as soon as they were gone, he would turn to any who might be present, and say, "Did I not seem to be in a passion?" and instantly resume his previous serenity of expression.

27 The remedies against anger are: 1. To forestall its movements, if possible, or at least to cast them aside

quickly, by turning the thoughts to something else. 2. In imitation of the Apostles when they saw the sea raging, to have recourse to God, whose office it is to give peace to the heart. 3. During the heat of passion, not to speak, nor take any action as to the matter in question. 4. To strive to perform acts of kindness and humility towards the person against whom one is incensed, especially in reparation for any of a contrary nature.

—ST. FRANCIS DE SALES

This good Saint was often wrongfully assailed by others with insulting words. To avoid yielding to anger in such cases, he would sometimes think of some good quality they possessed, to excite a sentiment of love for them; or again, he would be silent and let them talk, if he had tried sweetness and courtesy in vain. To a gentleman who had been an astonished witness of his heroic patience, he once said: "You see I have made a compact with my tongue, that when anything is said against me that may excite me to anger, it will beware of uttering a word."

If St. Vincent de Paul was at any time moved to anger, he abstained from speaking and from acting; and above all, he never resolved upon anything until he felt that his passion had subsided. He often said that actions performed under excitement may appear good, but can never be perfect, as they are not fully directed by reason, which is then perturbed and obscured, and that in spite of all the ebullitions of anger and all imaginable pretexts of zeal, we should speak only soft and courteous words, that we may gain our neighbors to God. Therefore, while the

emotion lasted, he made every effort to hinder any trace of it from appearing on his countenance, and if, on rare occasions, there escaped him any word or gesture which might indicate impatience or severity, he immediately asked pardon. One day he spoke with a great deal of decision to a lay-brother who had excused himself under various pretexts for giving lodging to a stranger. Though he had done this with the best intention, and the brother recognized his error, he yet humbled himself for it that same evening, and wished to kiss the lay-brother's feet. Another time he feared that he had offended a lay-brother by telling him to have patience and wait a little for the solution of certain doubts that he had proposed to him. In this uncertainty he would not say Mass until he had asked his pardon.

When the venerable Monseigneur de Palafox felt his emotions of anger or excessive zeal springing up in his mind while he was giving a reproof, he would instantly raise his heart to God and say: "O Lord, hold fast in this tempest the rudder of my reason, that I may not transgress Thy holy will in anything."

A great philosopher gave Augustus Caesar this advice: "When you feel any emotion of anger, do not say or do anything until you have run over in your mind at least the 26 letters of the alphabet."

Plutarch tells of a certain king of Thrace who was remarkable for his violent temper and the cruel punishments he inflicted on his servants. One of his friends gave him some vases, which were fragile but beautifully wrought. He gave his friend a handsome present in return, and then broke the vases. When someone expressed amazement at this latter action, he said: "I did this

so that I might not come to inflict my usual cruelties on anyone who should break them."

28 Accustom your heart to be docile, manageable, submissive, and ready to yield to all in all lawful things, for the love of your most sweet Lord; so will you become like the dove, which receives all the colors which the sun gives it. For this end, put your soul every morning in a posture of humility, tranquillity, and sweetness, and notice from time to time through the day if it has become entangled in affection for anything; and if it be not quiet, disengaged, and tranquil, set it at rest.

—ST. FRANCIS DE SALES

This holy prelate was so remarkable for accommodating himself to the dispositions of all that Alexander VII, in his eulogy, could find no way to describe him better than to say that God had willed to make him all to all. Among the innumerable proofs of this, it will be enough to mention one connected with St. Jane Frances de Chantal. She was afraid of losing him on account of his excessive application to his work and the little care he took of his health, and so she entreated him to take more care of himself. Equally humble and yielding, he answered her: "I take care of myself as much as possible, more because you tell me to than from any inclination I have to this sort of attention. I imagine, however, that it is God's will that I should desire something for your sake, and now let Him do with me according to His good pleasure." On other occasions also he gave her the same assurance.

St. Vincent de Paul had the habit deeply rooted in his nature of being pliable and ready to follow everyone's will in indifferent matters.

The Abbot Agatho declared that he had never retired to rest without having first stifled every emotion of anger, even against himself, and that he did so to fulfill the precept: *Diverte a malo et fac bonum; inquire pacem et persequere eam*—Turn away from evil, and do good; seek peace, and pursue it.

29 A most important means of acquiring interior mildness is to accustom ourselves to perform all our actions and to speak all our words, whether important or not, quietly and gently. Multiply these acts as much as you can in the time of tranquillity, and so you will accustom your heart to gentleness.

—ST. FRANCIS DE SALES

The Saint himself practiced this advice well, for he never seemed hurried on any occasion. When a person once asked him about this, he answered: "You ask me how I manage not to be hurried and troubled when everyone else is. How shall I answer you? I did not come into the world to bring perplexities; are there not enough in it already?"

30 To keep the soul continually in a state of gentle calm, it is necessary to perform every action as being done in the presence of God, and as if He Himself had ordained it.

—ST. FRANCIS DE SALES

216

This is the reason why St. John Berchmans performed all his actions so regularly and was so even-tempered on all occasions, without any alteration or perturbation. It was because he constantly enjoyed the Divine Presence, and was accustomed before beginning any action to plan it with God, and to remain in His sight while doing it.

When one of the Fathers of the Desert was asked how he contrived to lead a life so well-ordered and so perfectly even, he answered: "I keep my eyes always upon my guardian angel, who stands ever at my side, assisting me in every work, teaching me in all circumstances what I have to say and do, and noting carefully every one of my actions. Thence arise in me such fear and respect for him as make me ever attentive not to say or to do anything that can displease him."

31 One great means of preserving a constant peace and tranquillity of heart is to receive all things as coming from the hands of God, whatever they may be, and in whatever way they may come.

—ST. DOROTHEUS

St. Catherine of Siena once asked the Lord the way to obtain true peace of heart, and He answered: "It is to believe that all that happens in the world comes by the order and disposal of God, and that He never makes anything happen to anyone that is not best for him."

It is told of St. Macarius that he was never seen angry or melancholy, but that he always appeared cheerful and possessed of a heavenly gaiety. The cause of this was that he received all

that happened to him as coming from the hands of God. Severus Sulpicius, who spent much time with St. Martin, says the same of him.

When the servants of David wished to avenge him upon Semei, "No," he said, "for it is God who has commanded him to curse me; and who shall ask Him why He does it?"

St. Francis de Sales was once shamefully abused by a certain gentleman, in presence of a Religious, who was so amazed at his patience that he took the first opportunity of asking him how he could bear so many insults with so much tranquillity. "Do you not perceive," he replied, "that God has foreseen from all eternity the grace He would bestow on me, that I might bear these reproaches willingly? And would you not have me drink this chalice, which has been prepared for me by the hands of so good a Father."

"I never," said an illuminated soul, "had fully understood this truth, so often repeated again and again, that not a hair falls from our heads without the will of our Heavenly Father. To understand this clearly and fully makes the soul a sharer in celestial joys while still on earth, and the cross which was before a hell, becomes for her a paradise. All this is because she tastes the marvelous sweetness that lies hidden for pure souls in a command of God. And it is enough that anything should be His command, to cause her to find in it peace and tranquillity."

We read of the venerable Mother Seraphina that in any trial or misfortune that happened to her, all she did was to praise and bless God. She often said: "God is our Father, and whatever He does, all is for our advantage. If this had not been for our good, it would not have happened." News was once brought to her

that a ship loaded with provisions purchased in Salerno for her convent had been wrecked. She immediately took her daughters with her to the chapel, and there she praised and thanked the Lord for this act of His providence; and she said that it was as pleasing to her as if she had done it with her own hands and by her own choice, nay much more so as it had been done by the hand of God.

Obedience

---

*All things whatsoever that they command
you, observe and do.*—MATT. 23:3

---

1   We all have a natural inclination to command, and
a great aversion to obey; and yet, it is certain that it
is more to our advantage to obey than to command.
It is for this reason that perfect souls have so great
an affection for obedience, and find in it all their
delight.

These are the words of St. Francis de Sales, and in fact this
Saint exercised himself much in this virtue, although he was a
Bishop and Superior of so many houses. He even obeyed his
chamberlain in regard to rising and retiring to rest, dressing
and undressing, as if he had been the servant instead of the
master.

St. Teresa often said: "One of the greatest graces for which I feel bound to thank Our Lord is that His Divine Majesty has given me a desire to be obedient; since in this virtue I experience the greatest consolation and content, as the one which Our Lord enjoined upon us more than any other; and therefore I desire to possess it more than anything else in the world."

St. Mary Magdalen de' Pazzi had so great a love for obedience that even though a command might be very difficult to execute, or her weariness extreme, she never appeared reluctant or showed the least sign of discontent, but accepted everything with a cheerful countenance, as if the most agreeable proposal had been made to her. It even occurred to her to doubt of her own merit in obeying, on account of the great ease and delight which she experienced in it. But she did not content herself with submission to her Superioress. Of her own accord, she subjected herself also to her companions, and even to her inferiors. With this intention she chose one of her Sisters, whose permission she asked for even the most minute things which she desired or found it necessary to do, and obeyed her in everything in spite of all difficulties. If she could not have access to this particular Sister, she would ask the permission of some other; and whoever was her companion in any employment, she always yielded precedence to her, and followed her plans and methods.

2 Obedience is, without doubt, more meritorious than any austerity. And what greater austerity can be thought of than that of keeping one's will constantly submissive and obedient?

—ST. CATHERINE OF BOLOGNA

When St. Mary Magdalen de' Pazzi was sick, she was accustomed to refuse any delicate food or costly medicine that was offered her; but if the bringer required her to take it as an act of obedience, she made no further objections; but saying only "Blessed be God," she would instantly take it.

As St. Dositheus was not able to practice austerities or even the ordinary exercises of religion on account of his feeble health, he turned his attention wholly to the practice of obedience, and after five years spent in this manner it was revealed to him that a crown like that of the great St. Anthony awaited him in Heaven. When some of the hermits who had been most fervent in penances and in all the other exercises felt aggrieved at this, Our Lord signified to them that they had failed to understand the full merit of obedience.

3   Obedience is a penance of the soul, and for that reason a sacrifice more acceptable than all corporal penances. Thence it happens that God loves more the least degree of obedience in thee, than all the other services thou mayest think to render Him.

—ST. JOHN OF THE CROSS

This Saint, having finished his studies and returned to the monastic life, showed that he had a high opinion of himself on account of his great learning. To cure him, his director gave him a catechism, telling him to lay aside all other books and read this alone, picking out the words syllable by syllable, like a child. He continued to do this for a long time, and with great application, and afterwards confessed that he derived from it not only a high degree of obedience, but many other virtues as well.

We read in the Lives of the Fathers that four monks once visited the Abbot Pambo, and each of them told him in private of the virtues of the others. One fasted severely; another did not possess the smallest thing; this one glowed with the most fervent charity; while that one had lived in the practice of obedience for twenty years. When the Abbot had heard these things, one after the other, he said: "The virtue of this last is greatest of all, for the rest followed their own will, but he has made himself the servant of another's will."

4 A little drop of simple obedience is worth a million times more than a whole vase full of the choicest contemplations.

—ST. MARY MAGDALEN DE' PAZZI

We read of a holy nun who was one day enjoying the company of the Infant Jesus in her cell when she was sent for by the Superioress. Begging Him to wait for her, she went to obey the summons, and when she returned she found Him no longer an infant, but wearing the form of a full-grown youth. By this He intended to show her how much her prompt obedience had caused Him to grow spiritually in her heart in so short a time.

One day when St. Frances of Rome was reciting the Office of the Blessed Virgin, she was interrupted four times while repeating a single antiphon by the voice of her husband calling her. Each time she answered promptly, and when she returned the fourth time she found the antiphon written in letters of gold.

5 To pick up a straw from the ground through obedience is more meritorious than to preach, to fast, to use the discipline to blood, and to make long prayers, of one's own will.

—ST ALPHONSUS RODRIGUEZ

A Cistercian monk, having gathered up a few crumbs at the close of a meal, had not had time to eat them as the signal for leaving the table was given and grace was said. He was unwilling to waste them, but his rule forbade him to eat anything except at the regular repasts. He therefore went to his Superior, and kneeling, asked what he should do. But when at his Superior's command he opened his hand to show him the crumbs, they were changed into precious gems.

6 All the good of creatures consists in the fulfillment of the Divine Will. And this is never better attained than by the practice of obedience, in which is found the annihilation of self-love and the true liberty of sons of God. This is the reason why souls truly good, experience such great joy and sweetness in obedience.

—ST. VINCENT DE PAUL

The Saint just quoted had himself gained so complete a submission to the Divine Will that he cheerfully obeyed whoever had authority over him, as the Pope, Bishops, priests and civil rulers as well, and evinced special respect and veneration for each of them. An incident in his relations with his director deserves notice here. Having with his concurrence left the house

225

of Condé to avoid the high esteem in which he was held there, he could not be induced to return, though entreated to do so by many men of high rank. At last there came a letter from his director, not commanding his return, but merely mentioning the desire which these nobles had for it. Immediately a doubt arose in his mind as to what he ought to do, and this could not be quieted except by a personal interview with the director, who then exhibited some preference for his return. Upon this he went back without hesitation.

St. Mary Magdalen de' Pazzi had such great affection and regard for obedience as a safeguard from the danger of doing one's own will, that the thought of acting under it was sufficient to restore her peace and serenity when she was burdened by an unusual trial or labor.

7 Whoever has not the virtue of obedience cannot be called a Religious. Whoever, then, is under obedience by vow, and fails therein, not using every exertion to observe her vow with the utmost perfection, I cannot understand why she remains in the convent.

—ST. TERESA

St. Margaret of Hungary, a Dominican nun, was in the habit of taking all directions that were given to the community as addressed to herself, and as if their observance depended upon her.

St. Jane Frances de Chantal once gave permission to a Sister, in a case of urgent need, to use some money which St. Francis de Sales had put into her hands to be employed for the sick alone.

Though the Sister was sure to replace it from a gift that had been promised her, Mother de Chantal began to fear that she had failed in obedience, and sent for St. Francis, who came the next morning to the convent. She immediately threw herself at his feet, and, weeping, confessed her fault; and she herself said afterwards that she could never think of it without tears.

8 Would you know who are true monks? Those who by mortification have brought their will under such control that they no longer have any wish except to obey the precepts and counsels of their Superior.

—ST. FULGENTIUS

St. Francis once gave the blessed Egidius full freedom to choose whatever province or monastery he might prefer as a place of residence. After four days of this liberty, Egidius was surprised at finding himself much troubled in mind. Then returning to the Saint, he earnestly entreated him to fix his abode for life, for he knew that this liberty would banish all peace from his soul.

9 Every Sister, on entering religion, should leave her own will outside the gate, in order to have no will but that of God.

—ST. FRANCIS DE SALES

St. Dositheus said of himself that from his first entrance into religion he completely gave up his own will, subjecting it in everything to that of his Superior, to whom he also revealed all his temptations and all his desires. And he added that in this way

he had attained such peace of heart and tranquillity of mind that nothing could ever disturb him.

10 Many Religious and others have been saints without meditation, but without obedience no one.

—ST. FRANCIS DE SALES

A lay-brother of St. Bernard's Order being dangerously ill, the Saint visited him and encouraged him with the hope that he would soon pass from labor to eternal rest. "Yes," replied he, "I confide in the Divine Mercy, and feel certain that I shall soon go to enjoy God." The Saint, feeling that this might be presumption, said reprovingly: "What do you mean, brother? When you were so wretched and had nothing to live on, God put you in this place, where you have lived so well; and instead of being thankful for this favor, do you now claim His Kingdom, as if it were your inheritance?"

"Father," replied the sick man, "what you say is true, but have you not preached that the Kingdom of God is purchased not by riches or nobility, but by the virtue of obedience? Now, I have kept these words in mind, and have never failed to obey anyone who has given me an order, as all in the monastery will tell you. Why, then, have I not reason to hope for what you have promised me?" The Saint was much pleased at this, and told it to all in the house after the brother's death.

11 Obedience is the summary of perfection and of the whole spiritual life, and the securest, shortest, least laborious and least dangerous way of becoming

enriched with all virtues, and arriving at the goal of our desires—eternal life.

—ALVAREZ

St. Teresa was fully persuaded of this truth, which led her to say that if all the angels together told her to do one thing, while her Superior commanded the contrary, she would always give the preference to the order of the Superior. "Because," she added, "obedience to Superiors is commanded by God in the Holy Scriptures, and consequently it is of faith, and there can be no deception about it; but revelations are liable to illusion." And, in fact, she often disclosed to her director things revealed to her by God, and when he disapproved of them, she immediately let them pass.

St. Frances of Rome, on many occasions, received commands from God to do certain things, but she never did them without first having the consent of her confessor, which was very pleasing to Our Lord.

On her deathbed, St. Mary Magdalen de' Pazzi said that nothing in the review of her whole life gave her so much comfort as the certainty that she had never been guided in anything by her own will and judgment, but always by the will and judgment of her Superiors and directors.

St. Paul, surnamed the Simple, received grace to perform miracles, after serving God only a short time in perfect obedience.

12 The devil, seeing that there is no shorter road to the summit of perfection than that of obedience, artfully

insinuates many repugnances and difficulties under color of good, to prevent us from following it.

—ST. TERESA

On account of St. Bridget's extreme attachment to penances, her spiritual father once forbade her to perform so many. She obeyed, but with reluctance, for she feared the loss of a spirit of mortification. The Blessed Virgin then appeared to her and said: "Suppose, my daughter, that two of my children desire to fast on a certain day. One, being mistress of her own actions, fasts; the other, who is under obedience, does not fast. The second gains two rewards—one for her desire, the other for her obedience." This instruction completely reassured the Saint.

13 The more we see of failure in obedience, the stronger should be our suspicion of temptation and illusion. For when God sends His inspirations to a heart, the first grace He sheds upon it is that of obedience.

—ST. TERESA

When a nun wrote to St. Francis de Sales that she was very unwilling to do some things prescribed by the rule of obedience, he answered in this manner: "To wish to live according to one's own will, in order better to perform the will of God—what a wild idea is this! That an inclination, or rather a caprice, fretful, changeable, bitter, and obstinate, should be an inspiration— what a contradiction this would be!"

Surius relates of the blessed Giordano, General of the Dominicans, that when he was ill of a fever in a Piedmontese city, where

there was no house of his Order, the Bishop received him and gave
him a magnificent bed, soft, and richly curtained. The humble servant of God did not wish to rest so luxuriously, but submitted at the
wish of a prior of the Order, who had charge of him at the time, on
account of his medical skill. The demon, however, seeing so good an
opportunity, appeared to him the first night in the form of a shining
angel, and gazing on him with wonder, reproved him, saying that
he could not understand how he could repose in such luxury, and
how he could so soon abandon his usual mortifications, without
thinking of the grave scandal that he would thus give to his Order.
After adding that he ought rather to sleep on the bare ground, he
quickly disappeared. The holy man, instantly springing from the
bed, stretched himself upon the floor. When the prior returned in
the morning, he was much astonished at the condition of things,
and immediately ordered his chilled and shivering patient to return
to bed, if he did not wish to commit suicide. The demon, however, did not lose courage, and appeared again the next night, under
the form of an angel of light. "Oh," said he, "I had believed that a
warning from Heaven would suffice to bring you back to regular
observance! But I see that self-love is very strong in you. How do
you dare to rebel against the light of Heaven? Obey at once the voice
of God, who requires you to leave this effeminacy, to cure you amid
the austerities suited to your state!" Strangely enough, the good man
allowed himself to be persuaded again to exchange his bed for the
bare floor. But when the prior visited him the next time and found
him benumbed and half-fainting, he exclaimed sharply: "What
oddity or what spirit of rigor is this?" But the Saint interrupted him,
saying that he was lying thus not by his own caprice, but by command of the angel of the Lord, who had expressly informed him

that it was the will of God that he should not remain in such a luxurious couch. "No, Father," returned the good prior, "it cannot be an angel of the Lord that has taught you to disregard obedience. This is the malign spirit, who desires to destroy your life, or at least to prolong your illness, that he may hinder your plans for the glory of God; if he comes again, show him no favor." With these and similar words he persuaded him to return to bed and allow himself to be cared for. When the demon came back on the third night, the reception he met with showed him that he was discovered, and he instantly fled in a paroxysm of disappointment and rage. This sick man soon began to recover, and afterwards pursued his apostolic labors with such success that his name became terrible to Hell, and very glorious throughout the world.

14 That obedience may be complete, it must exist in three things: in execution, by doing promptly, cheerfully, and exactly whatever the Superior orders; in will, by willing nothing but what the Superior wills; in judgment, by being of the same opinion as the Superior.

—ST. IGNATIUS LOYOLA

Whatever command was laid upon St. Mary Magdalen de' Pazzi, she accepted it always with a cheerful countenance, and executed it with promptness and exactness. And, what is more, she obeyed blindly, without stopping to inquire about the purpose and reason of the order, and whether that or something else would be better; for, as she said, she would not consider herself obedient, though she performed what was required, if she did

not subject her own judgment to that of the Superioress. And so, when she received an order, she first applied herself to judge and feel as the Superioress judged and felt, then she inclined her will to desire what she desired; therefore, she found no difficulty in performing anything, whatever it might be. Once Our Lord ordered her to live on bread and water, to go barefooted, and to wear a single poor and patched garment; but as the Superioress did not consent to this, she put on stockings, shoes, and her ordinary dress, and ate the usual food, as far as she was able, until by an evident miracle God changed the will of the Superioress. By this she showed that she trusted more to the judgment of Superiors than to her own, or even to revelations.

The Abbot Silvanus loved one of his monks, named Marcus, with a special affection. When a person came one day to tell him that the others were much offended at this, he brought him to the cells of the monks, and called them, one after another, by name. All were slow in appearing, except Marcus, who instantly came out. The Abbot and his companion then entering his cell, found that he had been writing, and had left a letter half finished that he might not delay in answering the voice of his Superior. This proved to all how reasonable was the Abbot's preference for him.

"I take for my model," said St. Francis de Sales, "the little Babe of Bethlehem, who knew so much, could do so much, and allowed Himself to be managed without a word."

15 Obedience consists not alone in doing what is actually commanded, but also in a continual readiness to do on any occasion whatever may be imposed.

—ST. VINCENT DE PAUL

St. Francis Xavier was so ready for any act of obedience that though he was working so fruitfully in India, and with so much satisfaction to himself, he said that if at the beginning of a promising mission he should receive an order from St. Ignatius, his Superior, to return to Italy, he would instantly break off his work and set out.

St. Felix the Capuchin excelled greatly in this virtue. At the least sign from his Superiors, he showed himself ever prompt and ready to execute all their directions, however arduous, difficult, and varied they might be, without excepting any. This was so well known that Superiors were careful not to mention any wish of theirs in presence of this holy man without real need, for he would be sure to consider a mere remark as a rigorous precept, and immediately proceed to execute it.

16 True obedience manifests itself in executing gladly and without any repugnance, things which are objects of antipathy or contrary to one's interests.

—ST. ALPHONSUS RODRIGUEZ

St. Teresa tells of herself that when the prioress ordered her to leave a certain foundation which she had begun by divine command, and for which she had labored much, she instantly left it with perfect willingness; for she judged this to be a proof that she had done all she could, and that nothing more was required of her. But even her confessor would not believe in this resignation, thinking that she must be afflicted at so great a disappointment.

In the convent of the venerable Sister Maria Crucifixa it was the rule to receive male visitors veiled. A special direction to the

contrary was at one time given to her, which she obeyed readily, though with feelings of extreme repugnance.

St. John Berchmans was appointed to serve a High Mass at an hour very inconvenient for his studies. He accepted the duty gladly, and served the Mass for many months without a word of complaint, or an attempt to be relieved from the charge.

We read of St. Felix the Capuchin that he was always prompt in giving up his own preferences, and especially for actions in themselves virtuous and meritorious, which even pious persons find it difficult to abandon, from motives of charity or mortification. But if these acts ceased to be approved by his Superiors and directors, they no longer attracted him. And so, a simple prohibition was sufficient to make him forsake any austerity or spiritual exercise, not only without repugnance, but with the greatest tranquillity. For example, he had for years gone barefoot with the consent of his Superiors. But in his old age the Cardinal Protector, at the request of one of his companions, ordered him to put on sandals again. This he immediately did, without complaint or inquiry as to who had made the suggestion to the Cardinal and without considering how much his reputation would suffer among seculars, who would suppose that he had relaxed in virtue.

17 A truly obedient man does not discriminate between one thing and another, or desire one employment more than another, since his only aim is to execute faithfully whatever may be assigned to him.

—ST. BERNARD

St. Jerome wrote that when visiting hermits in the desert, he found one who for eight years had carried a heavy stone on his shoulders twice a day for a distance of three miles, by order of his Superior. Asking him how he could be willing to perform such an act of obedience, he replied that he had always done it with the greatest contentment, as if it had been the loftiest and most important occupation in this world. These, concludes the Saint, are the ones who make profit and grow in perfection, for they nourish themselves with "the flour of wheat"—that is, with doing the will of God; and he testifies that he was himself so moved by the reply he received, that from that hour he decided to become a monk.

18 The chief merit of obedience consists not in following the will of a mild, amiable Superior who asks rather than commands, but in remaining patiently under the yoke of one who is imperious, rigorous, harsh, ill-humored, and never satisfied. This is a pure fountain of water gushing from the throat of a bronze lion.

—ST. FRANCIS DE SALES

St. Jane Frances de Chantal used to say that she should feel greater satisfaction in obeying the lowest Sister, who would do nothing but vex her and order her about roughly and sharply, than in following the directions of the ablest and most experienced in the Order; for, she said, where there is least of the creature, there is most of the Creator.

St. Athanasius relates of the ancient monks that they sought for harsh and unamiable Superiors who would never be pleased

with what they did and who would reprove them for their good, as St. Pacomius did his disciple Theodosius; and the harder and more unattractive the Superior was, the more perfect was their obedience.

St. Catherine of Bologna desired that her Superioress should treat her always unkindly and impose upon her the hardest tasks. She said that her own experience had proved that obedience in ordinary matters is indeed very useful, but that obedience in things difficult or harshly commanded in a short time fills the soul with virtues, and unites it to God.

19 If you will not do violence to yourself and will not be indifferent as far as your own interests are concerned, as to who is your Superior, do not flatter yourself that you will ever become a spiritual man and a faithful observer of your vows.

—ST. JOHN OF THE CROSS

St. Francis of Assisi said that among the graces he had received from the Lord was this, that he was as willing to obey a novice who had been in the house but an hour, as the most worthy of the seniors.

St. Francis Borgia showed the greatest veneration for all Superiors, not only while in office, but after they had retired from it. And when St. Ignatius appointed a lay-brother to take charge of his health, he yielded the same obedience to him that he would have to the Saint himself.

20 Remember that thou hast given thyself to the Superior for the love of God, and to obtain the Kingdom

of Heaven, and consequently, thou art no more thine own, but his to whom thou hast given thyself. Therefore it is not permitted thee to do anything of thyself, and without his will, since he—not thou—is the master of thy will.

As far as St. Mary Magdalen de' Pazzi was able, she did nothing without seeking the command or permission of the Superior or Mistress.

The venerable Pudenziana Terziaria, a Franciscan nun, said to her confessor just before her death: "Father, since I gave myself into your hands, by the divine help I have never so much as uttered a sigh which had not the seal of obedience. I have now but to draw my last breath, which I desire should have the same merit. Give me, then, permission for it!" The Father, astonished at so strange a request, paused for a moment, and then answered: "My daughter, I do not wish you to go yet." She inclined her head, and turning to the crucifix, "My Lord," she said, "Thou seest I am detained. Do not compel me, for I cannot consent." A little while after, she renewed her request to the Father, with the same result. But finally, moved with pity, he said: "Depart, O blessed soul, to the eternal repose!" She said quickly, "Bless me, Father," and after receiving the usual benediction, she turned her eyes upon those around, as if bidding them farewell, clasped and kissed the crucifix, and saying, with a smile, "I am going," she expired.

21 Beware of paying any attention to the wisdom, skill, or intelligence of a Superior; if not, you will

exchange divine obedience for human; for you will be led to obey for the sake of the qualities you perceive in him, and not for the sake of God imperceptibly present in his person. Oh what great havoc the devil works in the hearts of Religious, when he succeeds in making them regard the qualifications of Superiors.

—ST. JOHN OF THE CROSS

Father Peter Faber never looked at the defects of a Superior, but always at his virtues, that he might honor him in truth. And if he met one full of faults and destitute of virtues, he would still strive to honor and obey him faithfully, for the love and fear of God, and for his own perfection.

St. John Berchmans saw God in his Superiors, and never their own qualities. This caused him to treat them always with great veneration, and he said that he had never the least dislike for any one of them.

22 When the Superior orders anything, consider that it is not he that speaks, but God, so that the Superior is but a trumpet through which the voice of God sounds. And this is the true key to obedience, and the reason why the perfect obey in everything so promptly, and make no difference between one Superior and another, and submit to the lowest in authority as well as to the highest, and to the imperfect as well as to the perfect; for they regard not the persons nor the qualities of Superiors, but God

alone, who is always the same, of equal merit, and of equal authority.

—ST. ALPHONSUS RODRIGUEZ

St. Aloysius Gonzaga said that he did not remember ever to have disobeyed the slightest order of a Superior. He even showed as much reverence and submission to the beadle as to the General himself.

The blessed Solomea observed the orders of Superiors with as much exactness as if they had been given by God Himself—for this reason, that he regarded them as originating from God, and only promulgated by the voice of the Superior.

The venerable Mother Seraphina sometimes had confessors who possessed but little wisdom, yet she obeyed them with the same exactness as she did the others; and she often said that when they did not command anything sinful, it was always necessary to obey them, without seeking a reason for their orders.

23 Do you know how it happens that many who have lived long in religion, and practiced daily so many acts of obedience, have by no means succeeded in acquiring a habit of this virtue? Because, not every time they obey, do they do it because such is the will of God (which is the formal reason of obedience); but they obey, now for one cause, now for another, so that their actions, being destitute of mutual similarity, cannot unite to form a habit of this virtue.

—ST. ALPHONSUS RODRIGUEZ

St. Mary Magdalen de' Pazzi never regarded the person who was her Superior, or who gave her orders, whoever she might be, but recognized in her the person of God; nor did she obey for any other reason than because she believed it to be the will of God. She considered whatever was imposed on her as ordered by divine authority, and so she obeyed the cook as willingly as the prioress, and experienced equal joy and satisfaction in doing so.

The same is narrated of the monks of Egypt, who performed promptly, without any discussion or objection, whatever duty was laid upon them, as if the order had come directly from God, whose will they were accustomed to recognize in that of the Superior.

24 If you ever are conscious of impulses, thoughts, and judgments opposed to obedience, though apparently good and holy, do not admit them on any account, but reject them promptly, as you would thoughts against chastity or faith.

—ST. JOHN CLIMACUS

St. John Berchmans once had a philosophical thesis to defend on which he was only partly prepared, when he was called to join a brother who was going out. He felt interiorly a slight repugnance to leaving his work; but without giving any outward sign of it, he turned his thoughts in another direction. When he came home, he reflected seriously on the emotion he had felt, and for some days recalled it at his particular examen, and made it a subject of mature reflection. Finally, by the grace of God, he

was able to tell his Superior that he had obtained a victory over himself; and he was never again disturbed by any repugnance.

The Venerable Maria Seraphina had permission from her director, who was living in Naples, to Communicate every day. But to avoid singularity, he advised her to ask permission each time from the ordinary director of Capri. When he refused it, as often happened, she submitted, though with much grief. On one of these occasions, as she was hearing Mass, the Lord appeared to her after the Consecration and seemed to invite her to go to Communion, which enkindled in her heart a most vehement desire to do so. But she would not yield to it, as she was persuaded that there might be an illusion in regard to the vision, while there could be none as to the command of the confessor.

25 Beware of examining and judging the orders of Superiors, and considering why such a thing was commanded, or whether another course would have been better. All this belongs not to the subject, but to the Superior.

—ST. JEROME

One very warm summer day, St. John Berchmans went out three or four times having been given by the Superior as a companion to several Brothers in succession. His roommate, feeling sorry for his evident suffering, advised him to use a little more discretion and prudence, for otherwise the intense heat would surely make him ill. But he answered with much gentleness: "Brother, I must leave prudence to him who gives me the orders. I am bound to nothing but obedience."

When the Bishop of Capri was going to celebrate Mass one morning at the convent of the venerable Mother Seraphina, he sent her word that he did not wish to give Communion to the nuns at the usual grating, but at the altar, and that they must therefore all come into the church. The servant of God was then in her cell, and without stopping to consider how painful was such a direction on account of the great irregularity it involved, she threw herself on her knees before her crucifix and kissed the ground; then rising, she kissed the Lord's feet, saying affectionately: "He was made obedient unto death." Without further delay, she left her cell and went to beg of her Sisters to obey the order of the Prelate. After receiving Holy Communion, they all went into the choir to make their thanksgiving. There the Mother had an ecstasy, in which Our Lord told her how much He had been pleased with this act of obedience. She told her companions of this when they were assembled at the general recreation. But when some dwelt on the repugnance they had felt, she said: "For me, the Lord gave me this morning a great reward for my blind obedience; and though the action in itself may not have been good, certainly the obedience was good."

26 It is not enough for obedience to do what is commanded. It must be done without debate, and must be looked upon as the best and most perfect thing possible, though it may seem and may even be the contrary.
—ST. PHILIP NERI

Father Alvarez was accustomed to subject himself willingly to obedience in all things. For he said that he had noticed that

even when it seemed desirable for him to do something contrary to what obedience required, yet by obedience he always succeeded best.

What did Our Lord do to cure the blind man? He anointed his eyes with clay, and told him to go and bathe in the pool of Siloe. This blind man might have said that this was a remedy better adapted to take away sight than to restore it, and he might have objected to the journey. But as he obeyed without cavil, he was cured.

St. Columbano the Abbot, having most of his monks sick, ordered them all to go to the barn and thrash the grain. It seemed a very hard and indiscreet thing to oblige men who were almost too weak to stand, to perform such laborious work, and to expose them to the rays of a scorching sun; but they all went out to execute the order, except a few prudent and cautious ones, who thought it safer to remain in bed. But what was the result? Those who blindly obeyed were cured instantly, while the others who reasoned about the matter remained sick of the fever for a whole year.

The Blessed Virgin, appearing to a nun, told her that by means of obedience the ends of Divine Wisdom are accomplished; which, often by ways sublime and not penetrated by human prudence, moves on to the aims it seeks without any hindrance.

27 Whoever wishes to be a good Religious must make himself like the ass of the monastery. This animal does not choose what burden he is to bear, nor go by the road he prefers, nor rest when he likes, nor do what he wishes; but accommodates himself to all

that is chosen for him. He walks, he stops, he turns, he goes back, he suffers and labors day and night, in all kinds of weather, and bears whatever burden is put upon him without saying, "Why?" or "What for?" "It is too much;" "It is too little;" or the like.

—ABBOT NESTERONE

This holy Abbot, as is told in the Lives of the Fathers, at his very entrance into religion made this beautiful resolution: I and the ass are one. I will consider myself to be the monastery ass. And so, he became one of the best Religious.

St. John Berchmans considered himself in the same light. Whatever was commanded him, he never refused to do, nor excused himself, nor gave any sign of discontent or discouragement, but accepted all cheerfully and executed it promptly and faithfully. And so, when the Superiors were in perplexity as to assigning some difficult task or finding a companion for a brother who was going out, he was always their resort. Thus, it sometimes happened that he had scarcely returned home with one, when he was appointed to go out with another; and this might occur three or four times in one day. And with these companions he would go back and forth, in one direction or another, stop anywhere and as long as they pleased, without objecting or complaining of the loss of time, or of not being as well treated as others; for his only aim was to obey and serve.

But St. Felix the Capuchin put on this character most completely of all, for he did it not only in his own mind, but by an avowal that others might have the same opinion of him; and he even valued the title of ass. Sometimes he was passing through a

crowded street with baskets full of bread or wine, when he would shout: "Make way for the ass!" And if anyone should say that he did not see any ass, he would answer: "Do you not know that I am the Capuchins' ass?" As he was walking one day in the city, he fell down by accident in the mud, and not being able to rise he said to his companion: "Do you not see that the ass has fallen? Why do you not put on the whip and make him rise?" When any Religious called him by his own name, he would often answer, "You are mistaken, Father; my name is Brother Ass." Nor was all this a mere matter of words; for the Superior could employ him at all times and places, precisely as if he had been an ass, and give him whatever he pleased to do, without the risk of a word of excuse or the slightest sign of reluctance.

28 Whoever lives under obedience ought to allow himself to be ruled by Providence, through his Superior, like a dead man. It is a sign of death not to see, not to feel, not to answer, not to complain, not to show any preference, but to be moved and carried anywhere at the will of another. See how far your obedience falls short of this.

—ST. IGNATIUS LOYOLA

A man of this type was St. Paul the Simple, a disciple of St. Anthony. He one day asked his master whether Christ was before the Prophets; upon which the Saint commanded him not to speak, as he was able to talk nothing but nonsense; and for three successive years the disciple observed perpetual silence. After that St. Anthony, wishing to try his obedience still further,

commanded him to do many absurd and useless things such as drawing water from a well and then pouring it out, making garments, then ripping them to pieces, and the like. St. Paul regarded all these things as necessary, at least because they were commanded, though they might be frivolous and of no account in themselves. He performed them, therefore, cheerfully, promptly and with all possible diligence, without making the least reflection about them.

The same spirit was shown by a certain disciple of the Abbot Martin who, having a dry rod in his hand, planted it in the ground and bade his disciple to water it until it blossomed. The latter did this regularly for three years, going daily for water to the Nile, which was two miles distant; and he never complained nor was discouraged by seeing that he had labored so long in vain. Finally the Lord deigned to show how much this labor pleased Him, for the rod grew green and blossomed. This anecdote is related by Severus Sulpicius, who says that he had himself seen the tree, which was preserved up to his time as a memorial in the court of the monastery.

On the day when St. Mary Magdalen de' Pazzi received the habit, she prostrated herself humbly and with true feeling at the feet of her Mistress and resigned herself wholly to her will, saying that she gave herself into her hands as if dead, and that hereafter she might do with her whatever she pleased, for she would obey her in everything. She also entreated her not to show her any favor in regard to humiliations and mortifications. She made the same protestations to a second Mistress afterwards appointed to succeed the first. And she did, in fact, live thus wholly submissive to their will, obeying them promptly

in everything, and allowing herself to be employed by them in whatever they wished, without ever contradicting or giving any sign of disapproval, whatever they might say. In this manner she succeeded so far in despoiling herself of her own will and judgment that she seemed no longer to have any, and they might be called dead in her.

29 The perfection of a Religious consists in exact obedience to his Rules; and whoever is most faithful in their observance will be, by this fact alone, the most perfect.

—ST. ALPHONSUS RODRIGUEZ

St. Vincent de Paul was most exact in the practical observance of all the rules of the Congregation, to such a degree that he scrupled to transgress even the smallest, such as that of kneeling on entering or leaving his cell, though in the last years of his life this became very painful to him, on account of a disease which had settled in his limbs. He was also usually the first to be present at the general exercises, particularly meditation.

Father Joli, Superior of the Congregation of the Mission, was most exact himself in the observance of the Rules and inflexible as to others, yielding neither to reasons nor to entreaties, so far as to permit the least want of observance. A Superior having once written to him to ask a certain permission, this was his reply: "Our Rule is opposed to this, and we ought to be most strongly attached to our Rule. This is the best of all reasons." In a discourse to his Community he said one day: "We ought to regard as our chief duties the Rules and holy practices of the Congregation,

disregarding, to observe them, all our own particular devotions. For example, we should consider it more meritorious not to speak without permission to persons of our acquaintance whom we may meet in the house, than to take twenty disciplines of our own will."

St. Jane Frances de Chantal had the observance of her Rules so much at heart, and kept such strict watch over herself, that she might not transgress the smallest, even when a Superior, and much advanced in years, that her practice served as a living and most efficacious rule to rouse and incite all the others to a most perfect observance. It happened once that she came into recreation from the parlor, much prostrated on account of her great age. Some companions begged her to rest for the short time that remained before the close of recreation. "But what shall we do," she answered, smiling, "with the Rule, which requires us to work in recreation?"

St. Aloysius Gonzaga was never seen to transgress the least rule of the Institute. He was so exact in this that he could not bring himself to give a companion half a sheet of paper or to receive any little picture that might be offered to him without first obtaining permission from the Superior, as the Rule prescribed.

One night the devil tormented a lay-brother in the Dominican monastery at Bologna with so much cruelty that the noise of blows and struggles aroused the Religious. When St. Dominic, who was there, commanded the demon to tell why this was, he answered that it was because the brother had taken something to drink on the previous evening without permission and without asking a blessing, as the Rule enjoined.

St. Gregory relates that an evil spirit entered into a nun and tormented her grievously because she had eaten lettuce without asking a blessing, according to the requirement of the Rule.

30 The predestination of Religious is inseparably connected with love for their Rule, and the careful performance of the duties of their vocation.

—ST. FRANCIS DE SALES

St. Bonaventure wrote these words in a notebook: "I have come into religion to live not as others live, but to live as all ought to live, in the spirit of the Institute and full observance of the Rule; for, at my entrance, the Rules were given me to read, and not the lives of others. The Rules were then accepted by me voluntarily and as the basis of my life, and therefore I ought to observe them all exactly, although I should see that no one else observed them."

St. Francis de Sales gave high praise to a certain General of the Carthusians, for his great regularity in the observance of his Rule; for, he said, he was so exact even in things of the least importance that he did not yield the palm even to the best novices.

St. John Berchmans was so devoted to the observance of the Rules that during all the time he lived in religion, no person ever saw him violate one of them. And so, when he came to die, he asked for the little book of his Rules, and clasping it in his hands he said, "With this I die willingly."

JULY

Simplicity

Be simple as doves.—MATT. 10:16

1 Among those who make profession of following the maxims of Christ, simplicity ought to be held in great esteem; for, among the wise of this world there is nothing more contemptible or despicable than this. Yet it is a virtue most worthy of love, because it leads us straight to the Kingdom of God, and, at the same time, wins for us the affection of men; since one who is regarded as upright, sincere, and an enemy to tricks and fraud is loved by all, even by those who only seek from morning till night to cheat and deceive others.

—ST. VINCENT DE PAUL

This Saint himself truly had great esteem for simplicity, and loved it much. Therefore he not only kept himself from any transgression against it, but could not suffer those under his authority to commit any. If at times they were guilty of doing so he would be sure to correct them for it, though with great mildness.

St. Francis de Sales, also, was full of respect and love for this virtue, as he once declared to a confidential friend, in these words: "I do not know what that poor virtue of prudence has done to me, that I find so much difficulty in loving it. And if I love it, it is only from necessity, inasmuch as it is the support and guiding light of this life. But the beauty of simplicity completely fascinates me. It is true that the Gospel recommends to us both the simplicity of the dove and the prudence of the serpent; but I would give a hundred serpents for one dove. I know that both are useful when they are united, but I think that it should be in the proportion observed in compounding some medicines, in which a little poison is mixed with a quantity of wholesome drugs. Let the world, then, be angry—let the prudence of the world rage, and the flesh perish; for it is always better to be good and simple, than to be subtle and malicious."

St. Phocas the Martyr was greatly to be admired for his simplicity, according to what Surius relates. He cultivated a little garden, less to provide food for himself than to supply with vegetables and fruit those travelers and pilgrims who had heard of his liberality and stopped at his house; for no one ever knocked at his door who was not received with great charity and courtesy. This holy man was denounced for aiding and abetting Christians, to the governor of the province, who, resolving upon his death, sent soldiers privately in search of him with orders to kill

him. They arrived one evening at his house, not knowing that it was his, entered it, and with the usual freedom of soldiery, demanded food. According to his custom, he received them willingly and kindly and gave them what little he had. He served them, too, at table, with so much charity and courtesy that they were delighted and captivated, and said between themselves that they had never met such a good-hearted man. And so they were led by his great simplicity and candor to ask him with confidence whether he knew anything of a certain Phocas, who helped and harbored Christians, and upon whose death the imperial prefect had resolved. The Saint replied that he knew him very well, and that he would willingly point him out to them so that they might go to rest quietly, without further inquiry, for on the next day he would show them an easy way of capturing him. He then spent the whole night in fervent prayer, and when it was day he went to visit the soldiers, and bid them good morning with his usual cordiality. They answered by reminding him of his promise to deliver up Phocas, whom they were seeking. "Do not doubt," he returned, "that I will find him for you. Consider that you have him already in your hands."

"Let us go, then, and take him," they answered.

"There is no need of going," he replied, "for he is here present. I am he. Do with me what you please." At these words, the soldiers were amazed and stupefied, both on account of the great charity which he had welcomed them and of the ingenuous sincerity with which he revealed himself to his persecutors, when he could so easily have escaped death by fleeing in the night. They gazed at each other in amazement, and neither of them dared to lay hands on one who had been so kind to them. They

were more inclined to give him his life, and to report to the prefect that after long search they had not been able to discover Phocas.

"No," said the Saint, "my death would be a less evil than to concoct such a fiction, and tell such a falsehood. Execute, then, the order you have received." So saying, he bared his neck and extended it to the soldiers, who severed it with one stroke and gave him the glorious crown of martyrdom. This most candid fidelity was so agreeable to God that He immediately began, and still continues, to signalize it by illustrious miracles, especially in favor of pilgrims and sailors, to whom—in death as in life—the Saint has been most liberal of benefits and miraculous helps. In recognition of this, a custom came into use among travelers by sea, of serving to him every day at meals a part of the first dish, which was called the portion of St. Phocas. This was each day bought by one or other of the voyagers, and the price deposited in the hands of the captain; and when they came into port, the money was distributed among the poor, in thanksgiving to their benefactor for their successful voyage.

2   Simplicity is nothing but an act of charity pure and simple, which has but one sole end—that of gaining the love of God. Our soul is then truly simple, when we have no aim at all but this, in all we do.

—ST. FRANCIS DE SALES

St. Mary Magdalen de' Pazzi once said: "If I thought that by saying a word, however indifferent, for any other end than

the love of God, I could become a Seraph, I certainly would not say it."

The devil, envying a young monk who was making good progress, appeared one night to his Master of Novices under the form of a good angel, and informed him that his disciple was already reprobated and that whatever good he did was of no use to him. The Master of Novices was much grieved at this and could not refrain from tears whenever he met the young man, who one day asked him the reason of his grief. When he told it, the novice said: "Father, do not grieve for this. If I am to be damned, I shall be damned; if I am to be saved, I shall be saved. I serve God not for the Kingdom of Heaven, but for His goodness and love towards me, and for the Passion He has suffered for me. If, then, He chooses to give me His Paradise, He can do it: and if He wishes to give me Hell, He can indeed do it; I am content that He should do with me what pleases Him." The following night, a true angel appeared to the Master of Novices and told him the one he had previously seen was a devil, and that his disciple had merited more by his act of resignation than by all the good life he had hitherto led.

3 The office of simplicity is to make us go straight to God, without regard to human respect or our own interests. It leads us to tell things candidly and just as they exist in our hearts. It leads us to act simply, without admixture of hypocrisy and artifice—and, finally, keeps us at a distance from every kind of deceit and double-dealing.

—ST. VINCENT DE PAUL

This Saint always held it as of the utmost importance to have God as his only object in all he did; neither could he bear that those under his charge should swerve in the least from this aim. When one of them was publicly accused of having done something from human respect, he reprimanded him severely, saying that it would be better to be thrown into the fire with feet and hands tied than to work to please men. Answering a letter from one of his priests, he writes thus: "You write to me that when you speak highly of a certain person in your letters, it would be well for his friends to know it, that he may come to know it too. What thoughts for you to have! Where is the simplicity of a missionary, who ought always look directly to God? If you do not see good in certain persons, do not speak of it; but if you find it, speak of it to honor God in them, since from Him all good proceeds. Our Lord reproved one who called Him good, because he did not call Him so with a good intention. With how much greater reason might you be blamed, if you praise sinful men to please them, and to gain their favor, or for any other earthly and imperfect motive? Remember that duplicity does not please God, and that to be truly simple, we ought to have no aim but Himself."

As to his own language, it was candid and simple, and so far from all evasion and craftiness that no one could ever fear being deceived by him. He also avoided high-flown compliments, which, as they are usually united with dissimulation, are not in conformity with the rules of Christian simplicity. Therefore he conversed with all simply and cordially, omitting useless demonstrations, as he desired also that his priests should do.

The venerable Sister Crucifixa possessed most remarkable candor and sincerity, by which she showed her hatred of all

dissimulation and duplicity. The slightest untruth never escaped from her lips, either in the way of civility or of jest, although at recreation she would often employ irony or other diverting forms of expression to enliven the conversation.

St. Charles Borromeo showed plainly that he was full of this holy virtue on several occasions, especially in the election of Pius V as Pope. As his uncle, Pius IV, had always disliked St. Charles, there was every reason to believe that the nephew would be opposed, or at least not very friendly, to him so that he might be taxed with want of prudence in giving power that would be likely to be used for his own ruin. Nevertheless, having before his eyes only the glory of God and the greater good of the Church and paying no regard to his private interests, he brought about his election. But God took care of him and caused him to be much favored and esteemed by Pius V. In his speech, St. Charles was extremely candid and utterly opposed to all artifice and duplicity, and he wished those of his household to be the same, as he once said to one of them who, in talking of a certain affair, allowed these words to escape him: "I will tell you sincerely what I think about it." The Saint interrupted him quickly, saying: "Then you do not always speak sincerely! Now, be sure that he cannot be my friend, who does not speak always with sincerity, and say with his lips what he means in his heart."

4 God loves the simple and converses with them willingly and communicates to them the understanding of His truths, because He disposes of these at His pleasure. He does not deal thus with lofty and subtle spirits.

—ST. FRANCIS DE SALES

St. Vincent de Paul was of the same opinion, the truth of which, he said, experience daily confirms; for it is but too clear that the spirit of religion is not ordinarily to be found so much among the wise and prudent of the world as among the poor and simple, who are enriched by God with a living and practical faith, which makes them believe and appreciate the words of eternal life. So they are usually seen to suffer their diseases, their poverty and all their trials with more patience and resignation than others.

St. Ambrose, in the funeral oration which he pronounced over his brother, St. Satirus, greatly exalts among his other virtues his childlike simplicity, "which," he says, "shone in him like a mirror, so that he could not have failed to please God; for He, as a completely simple being, loves what is simple, and hates and punishes all adulteration."

It is related in regard to St. Gertrude that the Lord once appeared to a holy soul and said, "Know that there is not a soul in the world which is nearer and more closely united to Me by simplicity, than that of Gertrude, and so there is none to which I feel Myself so much drawn as to hers."

5 True simplicity is like that of children, who think, speak and act candidly and without craftiness. They believe whatever is told them; they have no care or thought for themselves, especially when with their parents; they cling to them, without going to seek their own satisfactions and consolations, which they take in good faith and enjoy with simplicity, without any curiosity about their causes and effects.

—ST. FRANCIS DE SALES

St. Mary Magdalen de' Pazzi resembled in her behavior a simple girl, acting without craftiness, and with great candor and simplicity of heart—accompanied, however, with prudence and such gravity as made her loved and respected by all.

The venerable Sister Maria Crucifixa was truly remarkable for this virtue. Though gifted with heavenly illumination, she appeared precisely like a simple little girl, without a vestige of artfulness. She told everything candidly and as it seemed to her, and she thought others did the same; for she could not believe that a Christian would be capable of telling lies. Some examples will show this more clearly.

On account of the opinion generally entertained of her sanctity, a great number of letters came to her from many places. She believed that this was owing to the high standing of the convent, and that her companions received as many; but she was much surprised to notice that they were not kept as busy in writing answers as she was. To satisfy herself about the matter, she went around asking them if they received many letters; and they, to favor her simplicity, answered, with polite exaggeration, that they received *ever so many*. "Why, then, do you not write?" she replied. "I will bring you the inkstand so that you can answer them." She went for the inkstand and a pen, and gave them to her companions; but seeing that they could not restrain their laughter, she was unable to understand what the joke was, and remained much puzzled.

Having received from Cardinal Tommasi, her brother, who often wrote to her, a letter in which he signed himself "a wretch," according to the frequent custom of the time, she would answer neither that one, nor many others that he afterwards wrote. Being

asked the reason, she replied that she did not wish to keep up a correspondence with wretches; and it required no little trouble to induce her to write.

But in another pretty incident the Lord was pleased to show how acceptable to Him was her simplicity. A linnet was given to her, which she named Fiorisco. She loved it very much, not only for its beautiful voice, but for the virtues which she said were shown in its actions. It happened once that she wished to pull out two of its feathers, to make a little pen to draw a certain design for an approaching Festival. She thought the linnet was rather unwilling to give them to her, and she was somewhat disedified by his want of devotion. A short time after a young canary, taking his first flight, rested on the cage of the linnet, which held him by one of his feet with his beak and began to pull out his feathers with his claws. Seeing what was going on, she hurried to the rescue, and exclaimed, "Ah, Fiorisco! We are growing worse and worse! Is this the way to observe charity?" Then turning to the image of the Virgin, she protested that in this bird she loved nothing except God, but that he had done very wrong that day, and she wished that he might be suitably punished. At these words, the linnet, as if he foresaw the coming punishment, stopped singing, and spent the rest of the day in a melancholy manner in a corner of the cage, with his feathers ruffled up. When evening came, a noise was heard from the cage, where poor Fiorisco was struggling grievously, with mournful cries. The servant of God hastened to the scene and saw the devil, in the form of an ugly crow, attacking her bird. Crying aloud "*Santa Maria*," she put him to flight; but she found that her linnet had lost a wing, which had been torn off at the shoulder, and fell on

the ground before her eyes; and the injured bird seemed on the point of drawing his last breath. She was grieved at the sight and prayed to the Lord, asking, as He did not desire the death of a sinner, but his conversion and life, that He would grant that her Fiorisco, though he had been punished, might not die. Nor was the prayer in vain; for after she had taken the bird in her hand and caressed it a little, it suddenly recovered its usual strength and appeared with a new wing, fully provided with bones and flesh and skin, in nothing different from the first, except that the feathers were handsomer.

6 Astuteness is nothing but a mass of artifices, inventions, craft and deceit, by which we endeavor to mislead the minds of those with whom we are dealing and make them believe that we have no knowledge or sentiment as to the matter in question, except what we manifest by our words. This is wholly contrary to simplicity, which requires our exterior to be perfectly in conformity with our interior.

—ST. FRANCIS DE SALES

When this good Saint was told by a friend of his that he would have been successful in politics, "No," he replied, "the mere name of prudence and policy frightens me, and I understand little or nothing about it. I do not know how to lie, to invent or dissimulate without embarrassment, and political business is wholly made up of these things. What I have in my heart, I have upon my tongue; and I hate duplicity like death, for I know how abominable it is to God."

St. Vincent de Paul, too, was utterly opposed to worldly pol-icy, and in his dealings with others was most careful to avoid all evasions and artifices. The very shadow of falsehood affrighted him, and he had a horror of equivocations, which deceive an inquirer by answers of double meaning.

7 When a simple soul is to act, it considers only what it is suitable to do or say and then immediately begins the action, without losing time in thinking what others will do or say about it. And after doing what seemed right, it dismisses the subject; or if, perhaps, any thought of what others may say or do should arise, it instantly cuts short such reflections, for it has no other aim than to please God, and not creatures, except as the love of God requires it. Therefore, it cannot bear to be turned aside from its purpose of keeping close to God, and winning more and more of His love for itself.

—ST. FRANCIS DE SALES

This holy Bishop having gone one evening to the Certosa at Grenoble, the General of the Carthusians—who was a man of great learning and piety—received him very courteously. After talking with him in his room for some time on spiritual subjects, he took leave of him, excusing himself for not remaining longer, on the ground that it was the Festival of a Saint of the Order, and he must assist at Matins that night. In passing through the corridors to his cell, he happened to meet the procurator, who hearing of the visit, said that he had done wrong to leave the Bishop, as no one could entertain him better than himself; that

as to Matins, he could say them whenever he wished, but it was not every day that they had prelates of such great merit in that desert. "I believe you are right," replied the General. He immediately went back to the Saint, related to him with great ingenuousness what had just been said to him, and asked pardon for the fault which he had committed, as he said, without intending to. The Saint was astonished at such great candor and simplicity, and said that he was more amazed at it than if he had seen a miracle.

8 The chief point is to beware not of men, but to beware of displeasing the majesty of God.

—ST. TERESA

This Saint once said that she used every effort to perform every one of her actions in such a manner as not to displease Him whom she clearly beheld always overlooking her.

St. Vincent de Paul said one day that from the time he had given himself to the service of God, he had never done anything which he would not have been willing to do in the public squares; for he performed every action with a vivid recollection of the presence of God, whom he feared more than men.

9 When one thinks he has done all that God requires of him for the success of any undertaking whether the result be good or bad, he ought always to remain in peace and great tranquillity of mind, contenting himself with the testimony of his own conscience.

—ST. VINCENT DE PAUL

When St. Ignatius had done what he could to repair any mistake that had been made, if he did not succeed, he neither lost courage nor grieved over the time as wasted; but content with having exerted all his powers, he rested in the unfathomable counsel of Providence.

10 If you happen to say or do something that is not well received by all, you should not, on that account, set yourself to examine and scrutinize all your words and actions; for there is no doubt that it is self-love which makes us anxious to know whether what we have said or done is approved or not. Simplicity does not run after its actions, but leaves the result of them to Divine Providence, which it follows above all things, turning neither to the right nor to the left, but simply going on its way.

—ST. FRANCIS DE SALES

This Saint himself acted in this manner, for he never sought to know whether his words or actions were acceptable to others or not. When it was reported to him that a certain action of his had been disapproved by some persons, he answered without any discomposure: "That is not to be wondered at, for not even the works of Christ our Lord were approved by all; and there are many, even at this day, who speak blasphemously of them."

11 Do not reason about afflictions and contradictions, but receive them with patience and sweetness, feeling

that it is enough to know that they come from the hand of God.

—ST. FRANCIS DE SALES

It is told in the Life of a servant of God at Naples, called Sister Maria di Sandiago, that one day when she was reflecting upon a trial which she was suffering, she heard these words from an interior voice: "Do you say that you trust in Me, and yet debate with yourself so much upon this?" She then understood that she ought to receive a trial with simple resignation, and not reflect upon it further; and changing her previous habit, she did so, and continued to do so for the future, with great profit and contentment.

However great were the trials and adversities of St. Vincent de Paul, he was never disturbed—neither did he show, or even feel, anger against anyone; for he took all from the hands of God without discussion.

12 These continual reflections upon ourselves and our actions are of no use except to consume time, which would be better employed in doing, than in scrutinizing so carefully what has been done. For this constant watching as to whether we are doing well, often causes things to be done badly. Those souls which make reflections about trifles act like silkworms, which impede and imprison themselves in their own work.

—ST. FRANCIS DE SALES

A nun having sent to this Saint an account of her interior, he wrote thus in answer: "Your path is excellent; I have only to

say that you watch your steps too closely, through fear of falling. You make too many reflections upon the movements of your self-love, which doubtless are frequent, but which will never be dangerous, if, without being vexed at their importunity, or frightened at their numbers, you will say 'No.' Walk simply, do not desire so much spiritual rest. If you have not much, why do you disturb yourself so greatly? God is good. He sees what you are. Your inclinations can do you no harm, however bad they may be; for they are only left you to exercise your will in making a closer union with the will of God. Raise your spirit aloft with perfect confidence in the goodness of the Lord. Do not be troubled about Him, for He said to Martha that He did not wish it, or, at least, that He preferred she should not be troubled at all, not even in doing well. Do not examine your soul so much as to its progress. Do not wish to be too perfect, but go on smoothly. Let your ordinary exercises and the action you have to perform from day to day, make up your life. Do not take thought for the morrow. As to your course, God, who has guided it until now, will guide it to the end. Rest in perfect peace in the holy and loving confidence which you ought to have in the kindness of Divine Providence."

A young monk, very desirous of perfection, set his heart upon purifying himself from every fault and therefore kept his eyes upon all his actions, looking at them again and again, before and after their performance and while they were going on—to do them well, and to see whether they had been well done. Therefore the more he sought to avoid faults, the more he committed them; and by guarding himself from slight defects, he fell into grave ones. In this way he only filled his soul with fear and disquiet, to

very little advantage. Finally he went to an old and very spiritual monk to ask his advice. This holy man merely suggested to him gently those two counsels of the Holy Spirit: *"Fili, in mansuetudine serva animam tuam; in mansuetudine profice opera tua"*— "Have a heart full of peace and confidence in God, and work tranquilly, without so many reflections, so you will accomplish your design." He took this advice and began to follow it, and by this new method of proceeding he quickly regained peace and in a short time made progress in perfection.

13   When one aims at pleasing his God through love, as his mind is always turned in that direction in which love urges him, he has neither heart nor opportunity to reflect upon himself, and to see what he is doing and whether he is satisfied with it. For such reflections are not pleasing in the eyes of God, and only serve to satisfy that wretched love and inordinate care that we have for ourselves. This self-love, it must be said, is a great busy-body, which takes up everything and holds to nothing.

—ST. FRANCIS DE SALES

This appears very plainly from what St. Catherine of Genoa relates of herself. "Scarcely," said she, "had my Divine Love taken possession of my soul, when I entreated Him to purify it from every interior and exterior imperfection. This He immediately began to do, but with such exactness and so minutely, that to my amazement, He caused me to look upon things as wrong and imperfect, which everyone would have considered right

and perfect. Oh my God! in everything He found defects, and in every action something to blame. If I spoke of the interior emotions I experienced in my heart, He said: 'This talk aims at your own consolation.' If I was silent, and remained grieving and lamenting interiorly, 'Ah, this grief and lamentation serves to give you some refreshment!' If I turned my thoughts upon the course things were taking, 'All these reflections only serve to satisfy self-love.' If I remained like an insensible thing and only paid attention when things like what I felt in my own mind were spoken of, 'And is not this desire to listen a form of seeking self-gratification?' When the inferior part of my soul thus beheld itself revealed, and perceived that it could not deny these imperfections, it finally owned itself to be conquered. Then the superior part began to experience an unspeakable peace, seeing that the inferior lay prostrate and could do no harm, and that it would itself reap all the advantage. But here again my Holy Love found something to reprove, and said, 'What do you think to do? I desire all for Myself. Do not imagine that I will leave thee a single good of body or of soul, or that I will ever rest until I have annihilated in thee all that cannot abide in the Divine Presence, and have fully revealed and utterly subdued these things to Myself.' And so, not knowing what to say or do in view of His clear-sightedness, I gave myself wholly into His hands, that He might strip me of all that was not pleasing to His most penetrating eyes. Then I saw that Pure Love wishes to be alone; where It abides, It cannot bear company; and therefore when It wishes to draw a soul to perfection, It marks as enemies all things beloved by it, and intends to consume them without compassion for soul or body, and if permitted, would take them all away at once. But

seeing the weakness of man, which could not support so great and so sudden a work, He cuts them off little by little, by which the soul constantly knows more and more of the operation of God and is every day enkindled with fresh flames of His love, so that this divine fire is insensibly consuming her desires and imperfect loves, until she remains stripped of every other love and entirely possessed by the pure love of God."

14 That we may not be deceived by self-love, in considering matters that concern us, we ought to look at them as if they belonged to others, and our only business with them was to give our judgment—not from interest, but in the cause of truth; and in the same way we should look on others' affairs as our own.

—ST. IGNATIUS LOYOLA

Seleucus, King of the Locrians, acted on this principle when, after his son had committed a crime which by the laws of the kingdom was punishable by the loss of both eyes, he immediately condemned him, as if he had been an ordinary subject. Nor can this be considered an act of thoughtlessness or cruelty, or a proof that Seleucus had lost the feelings of a father; for he showed his sensibility to his son's unhappy condition by his readiness to share the penalty with him, commanding that one of his own eyes should be put out, and one of his son's.

In the Lives of the Fathers it is narrated that a person asked a holy abbot how he ought to act when, in regulating the conduct or affairs of others, he was in doubt whether he should say or do

certain things. The Saint replied: "Before saying or doing those things, reflect as to what your own feelings would be if someone else should say or do them to you. And if you find that you would feel displeasure or resentment, use that same moderation and charity which you would desire to have practiced towards you. In such cases this is my rule."

It was the usual custom of St. Vincent de Paul to regard his own interests as if they belonged to others, and those of others as his own, as may be seen in various incidents of his life. It will be sufficient to mention two. Some of his relatives, who had been summoned before a high tribunal on a grave charge, asked him for letters which might exert an influence in their favor. But he, through zeal for justice, would not interfere in the matter. On the other hand, when some of his friends wished to intercede with the judges on their behalf, he entreated them not to expose themselves to the danger of hindering the course of justice, but rather to wait until their innocence was made certain—just as he would have done in any other similar case. In the conferences which he had with members of his Congregation, when any business affecting others was under consideration, he would often say: "Let us keep our eyes open to others' interests as to our own, and let us take care to deal uprightly and honorably with all." Here surely was a man who did not allow himself to be carried away by natural inclinations, either in his own affairs or those of others!

15 The dissatisfaction we often feel when we have passed a great part of the day without being retired and absorbed in God, though we have been employed in works of obedience or charity, proceeds from a very

subtle self-love, which disguises and hides itself. For it is a wish on our part to please ourselves rather than God.

—ST. TERESA

When we consider how many and how important were the occupations of St. Vincent de Paul, on account of his office of Superior General of his Congregation, the position of counsellor which he was constrained to accept in the court, the continual works of charity in which he voluntarily engaged, the numbers of people who resorted to him—some for advice, some for direction, some for help and relief—so that he was constantly engaged, continually absorbed, and almost overwhelmed by these various avocations—it seems that he could have had no time to think of himself, and we wonder how he found any, as he did, to perform his ordinary exercises of piety. And yet, we do not read that he ever complained of not being able to remain retired and absorbed in God, although he certainly desired it as much as anyone. Nor can any reason be assigned for this, except that all his care was to please God, and not himself.

Father Alvarez, once finding himself overwhelmed with a multitude of occupations, complained lovingly to God that he had no time to converse with Him intimately. Then he heard this reply in his heart: "Let it be enough for thee that I make use of thy work, though I do not keep thee with Me." With this he remained happy and contented.

16 What a great benefit it would be to us if God would plant in our hearts a holy aversion to our own

satisfaction, to which nature attaches us so strongly that we desire that others would adapt themselves to us, and all succeed well with us. Let us ask Him to teach us to place all our happiness in Him, to love all that He loves, and to be pleased only with what pleases Him.

—ST. VINCENT DE PAUL

St. Dorotheus, though he was a man of much learning and prudence, confessed that in all matters not of a moral nature he willingly followed the opinion of others, though it might often seem to him ill-judged; nor did he ever discuss in his mind circumstances over which he had no control; but after doing his part, he left the event to God, and was contented with any result. For he did not seek to have things arranged according to his desire, but he wished them to be as they were, and not otherwise.

A young monk asked one old in religion why charity was not as perfect as in earlier times. "Because," replied the latter, "the ancient Fathers looked upward, and their hearts followed their eyes; but now all bend towards the earth, and seek only their own advantage."

17 With those who are perfect and walk with simplicity, there is nothing small and contemptible, if it be a thing that pleases God; for the pleasure of God is the object at which alone they aim, and which is the reason, the measure, and the reward of all their occupations, actions, and plans; and so, in

whatever they find this, it is for them a great and important thing.

—ST. ALPHONSUS RODRIGUEZ

This is the reason why St. Aloysius Gonzaga, St. John Berchmans, St. Mary Magdalen de' Pazzi, and so many others were so observant even of the least Rule, so exact in all their ordinary occupations and so careful to perform well every work trusted to them, however trifling it might be.

It is stated that the celebrated Father Ribera kept up through his whole life the same exact observance which marked his novitiate.

18 When anyone has to choose a state of life, and wishes to know what he should do for the good of his soul, let him first strip himself of every inclination of his own, and place himself generously in the hands of God, equally ready for whatever He may call him to. Then let him apply some Gospel truths to the matter, draw from them their legitimate consequence, and see how they relate to the ultimate end for which God has created us. If he still remains uncertain, let him imagine himself on his death bed, or before the judgment seat, which will teach him to do what he will then wish he had done.

—ST. IGNATIUS LOYOLA

St. Vincent de Paul was once obliged to send a man of business to Tunis, on account of a commission entrusted to him. He fixed

upon a lawyer of high standing and wrote to him, explaining the advantages and disadvantages of the position and leaving him to decide whether he would accept it. The lawyer answered the letter in person, told his objections, and begged St. Vincent to manifest to him the will of God. The Saint preferred that he should take the advice of some other person; but as the lawyer insisted that he wished for no opinion but his, St. Vincent asked for a short delay. The day after, he gave this answer: "I offered your difficulties to God in the Mass, and after the Consecration I threw myself at His feet, praying Him to enlighten me. After this I considered attentively how I should wish to have advised you, if I were at the point of death; and it seemed to me that if I were about to die, I should be glad to have told you to go, and sorry to have dissuaded you from going. Such is my sincere opinion; but for all this, you can go or stay." The lawyer was much edified by such detachment.

A pious lady, being asked by a poor man for some clothing, ordered her servant to bring him a shirt. When she brought one that was coarse and torn, she told her to find a better one— adding that it would cause her much shame if Christ, on the Day of Judgment, should show that shirt to all the world.

19 There is a kind of simplicity that causes a person to close his eyes to all the sentiments of nature and to human considerations, and fix them interiorly upon the holy maxims of the Faith that he may guide himself in every work by their means, in such a way that in all his actions, words, thoughts, interests and vicissitudes, at all times and in all places, he may always recur to them and do nothing except by

them and according to them. This is an admirable simplicity.

—ST. VINCENT DE PAUL

Here this Saint, without perceiving it, described to the life his own simplicity, which may even be called his special characteristic.

20 In human life prudence is indeed necessary, that we may be circumspect in our actions and know how to adapt ourselves to the dispositions of others.

—ST. VINCENT DE PAUL

By this virtue the same Saint regulated his actions so well that he succeeded in every undertaking and therefore gained such a reputation for prudence that he was commonly considered one of the wisest men of his time. As a result, persons of every condition and state, even those most conspicuous for rank or learning, had recourse to him as to an oracle in all affairs of importance for direction and advice.

St. Jane Frances de Chantal was so remarkable for this virtue that many celebrated Bishops regulated their dioceses, and many also their own consciences, by her wise counsels. Even St. Francis de Sales, her beloved spiritual father, and St. Vincent de Paul, her director after him, consulted with her upon their most important business and depended much upon her wise decisions.

21 Prudence is of two sorts: human and Christian. Human prudence, which is also called the prudence

275

of the flesh and of the world, is that which has no other aim than what is temporal, thinks only of arriving at its end, and makes use of such methods and sentiments alone as are human and uncertain. Christian prudence consists in judging, speaking and acting that way in which the Eternal Wisdom, clothed in our flesh, judged, spoke and acted, and in guiding ourselves in all cases according to the maxims of the Faith, never according to the fallacious sentiments of the world, or the feeble light of our own intellect.

—ST. VINCENT DE PAUL

St. Francis de Sales was a sworn enemy to human prudence, as he declared to one of his penitents, writing to her in these terms: "If I could be born over again with the sentiments that I have now, I do not believe that anyone could make me waver in the certainty which I feel, that the prudence of the flesh and of the sons of this world is but a mere chimera, and a most certain folly."

St. Vincent de Paul never used any but the Christian kind of prudence, so that it is no wonder that he was considered to have a rare and solid wisdom. Though his intellect was keen and clear enough to penetrate things to the bottom and discover all their relations, yet he never trusted to his own light till he had compared it and found it to agree with the maxims taught us by Our Saviour, which are the only rule by which to form a sure and certain judgment. So he never began to do anything of importance, or gave answers or advice to others, without first turning his eyes upon Jesus Christ, to find some act or word of

His upon which he might securely rest the decision he was about to make. Having collected a company of priests outside of his Congregation, who were called the Ecclesiastics of the Conference and who were accustomed to give Missions in the country under his direction, he was asked that they might give one in a section of Paris. The Saint saw no difficulty in this; but they saw much, and told him that in such a place a very different sort of Mission would be required from those they had been giving in the country, for the simple and familiar discourses which had succeeded so well there would furnish little but subjects of ridicule among more cultivated people. But he, who was little accustomed to trust to means purely natural, answered that he felt sure they ought to use the same method they had employed elsewhere, and that the spirit of the world so triumphant in that quarter of Paris could not be better conquered than by attacking it with the spirit of Jesus Christ, which is a spirit of simplicity. He added that to enter into the sentiments of this Divine Saviour, they ought to seek not their own glory, but that of the Eternal Father; that, in imitation of the Redeemer, they ought to be ready to suffer contempt and to bear, if it were the will of God, opposition and persecution; that remembering the words of the Son of God, they might at least be sure that Jesus Christ would speak by them, and that so good and holy a disposition as he had described would make them fit to serve as instruments of His mercy, which penetrates the most hardened hearts and converts the most rebellious spirits. His advice was received by them as the advice of an angel, and laying aside all human considerations they followed it in giving their Mission, which proved most fervent and successful.

22 Let us beware of worldly sentiments, for often by the pretext of zeal or the glory of God they cause us to adopt plans which never proceeded from Him and will not be prospered by His Divine Majesty.

—ST. VINCENT DE PAUL

One of his priests having expressed the opinion to this Saint that it would have been well to begin the Missions on the estates of some well-known man of rank, he answered thus: "Your idea seems to me human, and contrary to Christian simplicity. May God keep us from doing anything for such low ends. The Divine Goodness requires of us that we should never do well to make ourselves esteemed, but that all our actions should be directed to God alone." To the Superior of a house recently established, who would have been glad to begin the exercises with a Mission that would make a stir, he wrote this reply: "It seems disagreeable to everyone to be obliged to begin so poorly; since to gain a reputation it would be necessary, as it seems, to appear even at the beginning with a splendid Mission, which would show what the Congregation can do. May God keep you from entertaining such desires! What is suited to our poverty and to the spirit of Christianity is to avoid such ostentation, to conceal ourselves and to seek contempt and confusion as Jesus Christ did. If we have this resemblance to Him, we shall have Him for the companion of our labors."

23 Ah, how true it is that we love ourselves too much and proceed with too much human prudence, that we

may not lose an atom of our consideration! Oh, what a great mistake that is! The Saints did not act thus.

—ST. TERESA

Father Martino del Rio, who in the world had been eminent both for rank and learning after becoming a priest and a Religious used to accompany the steward in a ragged dress throughout the city and carry home to the college whatever articles he bought.

St. Francis Xavier, when on his way to India as Apostolic Legate, used to wash his own linen on board the ship. When someone told him that he was degrading his office by such work, he replied: "I consider nothing contemptible and unworthy of a Christian except sin."

24 When we have to deal with astute and crafty persons, the best way to win them to God is to treat them with much candor and simplicity. This is the spirit of Christ the Lord; and whoever is destined to glorify Him must act according to His spirit.

—ST. VINCENT DE PAUL

When this Saint was sending out one of his priests, he addressed him thus: "You are going into a region where the people are considered very crafty. If this is true, the best way of gaining them for God will be to act with great simplicity, since the maxims of the Gospel are utterly opposed to those of the world; and as you go for the service of Our Lord, you ought to behave in accordance with His spirit, which is full of uprightness and sincerity." For the same reason, when a house of the

Congregation was established some time after in that province, he purposely selected for it a Superior who was remarkable for candor and ingenuousness. And those in his Congregation who were of that stamp were always the most beloved by him.

25 May God keep us from vain praise, flattery, and everything intended to attract the goodwill and protection of others. These are very low motives and far from the spirit of Jesus Christ, whose love ought to be the principal aim of all we do. Let these, then, be our maxims: To do much for the love of God, and not care at all for the esteem of men; to labor for their salvation, and not concern ourselves as to what they say of us.

—ST. VINCENT DE PAUL

This Saint, though very courteous to all, never flattered anyone, saying that there was nothing so despicable and unworthy of a Christian heart and nothing more abhorred by spiritual persons than flattery. On the contrary, he refrained from praising people in their presence, except when he judged it necessary to confirm them in some good thing which they had begun, or to encourage the weak. He neither did himself, nor permitted his priests to do, anything to acquire the favor and protection of others; and so, in answering a letter written by one of them, he speaks thus: "I am pleased to hear that you have gained the friendship of those persons whom you mention, but not with the purpose for which you say that you did it; that is, that they might protect and defend you on occasion. Ah, your motive is

very low, and very far from the spirit of Jesus Christ, whose love should be our aim in all we do. Now you, on the contrary, are thinking of your own interests, and wish to employ the friendship and goodwill of these persons to secure your reputation. But if this reputation be not founded on truth, it is surely a vain thing; and if it be, what cause have you to fear? Remember that duplicity does not please God; and that to be truly simple, we ought to have no other end than to please Him alone."

26 If one happens to forget anything he ought to do, he should tell his fault candidly; and if he is asked about anything which he does not know or does not possess, he should openly confess his ignorance or poverty, leaving evasions to the prudent of this world.

—ST. VINCENT DE PAUL

It was in this manner that he acted himself. He sometimes happened to forget to do something that he had promised, and he then confessed his failure openly. He was many times asked for favors, even by persons of rank, which he did not consider it right to grant, and he told them with equal sincerity and respect that he could not oblige them. He was also sometimes thanked by persons for benefits which they were mistaken in supposing that he had conferred upon them. In such cases, he frankly avowed that he had nothing to do with these kindnesses. He was, then, wholly opposed to craft and dissimulation, and said that he had always prospered in telling things as they were, because God had blessed him in it.

In the same way, St. Charles Borromeo never flattered people with fine words, such as are used in courts, but when asked for an opinion, for advice or for any favor, simply stated his thoughts and intentions and never made a promise which he did not consider it advisable to fulfill. On the contrary he refused frankly, but at the same time gave his reasons for the satisfaction of the person he was obliged to disappoint. In this manner he treated people of all ranks, so that his word was trusted more than most men's bond, and the greatest personages came to ask his advice in grave and difficult affairs.

When a certain book, written by Fénélon, Archbishop of Cambray, was condemned in Rome by Pope Innocent XII, no sooner did the good prelate receive the condemnatory brief than, by an act of singular submission to the Supreme Pontiff, he not only read it publicly from his own archiepiscopal pulpit, but himself condemned and renounced his own propositions and forbade his people (who tenderly loved him, and who were weeping profusely) to read the book in the future, or to keep it in their houses.

27 The female dove has this peculiarity, that she does everything for her mate, so that when she sets, she leaves to him the care of herself and of whatever is needed and thinks of nothing but cherishing and protecting her dovelets, to please her mate and rear for him new offspring. Oh, what a pleasing rule is this—never to do anything except for God and to please Him, and to leave to Him all the care of ourselves!

—ST. FRANCIS DE SALES

Such was the spirit of St. Vincent de Paul, who occupied himself constantly in promoting the glory of God and in providing for the wants of others for His sake, without thinking of his own wants or of his Congregation, which he left entirely in the hands of the Lord.

Such also was St. Jane Frances de Chantal, of whom St. Francis de Sales said, on one occasion, that she was like those loving doves who bathe and plume themselves on the shore of brooks, adorning themselves not so much for the sake of being beautiful, as to please the eyes of their beloved mates; since she did not seek to correct herself in order to be pure and adorned with virtues, but rather to please her Divine Spouse; and if He had been equally pleased with ugliness and beauty, she would have loved one as well as the other.

28 There is a certain simplicity of heart which is the perfection of all perfections. This is found when our soul fixes her glance solely upon God and restrains herself that she may apply all her powers, simply and with complete fidelity, to the observance of her Rules and the methods prescribed to her, without turning aside to desire or wish to undertake any other thing. In this way, as she does not work by her own will or do anything unusual or greater than others, she has no great satisfaction or high opinion of herself, but God alone greatly delights in her simplicity, by which she ravishes His heart and unites herself to Him.

—ST. FRANCIS DE SALES

St. Jane Frances de Chantal practiced this simplicity won-derfully well, and experienced its effects abundantly. This was what she inculcated most, and most desired to see implanted and established in the minds of her daughters. And so this was the advice she gave to one of them, who asked her, by letter, for some counsel that would be useful for her perfection: "My daughter," she replied, "if you go on seeking every day to acquire perfection by so many methods, you will do nothing but lose time, and perplex yourself more and more. The best means that I can teach you is to put all your strength and diligence into the faithful observance of your Rules, and to perform with exactness what is assigned to you from day to day, banishing, meanwhile, all thoughts and desires of arriving at the goal until God shall be willing to grant you that grace."

29 Oh how lightly should we value a generous reso-lution to imitate the common and hidden life of Christ our Lord! It is easy to see that such a thought comes from God, as it is so utterly opposed to flesh and blood.

—ST. VINCENT DE PAUL

To imitate the hidden life of Christ was one of the dearest and most frequent occupations of this Saint, as it was his lot to lead a life in appearance low and common, in which nothing unusual or extraordinary could be seen exteriorly, though interiorly it was admirable and altogether heavenly. Christ could have made Himself known and adored in every place as the Son of God by making the rays of His glory shine through all Judea as He did

upon Tabor, yet He chose to pass for the simple son of a carpenter and for a man of no account. St. Vincent de Paul spoke of himself everywhere as the son of a poor peasant and sought to be considered as a simple country priest. He concealed, as far as he could, the lofty gifts of nature and of grace that he had received from God and which rendered him worthy of all veneration. He was an excellent theologian, but called himself a poor ignorant beginner. He avoided dignities and honors with greater care and earnestness than the most ambitious employ in obtaining them. He had a supreme abhorrence for ostentation, and found his complete satisfaction in abasement and humiliation.

30 The continual study of those, who, like missionaries, are destined to instruct others ought to be this: to take care to put off themselves and to put on Jesus Christ. For, as things, for the most part, produce results in accordance with their nature—if he who gives the spirit and form of life to others is animated by a merely human spirit, what can they do but imbibe the same spirit, and learn from him the appearance of virtue rather than its substance.

—ST. VINCENT DE PAUL

This Saint endeavored above all things to divest himself of the human spirit and to clothe himself with that of Christ. He sought to conform himself to Him, not only in external actions, but also in his interior dispositions, especially in his desires and intentions. And so he never desired or aimed at anything except what Jesus Christ had desired and aimed at; that is, that God

should be known, loved, and glorified by all, and that His most holy will should be entirely and perfectly fulfilled.

31 God is a Being most simple in His essence, admitting no composition whatever. If, then, we desire to render ourselves as much like Him as possible, we should endeavor to be by virtue what He is by nature; that is, we ought to have a simple heart, a simple soul, a simple intention, a simple mode of action. We ought to speak simply, and to act frankly, without deceit or artifice, always letting our exterior reflect our interior, and never regarding anything in all our actions except God, whom alone we endeavor and desire to please.

—ST. VINCENT DE PAUL

Such, in fact, was the simplicity of this Saint, for his exterior was always in entire conformity to his interior. Whoever heard his words could immediately know what was in his heart, which he always kept upon his lips. And however numerous and varied might be his occupations, they all had the same end, which was to please God alone. It might be truly said that he possessed this virtue to such a degree that the faculties of his soul were wholly steeped in it, and whatever he said or did proceeded from this source.

AUGUST

Diligence

He did all things well.—MARK 7:37

---

1 All our good and all our evil certainly lies in the character of our actions. As they are, so are we; for we are the tree, and they the fruit, and, therefore, they prove what each one is.

—ST. AUGUSTINE

A servant of God, at the point of death, once spoke thus: "Now I know that *totum opus nostrum in operatione consistit*—our actions are our sole concern."

St. Aloysius Gonzaga set down in writing a resolution that he would do all in his power that every one of his actions might be good, and bring him nearer to God.

St. Bonaventure used to excite himself and others to constant occupation in good works by often repeating this beautiful sentiment: Every hour that we waste in sloth, we lose a glory equal to the good works we might have performed in it.

2   It is not enough to do good things, but we must do them well, in imitation of Christ our Lord, of whom it was written: *Bene omnia fecit*—He did all things well. We ought, then, to strive to do all things in the spirit of Christ; that is, with the perfection, with the circumstances, and for the ends for which He performed His actions. Otherwise, even the good works that we do will bring us punishment rather than reward.

—ST. VINCENT DE PAUL

St. John Berchmans followed this precept in all his actions, however different and unequal they might be, so that anyone who saw him and who considered the work itself, and at the same time the manner and circumstances in which it was done, would be obliged to say that each action was performed in the best way possible. This was the case not only because his objects and aims were always perfectly correct, but because certain little details in performance were like an exquisite enamel which made all his actions perfect and finished in the eyes of God and men, and precious and meritorious in themselves. So, whoever should strip his actions of such adjuncts would rob them of their beauty and their value. For example, he never enjoyed games, but rather spiritual conversation or scientific discussions. But if he was in the country in vacation, he would play at billiards or quoits, when

invited, so as to be like the rest. In playing he would accept as a partner a newcomer or an unskilled player, though he might be sure it would make him lose the game. He played with the greatest attention, neither noticed nor spoke of anything else, and played well. When his turn came, he first made the Sign of the Cross openly, as he did before every action. He was never angry, and never raised his voice, whatever success he had. If he lost, he immediately knelt to say an *Ave Maria* for the victors. If he won, he was silent, showed no particular pleasure, and he did not exult over the losers. These circumstances, taken together, greatly elevated the action and made it spiritual, though, in itself considered, it was indifferent and trivial.

St. Ignatius asked a lay-brother who was doing his work with much negligence, for whom he did it. And when the latter replied that it was for God, "Now," said the Saint, "if you were working for men, it would not be so bad; but if you are working for so great a Lord as God, it is a very great fault to do it as you do."

3 Many believe that they can do no true penance for their sins except by giving themselves up to corporal austerities. But we know that he does a very good penance for his sins, who takes pains to perform all his actions well, to please the Lord, which is a matter of great perfection and great merit.

—ST. FRANCIS DE SALES

St. John Berchmans did no severe penances, but he placed his whole perfection in performing his ordinary actions well and with great exactness. To this effect he wrote upon a slip of

paper the maxim, "*Poenitentia mea maxima vita communis*—My greatest penance is the common life." And with this alone, how perfect and dear to God he rendered himself! The same thing is told of St. Stanislaus Kostka, St. Francis de Sales, and many others.

4 If man could see what reward he will have in the world above for well-doing, he would never employ his memory, understanding or will in anything but good works, without regarding at all what labor or trials he might experience in them.

—ST. CATHERINE OF GENOA

Blessed Boniface, a Cistercian monk, once desired on a Christmas Eve to see the Holy Infant, and the Blessed Virgin appeared to him and placed Him in his arms. Then the Child raised a veil which covered His face, at sight of which the monk exclaimed in ecstasy: "If there were nothing in Paradise but this blessed face, would it not be worthwhile to suffer all the tribulations in the world, to gain a sight of it?"

For this reason, St. Francis remained content in the midst of sufferings and said: "So great is the good which I expect, that every pain is a delight to me."

A servant of God, after her death, appeared to another and told her that the felicity and glory to which God had brought her in Heaven for her good works was so great that if she could possess in addition only as much as is given for an *Ave Maria* well said, she would be contented to return to earth and suffer all sorts of trials to the day of judgment.

5 Endeavor not to appear singular, but to be so. This is done by leading, in all respects, the common life, doing all things that are enjoined, but with exactness in the time, place, and manner prescribed. We must do common things not in a common matter, but in a manner more sublime and perfect than that in which they are commonly done. This is to appear externally like all the rest, and to be interiorly singular, which is a greater virtue and a treasure of merit.

—ST. BERNARD

This great praise is given to the same Saint himself: "*Erat in ordinariis non ordinarius*—In ordinary things he was not ordinary."

It is said of St. Francis de Sales that he was the most exact of men—not only at the altar and in choir, where he observed even the smallest ceremonies punctually and faithfully, but also in private, in reciting the Office and in all his duties.

6 Be not of those who think perfection consists in undertaking many things, but of those who place it in doing well what little they do. For it is much better to do little and do it well, than to undertake much and do it ill. Yes, little and good, this is the best. Therefore, if we wish to advance, or when we wish to give some special honor to Our Lord, we have to redouble not our exercises, but the perfection with which we perform them.

—ST. FRANCIS DE SALES

A devout young nun recited every day the complete Rosary of fifteen decades, but with little devotion, on account of its length. One day the Blessed Virgin appeared to her and told her to recite only the third part of it. "For," said she, "a few prayers said fervently are more acceptable to my Son and to me, than many said negligently and without devotion."

7 The Lord measures our perfection not by the number and greatness of the works we do for Him, but by our manner of doing them. And this manner is only the love of God with which, and for which, we do them. They are more perfect as they are done with more pure and perfect love, and as they are less mingled with the thoughts of pleasure or praise in this life or the other.

—ST. JOHN OF THE CROSS

When St. Bernard was assisting one night at Matins, he saw some angels who were carefully noting down the merit of each of the monks. The merit of those who were praying with much fervor, they set down in golden characters; of those with less fervor, in silver characters; of those with good-will, but without affection, in ink; of those with sloth and drowsiness, in water; but as to those who were in mortal sin or voluntarily distracted, they wrote nothing, but, standing motionless, they lamented their blindness.

St. Francis Borgia said that though his sermons often pleased neither himself nor others, through a wrong choice of arrangement of subject, yet they always produced fruit, because he did all he could for his own part, and always purely for God.

The same truth is illustrated by the incident of the two little copper coins which the widow in the Gospel cast into the treasury. Our Lord declared that she had put in more than the others, though perhaps there were some who gave gold or silver pieces. There could be no reason for this except that she must have given that small amount with more love than the rest, who, as the Lord Himself added, gave out of their superabundance while she, on account of her poverty, was obliged to subtract the little she gave from her daily living.

8 Doing our work well consists in a very pure intention and strong purpose of pleasing God alone. This may be called the principle or the soul of our actions, and it gives them all their value and renders them easy and pleasing to us.

—ST. FRANCIS DE SALES

St. Thomas Aquinas appeared with a most beautiful star upon his breast, after death, to one who had much devotion to him and said that it was given him as a reward for the perfectly pure intention with which he had performed all his actions.

St. Mary Magdalen de' Pazzi constantly taught her novices to offer all their actions to God, even the smallest. And to establish them firmly in this practice, she would sometimes ask them unexpectedly why they were doing whatever they were engaged upon; and if they answered that they were doing it without supernatural intention, she added: "Do you not see that you are thus losing merit? God does not accept such actions."

We read in Ecclesiastical History that the Abbot Pambo, seeing a dancing girl gaily dressed and adorned, began to weep. Being asked why he did so, he answered: "Because, alas! I do not use as much care and diligence in seeking to please God by my works, as this girl employs in adorning herself to please men."

9 What are the works upon which all our profit and all our perfection depends? All those which it is our lot to perform, but especially the ordinary ones that we do every day. These are the most frequent, and therefore upon these, more than upon others, we ought to fix our eyes and to employ our attention and diligence. The measure of their perfection will be the measure of our own. If we do them perfectly, we shall be perfect; if imperfectly, imperfect. Here, precisely, is the difference between the perfect and the imperfect Religious. It is not that one does different things from the other; but one does ordinary things with perfection, and the other with imperfection and tepidity.

—ST. ALPHONSUS RODRIGUEZ

When St. Gertrude was young she did nothing except what her companions did; indeed, she did less; for there were many things that she was not permitted to do, on account of her delicate health. Yet she was more perfect than they. Now, how did this Saint attain such lofty perfection? In this way: The very things that she did at the same time with the others, she did with greater perfection than they.

It is said of St. Stanislaus Kostka that though he did only the same things that others did, yet the excellence with which he did them made it seem that he did more.

10 Among our daily works, those which we ought to have most at heart are the spiritual. We should make every effort to perform them well, and let everything else yield to them, when necessity or obedience does not forbid; for they regard God most directly, and do the most to advance us in perfection. If we act otherwise, we draw upon ourselves the malediction fulminated by the Holy Spirit against those who do the work of God negligently.

—ST. VINCENT DE PAUL

St. Vincent himself lived by this rule. Though he was burdened with a great number and variety of important and urgent affairs, yet he was most exact in his ordinary spiritual exercises, which he performed always with great devotion and fervor.

When St. Philip Neri was performing or assisting at any spiritual exercise, such as a public ceremony or the reading of devout books, he was so penetrated with emotion that sparks of fire sometimes seemed to come from his face, and a torrent of tears from his eyes. One day, while they were singing Compline in the Dominican church, he was seen to weep so profusely that the tears drenched his clothing; and in reading the Lives of the Saints, especially in his old age, he wept constantly.

When the prophet Eliseus sent Gehazi with his staff to raise to life the son of the Sunamite by its means, he ordered him not

to give or return a salutation on the road. This was intended to show that when we are occupied in any spiritual exercise, we ought not be diverted to other things, even under pretext of civility.

11 The Mass is certainly a function the most excellent, the most holy, the most acceptable to God and useful to us, that can be imagined. And so, while it is going on, the angels assist in crowds, with bare feet, with earnest eyes, with downcast brows, with great silence, with incredible amazement and veneration. With what purity, attention, devotion, and reverence, then, ought the priest to celebrate it? He should approach the sacred altar as Jesus Christ, assist there as an angel, minister there as a Saint, offer there the prayers of the people as a high-priest, interpose there for reconciliation between God and men as a mediator, and pray for himself as a simple human being.

—ST. LAWRENCE JUSTINIAN

St. Cajetan prefaced the Mass always with a sorrowful confession and a long preparation, which often lasted eight hours, which he spent wholly in acts of love and contrition, by way of preparation and thanksgiving. The face of St. Ignatius used to glow while he was celebrating, and his heart became so inflamed that in many cases he could not stand after Mass, and was obliged to be carried to his room, to the wonder of all. St. Conrad was so enkindled that the fingers with which he touched the body of the Lord remained bright and glowing, so that in the darkness

of night they served him for a lamp. The venerable Father John Leonardi was, one morning, seen to come from the sacristy with his head surrounded by rays. A lady who saw him turned to the bystanders and said, "Now, surely, I can say that I have seen a Saint!" St. Thomas Aquinas, St. Francis Xavier and many others were often rapt in ecstasies at Mass.

St. Vincent de Paul pronounced the words of the Mass in a gentle voice, not very low nor very high, and in a manner at once unconstrained and devout. He recited them neither very slowly nor very rapidly, but as was suitable to the sanctity of the action, so that his Mass did not ordinarily exceed half an hour in length. But the interior spirit which accompanied his words and actions was singular, on account of its unusual tenderness. He said the *Confiteor, In spiritu humilitatis, Nobis quoque peccatoribus, Domine, non sum dignus* and similar prayers with great contrition and humility. His devotion rose especially while reading the Holy Gospel. When he came to any word spoken by Christ, he uttered it in a more tender and more loving voice; and when he met with the words *Amen dico vobis*, he gave marked attention to what followed. In fine, he did everything with such modesty, gravity and tenderness, as moved all present to devotion; and so, persons who did not know him were often heard to exclaim: "Ah! here is a priest who says Mass well! He must surely be a Saint!" After his own Mass he would serve another, from devotion, and he did this regularly, though overwhelmed with business, up to the age of 75 years, when he could no longer walk without a cane or kneel except with great effort.

But the glorious St. Philip Neri was conspicuous among all for this virtue. While others need long preparation in order to be

recollected and say Mass devoutly, he, on the contrary, needed first to amuse himself a little, so that often before going to celebrate he would have a book of stories read to him. In the act of celebrating, he was often noticed to heave deep sighs, and to melt into tears; sometimes he would pause, because he was unable to proceed; sometimes he would shiver and tremble, so as to shake the predella, and again, fall into such abstraction that it was necessary to pull his vestments to rouse him. When he reached the Offertory, the joy of his heart was so great while he was young, that his hand would rise of itself, and he could not pour the wine into the chalice unless he rested his arm firmly on the altar. In elevating the Most Holy Sacrament, he would remain with his arms stretched upward, unable for a time to lower them; and at other times he would rise a span and more from the ground. In taking the Body of the Lord, he enjoyed such sweetness that he seemed like a person who is tasting some delicious beverage; and in taking the Blood, he pressed the chalice between his lips so that he not only rubbed off the gold, but wore away the silver, upon which he left the marks of his teeth. For this reason, he was not willing that anyone should stand where his face could be seen—not even the server, whom he told to keep at a distance, and not bring him the purificator until he should receive a sign. If he was to give Holy Communion, his fervor increased to such a degree that thrills were seen to run through his whole body, to the great wonder of those present; and when he took the Ciborium in his hand, he trembled so much that the Sacred Particles were shaken above the edge; his face, meanwhile, seemed all on fire, and an abundance of tears flowed from his eyes. In saying Mass, he uttered the words with so much devotion that he often

made those weep who listened to him. When he had finished he withdrew immediately to his room, but with such abstraction that he often passed close to persons without perceiving them, and his face was so pale that he seemed rather dead than alive. His Mass, when said in public, was rather short than long, that he might not weary the people, so that those who were in haste were glad to see him come out of the sacristy; but when it was in his private oratory, it lasted not less than four hours.

12 The Divine Office is one of the most excellent works in which we can be engaged, as the Divine Praises are celebrated in it. It is an employment fit for angels, and therefore it ought to be recited not by constraint or custom, but by choice, and with the application of our whole soul.

—ST. MARY MAGDALEN DE' PAZZI

When this Saint heard the Office bell, she was glad to find herself summoned to praise God, and instantly laid aside whatever she was doing; and while she was reciting the Office, her face showed the attention and devotion of her mind. St. Augustine, during its recitation, banished every other thought and gave up his whole soul to it. Father Suarez says of himself that on taking up the breviary, every other thought vanished from his mind; and during the whole time of Office nothing, however important it might be, distracted him.

Father Alvarez never recited it in the streets, nor while walking, but always in a retired place, usually kneeling in the middle of his own room, and at the regular hours. He did it with great

calmness, with much reverence, and slowly. He would stop from time to time to dwell upon those pious sentiments which the Lord communicated to him, the greatness of which appeared in his exhortations and in the depth of his soul.

The venerable Father Daponte, when saying the "*Procidamus ante Deum*—Let us fall prostrate before God," prostrated himself at full length upon the ground, with the same feeling of devotion and veneration that he would have had in the visible presence of God. During all the time of the Office, he kept up the greatest attention and recollection, and never interrupted it for any cause, nor answered anyone who asked him a question.

Father Faber, in order to be attentive at Office, often imagined his guardian angel on one side, marking all the words said well, and on the other side a demon recording all distractions of mind. At the beginning of every Psalm he said: "*Pater coelestis, da mihi spiritum*—Heavenly Father, give me Thy Spirit." Then he bade his mind remain attentive through that Psalm. St. Francis Xavier said, with fervor, before each Hour, "*Veni, sancte Spiritus.*" St. Bonaventure imagined himself reciting it amid multitudes of angels, joining in their choir. St. Vincent de Paul did the same, and when he recited it privately he assumed the most humble and recollected posture that he could, by kneeling with uncovered head, until the last three years of his life when, on account of his great infirmity, he was obliged to remain sitting. But when he said it in choir, his elevation of mind was so great that he seemed as if unconscious of all things, and wholly wrapt in God.

All these, and many others, said their Office with great devotion, and, at the same time, with no ordinary consolation and fruit. Some of them were so filled with celestial delights

and sweetness, that they showed exterior signs of it. It is told of St. Augustine that he was often bathed in tears; of St. Ignatius, that he shed so many tears that he nearly lost his sight; of St. Julian the Monk, that he had thus spoiled his breviary, and made it nearly illegible; of two young monks whom St. Macarius saw, that at each verse a flame darted from the mouth of one, and, as it were, a lighted torch from that of the other; of St. Francis Xavier, that his great fervor made his heart palpitate so violently that he suffered frequent fainting fits; of St. Mary Magdalen de' Pazzi, that she had many ecstasies; of St. Catherine of Bologna, that she often remained immovable, with uplifted face and eyes fixed on the crucifix, and that her absorption was so great that she would not feel it if anyone pulled her habit; neither would she perceive any faults in the recitation, nor anything that happened in the chapel, nor who passed in or out; and she said that it was not possible to remember that one was in the midst of angels and singing praises with them, and at the same time to keep the heart on earthly things. St. Philip Neri, on account of the great union with God which he experienced while saying the Office, was always obliged to recite with another, for he could scarcely know how to bring it to an end alone.

13 The examination of conscience, which all good people are accustomed to make before going to rest, in order to see how they have passed the day and whether they have gone forward or backward, is of the greatest use, not only to conquer evil inclinations and to uproot bad habits, but also to acquire virtues and to perform our ordinary duties well. We

must, however, observe that its best use does not lie in discovering the faults we have committed in the day, but in exciting aversion for them, and in forming a strong resolution to commit them no more.

—FATHER M. D'AVILA

We read in monastic history that a holy monk said: "I do not think the devils have twice entangled me in the same fault." The cause of this was that in examining his first fall, he was so penetrated with shame for his disloyalty, and with abhorrence for the sin committed, and he impressed so deeply upon his heart the resolution of falling into it no more, that no second temptation to it had any power over him. All the Saints and masters of the spiritual life have set a high value on this examination, practicing it and recommending it as a most efficacious means to eradicate any vice or fault, and to advance in perfection. We may see this in reading the Lives of St. Dorotheus, St. Basil, St. John Chrysostom, St. John Climacus, St. Bernard, St. Bonaventure, St. Ignatius Loyola and many others. The last-named esteemed it so much that, in a certain way, he even preferred it to meditation; "For, by the examen," he said, "we put in practice what we draw from meditation." So at the beginning, he kept his companions occupied for a long time in their examination of conscience, and in frequenting the Sacraments, for he thought if these things were well done it would be enough to preserve them in virtue. He testifies, too, of himself that if he had gained anything, he knew that it had been acquired, in great part, by the diligence he had every day employed in making his examen.

Even the heathen philosophers knew the great utility of such an examen. St. Jerome relates of Pythagoras that among the instructions he gave his disciples, the one that he considered of the greatest importance was that they should have two times of day fixed, one in the morning, the other in the evening, when they should examine themselves upon three points: What have I done? How have I done it? What have I omitted that I ought to have done?—and that they should be pleased at the good which they discovered, and displeased at the evil. We read that Seneca, Plutarch, Epictetus and others, recommended the same thing.

14 How can the sun and moon praise God, as the Prophet exhorts them to? By performing well that task which has been imposed on them by the Lord. This is great praise which they give Him. Behold, then, an excellent way in which you can praise God at all times—by performing well your tasks and whatever you may have to do.

—ST. JEROME

St. John Berchmans was most diligent in every employment assigned to him. When he had the care of the Spiritual Father's room, he kept it so neat and so well provided with every little necessary that the Father was astonished, and never found another to equal him. And, what was more, he never disturbed him or said an unnecessary word. When he had charge of the lamps, he never once omitted to look them over and trim them; and if he was going out of town on a holiday, he would either attend to them before starting, or come back in time to have

them ready before it was dark. Once being afraid that he should lose this charge, he begged the Father Rector to let him retain it.

Father Alvarez faithfully fulfilled all the charges imposed on him, observing even the most minute rules, and continued this care and solicitude up to the last day and hour that he held them. When he was Rector he never failed to visit his subjects at the hour of prayer, and he did this up to the day when he left the house to become Provincial.

15 Never allow yourself to believe that time lost which is spent in performing your charge well. For this is a thing so acceptable to the Lord that He gives in a little time what He would otherwise be much longer in giving, and even doubles what has been abandoned in His service.

—ST. TERESA

This Saint relates that she had known a number of persons who had been long occupied entirely in works of obedience and charity, and who had yet advanced so much in the spiritual life that she was amazed. "I spoke with one in particular," she added, "who told me that for fifteen years in succession, obedience had kept her so much engaged in the guidance of others and in various employments that she did not remember having a day to herself; but she tried her best to snatch an hour for meditation, and to act with purity of conscience. She was a soul more inclined to obedience than any other I have ever met, so that she attracted to it all with whom she spoke. And Our Lord rewarded her richly, for in the end, without knowing how, she found herself with that

liberty of spirit which all the perfect have so earnestly prayed for, and which includes all the felicity that can be found in this life."

16 Do not fear that the occupations imposed by obedience will draw you away from union with God; for when they are performed for His glory, they have, instead, great power to unite us closely to Him. For how can those things separate us from God, which unite our will to His? The whole mistake arises from the failure to distinguish between being drawn away from God, and being drawn away from the sweetness found in the interior perception of God. It is true that in occupation this sweetness is not always enjoyed (though it is sometimes in the highest degree); but in depriving ourselves of this for the love of God, we gain instead of losing, while we leave the weak for the strong. While to quit or abandon our work to unite ourselves to God by prayer, reading, or recollection, by solitude and contemplation, would be to withdraw from God and to unite ourselves to ourselves and to our own self-love.

—ST. FRANCIS DE SALES

St. Mary Magdalen de' Pazzi performed all her exterior duties with so much spiritual delight, and with so pure an intention for God, that they were no hindrance to her interior retirement and did not distract her in the least from God. And so, on the instant after finishing any of them, she would retire to prayer and be wholly separated from all earthly things and completely wrapt

in God. Even in the midst of manual labor and employment she often fell into ecstasies, so that she once said: "It is the same to me whether I am told to go to prayer in the choir, or to any manual work, for I make no difference between them. Nay, were I to say that sometimes I find God more in such work than in prayer, I think I should tell the truth."

A Franciscan lay brother who was cook, when he had thoroughly performed the work of his charge, used to retire to prayer, in which he enjoyed many heavenly consolations. To enjoy more of these, he asked and obtained from his Superior permission to give up his distracting occupation; then giving himself entirely to prayer, he found in it nothing but aridity and distractions. Seeing his mistake, he returned to his former work, when the lost consolations immediately came back.

17 Even little actions are great when they are done well; so that a little action done with desire to please God is more acceptable to Him, and gives Him more glory, than a great work done with less fervor. We must, then, give particular attention to perform well the little works, which are easiest, and are constantly within our reach, if we wish to advance in friendship with God.

—ST. FRANCIS DE SALES

St. Ignatius said of a lay-brother who was a mason that he wrought for himself in Heaven as many crowns as he laid bricks or gave strokes of the hammer, on account of the pure and upright intention with which he animated these works.

It is told of St. Francis Xavier that he was very careful to do little things well, and that he used to say: "We must not deceive ourselves, for he who does not take pains to excel in little things, will never do so in great."

18 Much more is accomplished by a single word of the *Pater Noster* said, now and then, from the heart, than by the whole prayer repeated many times in haste and without attention.

—ST. TERESA

The Lord one day revealed to St. Bridget that He was more pleased with one who would recite with perfect faith and earnestness these three words: *"Jesu, miserere mei—*Jesus, have mercy on me," than with another who might recite a thousand verses without attention.

19 Whoever has not experienced it will not be able to believe how much we gain by being careful not to fail in little things; for the devil, by means of these, makes gaps and breaches through which great things can enter.

—ST. TERESA

When St. Louis Bertrand was Superior he used to reprove and punish very severely, at the Friday Chapter, the very smallest faults, such as failing in silence, oversleeping a little, or making a mistake in choir—only because he judged that advancement and religious discipline depended on these little things.

St. Lawrence Justinian took more pains to guard himself from slight faults than from grave ones; for he used to say that to beware of grave faults belonged not to Religious, but to seculars.

20 Be careful not to forget God in your occupations, from a belief that in this way you will accomplish more; for if He abandons you, you will not be able to take a step without falling prostrate on the ground. Rather imitate little children, who with one hand cling to their fathers, while with the other they pluck strawberries and mulberries along the hedges. Attend to what you are doing, yet not without raising a glance from time to time to your Heavenly Father, to see whether He is pleased with your plans and to ask His help. In this manner, you will accomplish even the most difficult business better and more easily. See how the Blessed Virgin quietly employed one hand in work, while she was holding upon the other arm Our Infant Lord.

—ST. FRANCIS DE SALES

St. Mary Magdalen de' Pazzi performed her exterior occupations with such abstraction that, as her companions said, it seemed her body only was engaged in them, and her soul was rather where she loved than where she lived. It was observed that at meals in the refectory, at the time when there is usually a pause in the spiritual reading, she showed by her motions that she was absorbed in some devout thought.

We read the same thing of the venerable Father John Leon-ardi, who in the midst of business seemed so absorbed in God that he appeared, like St. Paul, to have his "conversation in Heaven."

It is narrated of St. Rose of Lima that in all her employments she kept her mind uninterruptedly raised to God, so that in reading, embroidering, weaving, conversing with others, pro-viding for the wants of the family or walking in the street—in every action, in all times and places, she was beholding, as in a clear mirror, and lovingly contemplating, the fair countenance of her Beloved. What is more wonderful, this continual pres-ence of God occupied her interior powers with much sweet-ness, without interfering at all with the exercise of her senses, so that while she was interiorly conversing with God, she was exteriorly conversing with men, answering connectedly, giving advice or orders, planning and executing whatever was neces-sary, with as much ease and readiness as if she had no other thought in mind. This was a truly a wonderful gift granted to her by the Lord.

It is related of St. Anthony that while he was making bas-kets, he used to repeat from time to time the verse, *"Miserere mei Deus, secundum magnam misericordiam tuam*—Have pity on me, O God, according to Thy great mercy."

We read of the venerable Monseigneur de Palafox, that if a doubt occurred to him while writing he would turn to an image of the Infant Jesus and say, "O Lord, what can we say about this?" or again: "O Lord, teach me what I have to say!" or: "O Lord, give me light!" Sometimes, after he had written what he thought suited to the occasion, he offered it to God, saying: "O Lord, let this be for the good of souls. Give Thy spirit to it,

O Lord! Give life to these characters, O Life of all created things!"
If at times he felt pleased with his reasoning or his expressions,
he held the paper near the lamp and said: "My God, is it Thy
will that I should burn it? Nothing here is mine. Let every work
and every feeling of my own be consumed!" But then he received
interior light, which showed him that it would not be well to do
so, and he refrained.

21 Among the hindrances which prevent us from performing our actions well, the foremost is that while
we are doing one thing, we are thinking of another
which we have to do or which we have done; so that
our occupations interfere with one another, and
none is well performed. The way to do them all well
is to attend solely to the one we have in hand, taking
care to do it as perfectly as possible, and banishing
for the time the thought of every other; and when
this is finished, not to think of it any more, but to
think of what remains to be done.

—FATHER M. D'AVILA

At a time when God was shedding His heavenly graces
in abundance upon the venerable Sister Maria Crucifixa, and
calling her to enjoy the contemplation of Himself in solitude,
her Superioress heaped upon her the offices of sacristan, cook,
refectorian, and in certain novenas of great devotion, she had
charge also of the door and of the medicine room. She did
everything with exactness and to the satisfaction of all, and yet
found time for her contemplation. This was her method: When

she was in the sacristy, she said to herself, "Now be nothing but a sacristan"; and when she came out of it, she would say, "Now do not be a sacristan any longer"; and the same with the rest of her employments.

22 Perform faithfully what God requires of you each moment, and leave the thought of everything else to Him. I assure you that to live in this way will bring you great peace.

—ST. JANE FRANCES DE CHANTAL

The Saint herself was an example of this course of conduct. So was St. Francis de Sales also, of whom it was said that when he was doing any work or transacting any business, he gave his whole mind to it, as if he had nothing else in the world to think of.

Nazianzen relates of his mother that she threw herself wholly into whatever she was doing and did everything to perfection, so that seeing her in the midst of her household occupations one would think she cared for nothing else; but when she was attending to her spiritual duties, she showed that they were receiving her whole attention; and she felt as much interest in every occupation as if she had no other.

23 The second hindrance is haste. Beware of it, for it is a deadly enemy of true devotion; and anything done with precipitation is never done well. Let us go slowly, for if we do but keep advancing we shall thus go far.

—ST. FRANCIS DE SALES

It was thus that the Saint himself conducted all his operations. St. Philip Neri did the same, and recommended this course to his penitents, often saying: "You need not try to do everything in a day, nor to become a Saint in a month. Prudence does not advise it."

24 The works of God are performed, for the most part, little by little, and have their beginnings and their progress. We ought not to expect to do everything at once and in a hurry, nor imagine that all is lost, if success does not come in an instant, but we must advance quietly, pray much to God, and make use of the means suggested by His spirit, and never of the false maxims of the world.

—ST. VINCENT DE PAUL

St. Vincent de Paul had a habit of proceeding in all his affairs, both in undertaking and prosecuting them, with such tranquillity that he was regarded as too slow. But experience showed that his slowness did no harm, for to the wonder of all, he brought to a successful issue so many and such difficult affairs that many persons together would not have been able to do as much, even if they had given their whole minds to the work. What is more, he succeeded in this way in performing all his spiritual works with fervor, and all the indifferent ones with success.

25 The third hindrance is anxiety and solicitude. Be diligent and accurate in all the affairs of which you have charge; but, if possible, do not let them cause

you anxiety and vexation; that is, do not manage them with disquiet, solicitude, and eagerness. Do not worry in attending to them, for worry disturbs the reason, and hinders us from doing well even what does not trouble us. But great affairs do not disturb us so much as a great number of little ones; therefore, receive these also with calmness, and try to attend to them in order, one after another, without perturbation. Thus, you will gain great merit by them, for the time spent peacefully is doubtless most usefully employed.

—ST. FRANCIS DE SALES

This Saint passed many hours with poor people who occupied him about things of little account. When it was said to him that it was not well for him to lose so much time on trifles, he answered: "What do you think I ought to do? These things appear great to them, and they desire sympathy as much as if the case were really so. God knows well that I desire no greater employment, and that every occupation is indifferent to me, if only it regards His service. While I am engaged in this work, small as it is, I am not obliged to do any other. And is it not a sufficiently important employment to do the will of God?" To encourage one of his penitents to this practice, he wrote to her thus: "Whoever can preserve interior sweetness in a multiplicity of business, may be called perfect. Though few can be found even in the Orders who have arrived at this degree of felicity, yet there are some, and there have been some in every age. We must aspire to this high standard."

St. Jane Frances de Chantal faithfully followed this advice by doing everything with the greatest attention—but without any anxiety and without ever losing peace of heart—and so, all she did succeeded well; and she spoke of this freely to her daughters. To one of them she said one day: "Believe me, my dear daughter, I deeply love our poor Congregation, but without anxiety—without which, love ordinarily is not wont to live. But mine, which is not ordinary, lives without it." And to another who had sought from her a remedy for the constant perplexities she experienced in her employments, she wrote: "The origin of your trouble and perplexity comes from nothing but the anxiety you feel in seeking the good you aim at, and your want of patience and submission to the will of Him who alone can give it to you. So, if you desire your work to be better and less burdensome, you must correct this anxiety and solicitude, striving to work with fidelity, but, at the same time, with calmness and spiritual sweetness."

26 It is a characteristic of the spirit of God to work with gentleness and love; and the surest way of succeeding in whatever we undertake is to imitate Him.

—ST. VINCENT DE PAUL

This Saint managed all his own affairs in this way, whether they were important or indifferent, spiritual or temporal—with a great calmness and quiet, which appeared even exteriorly.

27 The fourth hindrance is a desire to do too much. There is no need of wearing ourselves completely out in the exercises of virtue, but we should practice them freely,

naturally, simply, as the ancient Fathers did, with good will and without scrupulosity. In this consists the liberty of the children of God: that is, in doing gladly, faithfully, and heartily, what they are obliged to do.

—ST. FRANCIS DE SALES

Such, in fact, was this Saint's manner of working—a manner free, simple, ready, devoid of artifice, proceeding by ordinary and natural means, arising rather from the heart than from the mind, and therefore pleasing to God, and very easy and meritorious for the Saint himself.

Though St. Jane Frances de Chantal was most exact in the observance of her Rules and in all her employments, she took precautions both for herself and others, that this exactness should not be accompanied by that spiritual constraint and oppression, which self-love often causes for faults committed through ignorance or inadvertence, and without malice. In everything she went on lovingly, happily, and in peace.

28 Among the many means of performing our actions well, one is to do each of them as if it were to be the last of our lives. At every action, then, say to yourself: "If you knew that you were to die immediately after this action, would you do it? and would you do it in this way?"

—ST. VINCENT DE PAUL

Whatever St. Francis de Sales did, he did it as if it were his last act in the world.

A certain priest was accustomed to go to confession every morning before saying Mass. Once, being dangerously ill, he was advised to make his confession in preparation for death. But he answered: "Blessed be God! I have made my confession in that way every day for the last thirty years, as if I were immediately to die; so I need do no more than make my ordinary confession, as if I were going to say Mass."

29 Another good method is to consider only the present day. One of the arts which the devil employs to ruin souls and to retard many in the service of God is to represent to them that it is a very difficult and insupportable thing to live for many years with so much exactness, circumspection and regularity. Now, to consider today only closes the path to this temptation, and at the same time lends much support to human weakness. For who is there that cannot for one day make a strong effort to do all he can, that his actions may be well performed? Let one say to himself in the morning, "This day I mean to perform my ordinary actions well." So, that becomes easy and tolerable, which might appear very difficult if it were taken in a general way, and with the thought that this effort was to be made for a lifetime. Meanwhile, by proceeding every day in this manner, little by little a good habit is formed, and no further difficulty is experienced.

—ST. ALPHONSUS RODRIGUEZ

A certain monk is mentioned in the Lives of the Fathers, who even early in the morning suffered intolerably from hunger and weakness. In order not to transgress the holy custom of the monks, which forbade any food to be taken before three o'clock in the afternoon, he adopted the following device. In the morning he said to himself: "Hungry as you are, is it a great thing to wait until tierce?" At tierce he said, "Truly I must make some effort, and not eat until sext." At sext he put the bread into the water, and said: "While the bread is soaking, I can wait till none; as I have waited so long, I do not mean, for the sake of two or three hours, to transgress the good custom of the monks." When the hour of none arrived, he said his prayers, and took his breakfast. So he went on for some days, beguiling himself by these short periods of time, until one day when he was eating at the regular hour, he saw a smoke arise from the basket of bread, and go out of the window of his cell. This was, no doubt, the evil spirit that had tempted him. From that time forward, he no longer felt hungry as before, so that at times he remained entire days without food, and without feeling any need of it.

In the same book another monk is mentioned who was for some time tempted to leave his monastery. Every evening he would say to himself, "Tomorrow I will go"; and when morning came, he would say, "Now, for the love of God, I will stay one day more." After continuing this practice for nine years, he was at last freed from the temptation.

30 It is a great error of certain souls otherwise good and pious that they believe they cannot retain interior repose in the midst of business and perplexities. Surely

there is no commotion greater than that of a vessel in the midst of the sea; yet those on board do not give up the thought of resting and sleeping, and the compass remains always in its place, turning towards the pole. Here is the point: we must be careful to keep the compass of our will in order, that it may never turn elsewhere than to the pole of the divine pleasure. This is the third means of performing our actions well.

—ST. FRANCIS DE SALES

St. Vincent de Paul excelled in this. He was never perturbed by the multiplicity of business, nor by the difficulties he encountered, but he undertook everything with inexhaustible spiritual strength and applied himself with method, patience and tranquillity, making the will of God his constant aim. This was especially visible when he had a seat in the king's council and at the same time the government of his own Congregation and of many other communities, assemblies, and conferences, together with other employments which almost overwhelmed him. One might have supposed that he would have been in a state of distraction, divided, as it were, among a hundred thoughts and cares and with his mind, in consequence, harassed and agitated. But no. In the midst of a constant ebb and flow of persons and employments, he appeared always recollected, self-possessed, master of himself, with as much evenness of temper, peace and tranquillity, as if he had only one thing to think about.

31 All that we do receives its value from conformity to the will of God. When I take food or recreation, if

I do it because it is the will of God, I merit more than if I went to suffer death without that intention. Plant this principle firmly in your mind, and then at every action fix your eyes upon it, in imitation of the carpenter, who brings every board under the square. Thus, you will do your work with perfection.

—ST. FRANCIS DE SALES

This truth was well understood by the good lay-brother who said that when he was sitting at table, he was preaching Xavier's sermons in India; for the best thing about Xavier's preaching was that he did the will of God by it, which the lay-brother was also doing.

St. Mary Magdalen de' Pazzi had this perfect conformity, not only habitual and implied, but also actual. So that while it seems to most spiritual persons a very difficult thing to direct every action actually to God, it was so easy and familiar to her that she thought it impossible for anyone to work without reflecting upon the will of God.

SEPTEMBER

Prayer

Oportet semper oras et non deficere—We must always pray, and not faint.—LUKE 18:1

1 There is certainly nothing more useful than prayer. Therefore, we ought to entertain great esteem and love for it, and employ every effort to make it well.

—ST. VINCENT DE PAUL

All the Saints have shown great love for this exercise. St. Cajetan used to spend in it eight hours in succession; St. Margaret, Queen of Scotland, and St. Stephen, King of Hungary, almost all night; St. Frances of Rome, all the time that was left from her ordinary occupations; St. Rose of Lima, twelve hours a day. At a very early age, St. Aloysius Gonzaga adopted the practice, which he never gave up, of occupying in it one, two or three hours a day. When he was at court he hid himself in

the woods, that he might not be interrupted, while praying, by his companions.

St. Mary Magdalen de' Pazzi, while still in the world and only nine years old, dedicated to this divine exercise one hour, then from two to four hours daily, and finally, whole nights; and after she entered religion, she spent in it all the time which the novices had left at their disposal.

St. John Berchmans, from the age of eleven, gave to it all the time that remained from his studies. Any corner of the house served him for an oratory, and he was often found by his family at midnight praying with bare knees upon the ground.

St. Philip Neri, from his childhood, gave himself to prayer so earnestly, advanced in it so far, and acquired such a habit of it that wherever he might be, his soul was always elevated to divine things. And so, when his room was full of people, and various affairs were under discussion, he could not sometimes refrain from raising his eyes or hands to Heaven, or uttering some aspiration, though he watched over himself carefully, that he might do nothing of the sort in the presence of others. When he went out of the house he was so abstracted that someone had to warn him when a salutation was to be returned; and sometimes, when his attention had been secured with great difficulty and by pulling his robe, he would make a gesture like a person who has just been roused from a heavy sleep.

2 Prayer well made gives much pleasure to the angels, and therefore it is much assisted by them; it gives great displeasure to the devils, and therefore is much persecuted and disturbed by them.

—ST. JOHN CHRYSOSTOM

The same Saint says that the angels have a high esteem for him who renders himself intimate with God by prayer; that while he is making it, they stand beside him in perfect silence; and when he has finished, they praise and applaud him.

St. Macarius, being present one night at the prayers of the Community, saw the place filled with black children who went among the monks and mocked them. They pressed two fingers on the eyes of some, and these immediately fell asleep; they laid a finger on the mouths of others, and these yawned; to some they appeared in the form of women; to others, in that of laborers at work; to these, of merchants selling goods; to those they seemed as if at play: and they produced in the minds of all a vivid picture corresponding to the outward appearance they assumed. But scarcely had they approached some, when they fell to the ground, as if violently repelled. When the Saint afterwards asked his companions what had happened to them at that time, he found they all had suffered the same temptations which he had seen.

3 Souls that have no habit of prayer are like a lame and paralytic body, which, though it has hands and feet, cannot use them. Therefore, to abandon prayer seems to me the same thing as to lose the straight road; for as prayer is the gate through which all the graces of God come to us, when this is closed, I do not know how we can have any.

—ST. TERESA

St. Teresa proved this by her own experience; for having abandoned prayer for some time, she began to fall into certain faults and defects from which, though they were slight, she could not free herself; rather, she went daily from bad to worse. She

was herself obliged to say that she was on the road to perdition, to which the Lord told her she would have come, if she had not resumed prayer.

4 The soul that perseveres in the exercise of prayer, however many sins, temptations and falls of a thousand kinds the devil may oppose to it, may hold it for certain, after all, that the Lord will sooner or later rescue it from danger and guide it into the harbor of salvation.

—ST. TERESA

St. Mary of Egypt confessed to the Abbot Zosimus that for seventeen years after her conversion, she suffered constant and frightful temptation; yet because she gave herself to prayer, she never fell. The same thing happened to St. Augustine, to St. Margaret of Cortona and to many others.

5 A man of prayer is capable of everything; therefore, it is of great importance that missionaries should give themselves to this exercise with particular earnestness; and as without it they will gain little or no fruit, so with its help they will become much more able to move hearts and convert souls to their Creator, than by learning and oratorical skill.

—ST. VINCENT DE PAUL

St. Francis Borgia was a man of much prayer, in which he would remain, as if in ecstasy, sometimes for six hours in

succession, which appeared to him but a moment; and the mere sight of him in the pulpit would rouse the people to compunction.

St. Thomas, St. Bonaventure and the Blessed Albertus Magnus confessed that they gained their learning more by prayer than by study. We read of St. Thomas, in particular, that not being able to understand a text of Scripture, he had recourse to prayer, and while he was praying with great fervor there appeared to him the holy Apostles Peter and Paul and explained the difficulty in a voice so clear and distinct that it was heard by his companion Brother Reginald.

6 When we have to speak to others on spiritual matters, we ought first to speak of them to God in prayer, and empty ourselves of our own spirit, that we may be filled with the Holy Spirit, which alone illuminates the mind and inflames the will. Superiors, especially, should do this, and endeavor to have continual communication with God, having recourse to Him not only in doubtful and difficult cases but in everything that occurs, to learn immediately from Him what they are to teach others, in imitation of Moses, who announced to the people only what the Lord had previously taught him. *Haec dicit Dominus*—Thus saith the Lord.

—ST. VINCENT DE PAUL

When this Saint was about to deliberate on some business, or take some resolution, or give some advice, he was accustomed before speaking and even before thinking of the matter

to raise his mind to God to ask light and help. On such occasions he usually raised his eyes to Heaven, then dropped them and kept them partly closed, as if consulting with God in his own heart before replying. When matters of importance were under consideration, he desired that time should be taken, to recommend them to God. And as he trusted wholly to the divine wisdom, and not at all to his own, he received from Heaven great lights and graces, by means of which he often discovered things which could not have been penetrated by the human intellect alone.

In grave matters, St. Ignatius never resolved upon anything without first recommending them to God in prayer.

When the Abbot Pambo was asked for advice, he used to reply, "Give me time to think." Then he made it a subject of prayer; and if he received any light from God, he communicated it; otherwise, he did not answer at all.

7 Mental prayer consists in weighing and understanding what we are saying, who it is to whom we are speaking and who we are to have the courage to speak to so great a Lord. To have these and similar thoughts is properly to make mental prayer. Their opinion, however, is not to be followed who believe that its whole essence consists in thinking, so that if they can keep their thoughts fixed by a great effort, then they consider themselves very spiritual and men of prayer; but if they are able to do this no longer, and their attention wanders a little, even to good things, they imagine they are doing nothing. No, the substance

of mental prayer, in my opinion, consists in nothing but conversing with God as with a friend. And so, to speak of this thing or of that to Him, who, we know, loves us, is mental prayer.

—ST. TERESA

When St. Ignatius was once traveling with his companions, each with a bundle on his shoulders, a worthy man, moved with compassion, offered to carry all their burdens, and did so. When they came to inns on their way, the Fathers tried to find some nooks, each for himself, to make their prayer; and the good man, seeing this, found a corner of his own where he remained kneeling, like them. When someone asked him what he was doing there, "I am doing nothing," he replied: "These are Saints, and I am their ass. Whatever they are doing, I would do. And I stay there offering this to the Lord." It is said that in this manner he succeeded in becoming very spiritual and attaining the gift of a very lofty contemplation.

The venerable Monseigneur de Palafox, having frequently considered in prayer who he was that was speaking, and to whom he was speaking, that it was the most unworthy of men to the Divine Goodness, a wretched worm to God, was so filled with humiliation that he wept. It grieved him that he had the temerity to speak. "What!" he exclaimed, "a little dust of the earth, the worst, the most miserable, the most abandoned, man in the world, speak to the Eternal, the Infinite, the Boundless!" Then he was afraid, and said: "O Lord, am I to speak to Thee? Am I to have the boldness to love Thee? a God infinite, a God all-powerful, Creator of all that is created! and I nothing, and

327

less than nothing, and, what grieves me most, wicked, and more than wicked! What is this? How can this be borne?" But again he would say: "O Lord, is it not just to love? Then ought I not to love Thee? O Lord, the worms adore Thee, and I am a worm; then I can adore Thee! O Lord, Thou camest to seek sinners—I am the greatest of sinners! O Lord, if Thou didst abase Thyself that we might adore Thee, might speak to Thee, might pray to Thee, why should I not adore Thee, speak to Thee, pray to Thee?"

8 If, while one is praying, he regards and considers the fact that he is conversing with God with more attention than the words that he utters, he is making vocal and mental prayer at once, which may be of much advantage to him. But if he does not consider with whom he is speaking, nor what he is saying, it may be thought certain that, however much he may move his lips, he prays very little.

—ST. TERESA

A certain bishop once saw an angel come down from Heaven, and collect the tears of a woman who was praying in a corner of the church. Astonished at this, he asked her, as they went out, what she had been doing at that time. She replied that she was reciting the *Pater Noster, Ave Maria,* and *Credo.*

9 After our affections have been moved in prayer, we need not multiply considerations, but stop a little and dwell upon those already made; then, from time to time, say

to Our Lord some word of compunction, love or resignation, according as we feel ourselves inclined. This is the best kind of prayer.

—ST. JANE FRANCES DE CHANTAL

St. Cyril of Alexandria made this clear and plain by a comparison. "Meditation," said the Saint, "is like striking the flint with the steel to draw out a spark; but when the spark has come and lighted the tinder, we lay aside the steel. So, by considerations and the use of the intellect, we strike the hard rock of our heart, until we kindle in it the love of God, and the desire of humility, mortification, or some other virtue; and when this is come, we rest upon it, and seek to establish ourselves in it firmly. This is certainly a better and more useful prayer than if we should make very lofty and farfetched considerations and arguments." It was in this way that the Saint, and all others who have profited by prayer, conducted it.

This truth was well understood by a good servant of God, who in his prayer, which was generally upon Our Lord's Passion, did not go very fully into speculations and reasonings. But after representing to his mind the mystery upon which he was to meditate as soon as he felt any affection such as love or gratitude towards God or sorrow for having offended Him, with the intention to offend Him no more, or perhaps a desire to imitate Christ in humility or suffering, or any similar affection—he rested upon it, and endeavored to warm and cherish it in his heart. When he perceived that it was growing cool, he tried to enkindle it again with the whole or a part of the consideration which had lighted it up at first, saying:

"What a great suffering was this! Who endured it? The Son of God—the Son of God! And for whom did He endure it? For me; and the Son of God endured to suffer so much for me! And I cannot endure to suffer a word, a little slight, for love of Him! How much has Jesus Christ done for me! and I never cease offending Him! Where are my ordinary human feelings! Ah, how sorry I am that I have grieved my God in this way! Surely I will offend Him no more! Behold, how much my good God has loved me! and I do not love Him, who loved me so much! Ah yes, I mean to love this God, who loves me so much!" So he continued dwelling on these affections and bringing them up afresh, and in this way became a man of great perfection.

10 Souls but little confirmed in piety advance well and happily when the Lord gives them consolations in prayer. But if He afterwards deprives them of these, they immediately become languid and discontented, like children who thank their mother when she gives them sweet things and cry when she takes them away, because they are children, and do not know that a long course of such things is hurtful to them and causes worms. Sensible consolations of the soul often produce the worm of self-satisfaction and that of pride, which is the poison of the soul, and corrupts every good work. This is the reason why the Lord, who gives them to us at first to encourage us, afterwards takes them away that they might not hurt us, and therefore merits

no less thanks in taking them away than in giving them.

—ST. FRANCIS DE SALES

A great servant of God said of himself: "For forty years I have exercised myself in prayer without any interior consolation, but with much advantage. My only comfort is that I have served God at my own expense."

St. John Berchmans often experienced great consolation in prayer, but from time to time, also great aridity. In such cases he never lost his courage or cheerfulness.

11 When the soul finds herself oppressed by aridity and sterility, she ought to make the prayer of reverence, confidence, and conformity to the Divine Will, standing in the presence of God like a poor man before his prince, making use of such words as express a loving submission to the divine pleasure.

—ST. JANE FRANCES DE CHANTAL

"I should never wish," said St. Teresa, "for any other prayer than that which would cause me to grow in virtue. So I should consider that a good prayer, which was attended by many aridities, temptations, and desolations, that left me more humble. Can he be said not to pray, who is in the midst of such trials? On the contrary, if he offers them to God and bears them with conformity to His holy will, as he ought, this is prayer, and very often much better than his who wearies his brain with various

reflections, and persuades himself that he has made a good prayer if he has squeezed out four tears."

St. Philip Neri considered it an excellent remedy in such case to imagine ourselves beggars, as it were, in the presence of God and the Saints, and, as such, to go now to one, now to another, to ask spiritual alms, with that feeling and earnestness which the destitute usually exhibit. He advised too, that this should be done even corporally at times by visiting the churches of different Saints, to ask some favor from each.

12 Whoever wishes to profit by prayers should not take account of spiritual consolations. I know by experience that the soul which has started on this road with a full determination not to consider whether the Lord gives or denies him consolations and tenderness, and really acts on this determination, has already made a great part of the journey.

—ST. TERESA

St. John Berchmans, when asked what remedies he made use of against aridity, replied, "I pray, I take care to be occupied, and I have patience."

St. Francis de Sales was never angry with himself on account of the desolations, aridities, or interior abandonment which he endured. He told St. Jane Frances de Chantal that when he was at prayer, he was not in the habit of reflecting as to whether he was in consolation or desolation, but if the Lord gave him any good sentiments he received them with profound reverence and simplicity; and if He gave none, he did not reflect upon it, but

remained still before God, with great confidence, like a loving little child.

13 There is another thing which greatly afflicts those who give themselves to prayer. It is the distractions which often come and carry their thoughts, and their hearts too, hither and thither. They come at times from the immortification of the senses; at times with the soul being distracted in itself, and often because the Lord wills it, to try His servants. Now in such cases we must recall our thoughts from time to time, by reviving our faith in the presence of God, and by remaining before Him with reverence and respect. If we do not succeed in fixing them on the prescribed point, we must bear those annoyances and vexations with humility and patience. It will not be lost time, as at first sight it may appear, but such a prayer will sometimes be more fruitful than many others made with recollection and pleasure. For all the actions performed to banish or to endure these distractions, as they are done in order not to displease God, and to become better qualified for His service, are so many acts of the love of God.

—ST. TERESA

St. Jane Frances de Chantal gave this advice to her daughters, which she surely also practiced herself. "When one is disturbed by distractions in the time of prayer, it is well to make the prayer

of patience, and to say, if possible, humbly and lovingly: 'O Lord, Thou art the sole support of my soul, and all my consolation!'"

St. John Chrysostom advised one who was easily carried away by distractions to arouse himself by this comparison: "What! I stand talking with a friend about news, trifles, reports, and I am all attention; now that I am conversing with God about the pardon of my sins, and the way for me to be saved, I am all torpor! Though my knees are bent, my mind goes wandering through the house and through the streets! Where is my faith? where, my reason?"

St. Aloysius Gonzaga possessed a gift of prayer that was no less worthy of wonder than of envy. We read of him that he reached such a point that he scarcely ever suffered from distractions. Once when he was giving an account of his interior, the spiritual Father asked him whether he suffered many distractions in prayer. He paused to think a moment, then answered that if he should put together all he had had for six months, he did not believe they would occupy as much time as one *Ave Maria*. A great gift, in truth! But the efforts he made to induce the Lord to grant it were not slight. By practicing continual mortification of all his senses; by never occupying his mind with any thoughts but such as might perfect him in piety and learning; by throwing himself at the time for prayer, wholly, with all his fervor, into it—thus he had so closed the way to distractions that they did not dare, so to speak, to approach him.

14 The whole aim of whoever intends to give himself to prayer ought to be to labor, to resolve, to dispose himself, with all possible diligence, to conform his

will to that of God. For in this consists all the highest perfection that can be acquired in the spiritual way.

—ST. TERESA

It was the principal object of all the prayers of this Saint, to conform herself in everything to the Divine Will. This also was the end that St. Bernard fixed for himself at the beginning of his prayer, when he encouraged himself to make it, as we read in his Life, by the hope of knowing and doing the will of God. The same thing is related of St. Vincent de Paul, and of many other servants of God.

15 Prayer ought to be humble, fervent, resigned, persevering and accompanied with great reverence. One should consider that he stands in the presence of a God, and speaks with a Lord before whom the angels tremble from awe and fear.

—ST. MARY MAGDALEN DE' PAZZI

St. Francis de Sales, even when he was alone, remained before God through the whole time of prayer, humble, abased, composed, motionless and with singular reverence, like a loving son.

St. John Berchmans remained always on his knees, with his eyes closed, his hands clasped on his bosom, without support, motionless as a rock, with a countenance full of joy and such ardor that others placed themselves near him, that they might gain fervor by looking at him.

St. Rose of Lima kept herself recollected, and so great was her attention and devotion that any object that presented itself before

her distracted her no more than if she were insensible. When she went to church she placed herself in a corner, with her eyes fixed upon the tabernacle. She would remain thus for many hours immovable, while the sight of persons passing near her and the general buzz and murmur of the crowd did not disturb her at all.

At the close of their prayers, many Saints showed exterior marks of their fervor. St. Gervasius, the Bishop, was often seen with rays around his head; the face of the venerable Father John Leonardi was so changed and glowing that he seemed transformed into a Seraph; and the Abbot Silvanus was transported to such a degree that all the things of the earth seemed to him vile and abject, and he covered his eyes with his hands that he might not see them, saying: "Close, my eyes, and seek not to look at the things of the world; for there is nothing in it worthy to be gazed upon."

St. Bernard, one morning, saw an angel going through the choir with a censer full of perfumes, censing the monks as they were at prayers. This censing produced in the hearts of the fervent a very sweet fragrance, but in those of the negligent and sleepy, a foul and sickening odor.

16 Try to disengage yourself from so many cares, and take a little time to think of God and to rest in Him. Enter into the secret chamber of your heart, and banish from it everything save your Creator alone and what can help you to find Him; then having closed the door, say to Him, with all your soul: "Lord, I seek Thy divine countenance—teach me to find it!"

—ST. AUGUSTINE

St. Francis de Sales called the center of his soul the sanctuary of God, where nothing enters save the soul and God. This was the place of his retirement and his ordinary abode; and therefore, in his soul there was nothing but purity, simplicity, humility, and union of the spirit with its God.

When St. Bernard was entering a church to pray, he would say to his thoughts: "Remain here outside, useless thoughts and disorderly affections, and thou, my soul, enter into the presence of thy Lord!"

17 Those who can shut themselves up in this little heaven of the soul, where He dwells who has created Heaven and earth, may believe that they are walking in an excellent way, and that they shall not fail to drink of the water of the fountain, for in a little time they will make great progress.

—ST. TERESA

St. Catherine of Siena, who was very fond of retirement, was loaded by her parents with cares and employments. But she built for herself a cell in her own heart, where she remained in constant retirement, even in the midst of the most active occupations, contemplating God and conversing familiarly with Him. Thus she succeeded in gaining a firm and constant union with His Divine Majesty, and she used to say that the Kingdom of God is properly in our hearts, where He fixes His abode.

A devout maiden having become a Religious, devoted herself to a peculiarly retired life, withdrawing herself more than usual from all communication at the grate. For this reason her relatives

endeavored to persuade her to rest and refresh herself with some innocent conversation; but she replied that she was constantly engaged in intercourse that kept her cheerful and happy, and it was communion with Jesus Christ.

"How much it helps me," said St. Teresa, "to remember that I have company in my heart, even God! and I remain there truly with Him."

18 In mental prayer, we are not obliged to employ our intellect all the time. We can occupy ourselves in the presence of God by conversing and consoling ourselves with Him, without the weariness of formal considerations and choice words. We can represent to Him simply our necessities, and the cause He has for showing us mercy. For example, when we think of some part of the Passion, it is a good thing to make a consideration first, by meditating on the pains which Our Lord suffered in it. But let not the soul weary itself by seeking too long for this; let it rather sometimes remain still with Christ, and keeping the intellect inactive if possible, let it occupy itself, in thought, in looking upon Him; let it accompany Him, ask favors of Him, humble itself and console itself with Him, and remember that He did not deserve to be there. This method of prayer has many advantages.

—ST. TERESA

This Saint testifies of herself that she frequently practiced this kind of prayer, and derived much advantage from it.

Gerson relates that a servant of God used to say: "For forty years I have practiced mental prayer with all possible diligence, and I have found no better nor easier method of making it well, than that of presenting myself before God as a child or a beggar, poor, blind, naked and abandoned."

It was thus that St. Francis prayed, when he passed whole nights repeating and dwelling upon these few words, "My God, who art Thou, and who am I?" Now exciting himself to love for so great a God, now to contempt for so vile and ungrateful a creature, he would sink into confusion and shame for his many failures, and ask pardon and help from the Lord.

19 In prayer it is well to occupy ourselves sometimes in making acts of praise and love to God; in desires and resolutions to please Him in all things; in rejoicing at His goodness and that He is what He is; in desiring His honor and glory; in recommending ourselves to His mercy; also in simply placing ourselves before Him, beholding His greatness and His mercy, and, at the same time, our own vileness and misery, and then to let Him give us what He pleases, whether it be showers or aridity; for He knows better than we what is most suitable for us. These acts do much to arouse the will and the affections. Be careful, when these sentiments come, not to leave them for the sake of finishing the ordinary meditation. For, to profit greatly in this course, the chief point is not to think much, but to love much. Therefore, whatever will arouse you to love, do it.

—ST. TERESA

Father Segneri the younger one day said with tears to an intimate friend, "Do not act as I have done; for, from the time I began to study theology, I always spent the hour for meditation in making various considerations to excite the affections, so that I had little time left for recommending myself to God. But finally the Lord deigned to open my eyes. Ever since, I have always tried to spend the whole time in recommending myself to Him; and if I have done any good either to myself or others, I think it is all due to this holy exercise."

We read of St. Jane Frances de Chantal that she found her delight and repose in the consideration of the vast perfections of God, and in the desire that this Supreme Good might be known and loved by all His creatures. It is related, too, of the blessed Egidius, a companion of St. Francis, that by meditating often upon the perfections, works and mercies of God, he became filled with such great love towards Him, that he could not speak of Him, nor hear Him spoken of, nor even think of Him, without immediately falling into an ecstasy.

20 It is well to imagine sometimes in prayer that insults or affronts are inflicted upon us, or that misfortunes fall upon us, and then to strive to accustom our hearts to pardon them and bear them all with patience, in imitation of our Saviour; for in this, much spiritual strength is gained.

—ST. PHILIP NERI

When St. Ignatius was once confined to his bed by illness, he began to think whether anything could happen which could

disturb him. After having imagined many troubles and trials, he found that nothing could afflict him and take away his peace, except to see the destruction of his Society. But after meditating several times upon the point, he gained the mastery over himself to such a degree that he thought if this should happen, a quarter of an hour spent in praying would suffice to make him tranquil and resigned.

21 We should set a high value on meditation upon the Passion of our Redeemer. For a simple remembrance or meditation upon this is worth more than if for a whole year one should take the discipline to blood, or fast on bread and water every week, or recite the whole psalter every day.

—BL. ALBERTUS MAGNUS

This was an ordinary subject of meditation with St. Francis Xavier, and a continual one with St. Casimir, even when hearing Mass, and he applied himself to it with so much intensity that he frequently became insensible. St. Bridget, too, made it almost always, and never without tears.

The Empress Leonora, from long meditations on the Passion, conceived so tender a love for Jesus Crucified that if she had been equally sure, as she said, of being saved in the midst of ease and honors, she would have chosen in preference the way of the Cross, that she might in some degree resemble her Lord. Thence she drew that generosity which enabled her to conceal her illness and bodily pains, and refrain from complaint or lamentation. And if anyone, in such cases, seemed to sympathize

with her, the humble servant of God would say: "This cross is very light and very dear to me; without it I could not be contented. I have very great need of it—I should otherwise be too presumptuous."

The venerable Monseigneur de Palafox often practiced the same exercise. Sometimes he represented his soul under the figure of a bird flying, and then becoming weary, and resting upon the nail which fastened Our Lord's feet to the Cross; then contemplating Him, and drinking with the greatest consolation the blood that flowed from His wounds. Again, he would take the figure of a bee, going as, from flower to flower, to one or another wound of Our Lord—to those of the head, the hands, the feet and especially to that of the side, into which he would enter and bathe himself. Sometimes, when weary of temporal things, such as writing or study, he would turn to the feet of Jesus, saying, "My Jesus, let me rest here!"

This devotion rose to a singular height in St. Philip Neri, who could not meditate, nor read, nor speak, nor hear of the Passion of our Saviour, without becoming pale as ashes and shedding a flood of tears. This was especially the case in Holy Week, and still more, if any mention was made of the love with which He suffered for us. One day, when he was preaching on this topic, he was overcome by extraordinary fervor and began to weep and sob so violently that he could not recover his breath, and was obliged to descend from the pulpit and leave the church. As this occurred many times, and could not be prevented, he was obliged for some years before his death to give up preaching on this subject; and he could not speak of it even in private. He even became so sensitive that at times, if he only

heard the words *Passion of Christ*, he would weep so as to be unable to utter a word.

A similar thing is said to have happened, on a Good Friday, to the venerable Father Louis de Grenada, when he went into the pulpit to preach on the Passion. Scarcely had he uttered the words, "*Passio Domini nostri Jesu Christi*," when he burst into a torrent of tears. After he had recovered his breath a little, he repeated the same words, but with the words the tears came back, and more abundantly than at first. Finally he made a vigorous effort to begin the sacred words for a third time; but a third time the fit of weeping returned, with such force and violence that it excited universal commotion through the audience, so that for a long time nothing was to be heard in the church but sobs and cries. And so the sermon ended without having begun.

22 As one friend often visits another, going to bid him good morning and good night, and looking in upon him at times during the day; so should you often visit Jesus in His Sacrament, and offer His precious blood many times in each visit to the Eternal Father, and you will see that your love will increase marvellously by these visits.

—ST. MARY MAGDALEN DE' PAZZI

St. Francis Borgia made seven such visits daily, and acquired by them such familiar affection that on entering a church he could tell by the sense of smell where the Blessed Sacrament was.

Every time St. John Berchmans went out to take a walk he was careful to visit some church, whether it was a time of

Exposition in it or not. On such occasions his recollection was so profound that he did not notice when his companion arose to go out, so that the latter was often obliged to come back from the church door and arouse him, and even call him aloud by name, so great was his abstraction.

St. Mary Magdalen de' Pazzi visited the Blessed Sacrament 33 times a day, to her great happiness and advantage; and St. Wenceslaus, Duke of Bohemia, used to pay visits to the churches barefooted, by night, through snow and ice, so that the pavements were stained with his blood.

St. Vincent de Paul made visits as often as he was able, and the rest that he took from his grave occupations consisted in staying, sometimes for hours, before the sacred Tabernacle. He remained there with an aspect so humble that it seemed as if he would willingly have sunk to the center of the earth, and with an exterior as modest and devout as if he were beholding the person of Jesus Christ with his own eyes, so that he inspired with devotion all who beheld him. When he had difficult business to transact, he had recourse, like Moses, to the sacred Tabernacle, to consult the oracle of truth. On leaving his house, he went to the chapel to ask a blessing, and on his return, to give thanks for the graces received and to humble himself for the faults he had perhaps committed. He did this not as a matter of form, but with true religious feeling.

23 We must not neglect to exercise ourselves in self-knowledge, for this is of great importance in the contemplative way. But this should be done with due regard to time and measure. I mean, that after

a soul has yielded and surrendered itself, and clearly understands that of itself it has no good thing, and is ashamed and confounded to stand before so great a King, and sees how little it returns for so many gifts—what necessity is there, under these circumstances, to occupy it and make it spend more time, in this? We must let it pass to other things which the Lord places before it, so that it may come forth from itself, and fly to consider the greatness of its God.

—ST. TERESA

From the time St. Francis Borgia first applied himself to prayer, he spent two hours every morning in self-examination. By this time he arrived at so humble an opinion of himself that he was astonished that everyone did not treat him with contempt.

St. Bonaventure tells of St. Francis that he used to pass whole days and nights in this brief prayer: "My Lord and my God, who art Thou, and who am I?" and on such occasions he was often seen to be lifted from the ground, and surrounded by a bright halo.

A story is told in the Lives of the Fathers of a young monk, who said to an old one: "Father, my heart tells me that I am good." But the old man answered: "Whoever does not see his sins, always thinks himself good; but when one sees them, his heart cannot persuade him of any such thing. It is necessary, then, to strive to know ourselves."

We read of the Abbot Isidore that one of his disciples entered his cell one day, and finding him in tears, asked the cause. "I am weeping," he answered, "for my sins." "But, Father, you

have no sins," said the disciple. "My son," returned the Abbot, "if God should reveal my sins to men, the world would be filled with terror."

A vision recorded by the venerable Sister Maria Crucifixa is well adapted to illustrate this point. "It was permitted me to enter," she writes, "by a spiritual glance, into the most secret recesses of the human heart. I was amazed at the sight of wonders of human ugliness and deformity, as I was shown the birthplace of sin. It appeared like a horrible subterranean cavern, wherein swarmed constantly vast troops of animals and insects, great and small, all frightful and loathsome. These typified mortal and venial sins and imperfections. By this terrible sight I penetrated the deep abyss of knowledge of myself and of my extreme misery, so that I perceived myself to be deserving only of scorn and ignominy, for I appeared like a mass of black and greasy soot, like foul and corrupt refuse, or an ugly and dangerous monster, which no one could behold without taking to flight." She had this vision on the day of her profession, and this sight of herself made so strong an impression upon her soul that it lasted a whole year. All this time she believed that her companions saw her as she saw herself, and was astonished at their self-control and virtue, and could not understand why they did not all abhor and fly from her. "I would willingly have buried myself alive," she writes, "if I could thus have hidden from their eyes my intolerable appearance. Therefore when I received wrongs and insults I thought they rather praised and honored me, for I felt that they were treating me better than I deserved, and it was impossible for me to think otherwise. So that if they had told me that I was ugly, stupid, without

talent or wit, I should certainly have wondered and said: 'Oh how little you know of my miseries! I am insufferable in the eyes of God by my extreme destitution, and you wonder that I am not rich in good qualities! What would a beggar do, who, while barely covered with rags, should hear himself reproved for not having a gold chain and a badge of knighthood? What would he do on hearing such reproofs? Instead of being angry, he would be amazed, and would say: I have not so much as a shirt, and you wonder that I am without a gold chain and a badge! In charity, give me a bit of bread, for I have nothing to do with chains and badges.'"

24 The great work of our perfection is born, grows, and maintains its life by means of two small but precious exercises—aspirations and spiritual retirement. An aspiration is a certain springing of the soul towards God, and the more simple it is, the more valuable. It consists in simply beholding what He is, and what He has done and is doing for us; and it should excite the heart, as a consequence, to acts of humility, love, resignation or abandonment, according to circumstances. Now, these two exercises have an incredible power to keep us in our duty, to support us in temptation, to lift us up promptly after falls and to unite us closely to God. Besides, they can be made at any time or place, and with all possible ease; therefore, they ought to be as familiar to us as the inspiration and expiration of air from our lungs.

—ST. FRANCIS DE SALES

Every time that the clock struck, St. Ignatius collected his thoughts and raised his soul to God.

Though he might happen to be in the company of men of rank, St. Vincent de Paul always uncovered his head when the clock struck, and raised some devout aspiration to Heaven. At other times, he often uttered some devout ejaculation or aspiration, most frequently this one: "O my Lord! O Divine Goodness! when wilt Thou give me the grace to be entirely Thine, and to love only Thee?"

St. Bartholomew the Apostle adored God by making a hundred genuflections each day, and as many in the night.

St. Thomas Aquinas used this kind of prayer many times a day—when he was at Mass, when he was studying, when he left his cell or returned to it and at all odd moments.

Cassian says that the monks of Egypt frequently employed this brief ejaculation, which is full of humility and confidence: "*Deus, in adjutorium meum intende. Domine, ad adjuvandum me festina*—O God, incline unto mine aid. O Lord, make haste to help me."

Monseigneur de Palafox, the Bishop, practiced it on all occasions. When anything seemed doubtful, he turned to God and said, "O Lord, what shall we do in this matter? counsel me, guide me Thyself, in danger. O Lord, rule me; let me not be presumptuous, but humble; do not permit me to stray a hair's breadth from what pleases Thee." When through human frailty he fell into some fault, or said or did some thing that was not suitable, he would say, "O Lord, raise me up! What is this, O Lord? Is it possible that I am to be always the same? Hold me, that I may hold to Thee!" Often, too, he would say in his heart: "I desire

nothing, I wish for nothing, I cling to nothing, except Thyself, my God and my All! Glory? it is Thine, and I seek it only for Thee! Honor? all my honor, my Jesus, is Thy honor. Satisfaction? my only satisfaction and pleasure is that Thou art satisfied and pleased"; and so on.

25 It is a great help to humility to accustom ourselves to draw from all things reflections suited to raise our hearts to God, by beholding in them all His perfections, or else the love He bears us, and our obligation to serve Him faithfully.

—SCUPOLI

Such was the practice of St. Francis de Sales. On beholding a beautiful landscape, he would say, "We are fields cultivated by God." If he saw magnificent and richly adorned churches, "We are the living temples of God; then why are our souls not as well adorned with virtues?" If he looked at flowers, "When will the time come that our flowers shall change into fruit?" If he saw rare and valuable pictures, "Nothing is as beautiful as the soul made in the image of God." If he walked in a garden, "When will that of our soul be dotted with flowers, filled with fruit, well arranged, and free from dust and rubbish?" If he came to a fountain, "Oh, when shall we drink our fill from the fountains of the Saviour?" If to rivers, "When shall we go to God, as these waters do to the sea?" Thus he made use of all visible things to raise his soul to God.

26 There is a certain method of prayer which is both very easy and very useful. It consists in accustoming

our soul to the presence of God, in such a way as to produce in us a union with Him which is intimate, simple, and perfect. Oh what a precious kind of prayer is this!

—ST. FRANCIS DE SALES

In all his actions and exercises, Rusbruchio kept his mind elevated to God so that, he confessed, he had obtained from the Lord this special favor, that he could without difficulty immerse himself at will in a most sweet contemplation of the Divinity, whether he was alone in his room or abroad in company with others.

St. Aloysius Gonzaga found nothing easier than to keep his mind constantly united to God, so that he had as much difficulty in turning his thoughts from Him, as others have in keeping them fixed in that direction.

27 If we persist in walking for a year in the presence of God, at the end of the year we shall find that we have reached unconsciously the summit of perfection.

—ST. TERESA

It is narrated in the Lives of the Fathers, that a holy Abbot instructed one of his novices that he should take care never to lose sight of God, and think of Him as always present. "For," said he, "this is the rule of rules, and the one which the Lord taught to Abraham, when He said, '*Ambula coram Me, et esto perfectus*—Walk before Me, and be perfect.'" This was so impressed on the mind of the young man that he practiced it wonderfully well; and from the reckless youth that he was, he became a monk so

perfect that when he died a few years after, he was seen to fly directly, and with great glory, into Heaven.

28 The greater part of the faults which Religious commit against their Rules, and in all the exercises of piety, arise from easily losing sight of the presence of God.

—ST. FRANCIS DE SALES

It is said of St. John Berchmans that he never lost sight of the presence of God, that he practiced it with rare facility and naturalness, and what is more wonderful, he was free from absence of mind, so that he was always attentive to whatever he was doing and ready and prompt to assist others. He performed his spiritual exercises, too, with so much devotion that he was never seen to transgress the smallest of his Rules, nor commit a fault of any kind.

29 There is a certain method of practicing the presence of God, by which, if the soul chooses, she may remain always in prayer, and constantly enkindled and inflamed with the love of God. This consists in realizing, in the midst of our occupations, that we are doing the will of God in each, and in rejoicing and being glad that it is so.

—ST. ALPHONSUS RODRIGUEZ

St. Francis de Sales, for many years before his death, had scarcely any time for prayer, as he was overwhelmed with other occupations. One day St. Jane Frances de Chantal asked him

whether he had made his meditation. "No," he replied, "but I am doing what is worth as much." In fact, he endeavored to keep himself continually united with God, and he used to say that in this world we must make a prayer of works and activities. Thus his life was a continual prayer, for he did not content himself with merely enjoying a delicious union with God in prayer, but equally loved to do His will.

30 The highest and most perfect prayer is contemplation. But this is altogether the work of God, as it is supernatural and above our powers. The soul can only prepare itself for this prayer, and can do nothing in it. The best preparation is to live humbly, and to give ourselves in earnest to the acquisition of virtues, and especially, of fraternal charity and the love of God; to have a firm resolution to do the will of God in all things; to walk in the way of the Cross, and to destroy self-love, which is a wish, on our part, to please ourselves rather than God.

—ST. TERESA

This Saint fulfilled all this with great perfection, and for that reason she was endowed with such lofty contemplation and rare gifts.

When St. Anthony the Abbot was asked how he could pass whole nights in prayer, he answered: "I never knew in what true contemplation consists as long as I had regard to myself. But when I succeeded in purifying my mind from every disorderly motion and separating my heart from every earthly affection,

then I began to enjoy that admirable fruit of the Divine Will which purified souls are wont to taste in contemplation."

The following words came from a soul that had received much light: "I know by experience that to learn mystic theology, it is more useful to study the crucifix than books; that is, instead of occupying ourselves with much reading, we ought to labor in the practice of virtue, in the imitation of Jesus Christ, in attention to purity of life, to prayer, and to fidelity in doing and suffering whatever God requires of us, as well as in dying to ourselves."

OCTOBER

Confidence

Ecce ego vobiscum sum—
Behold I am with you.—MATT. 28:20

---

1   As the omnipotence of God is infinite, nothing is impossible to Him; as His wisdom is infinite, nothing is difficult to Him; as His goodness is immeasurable, He has an infinite desire for our well-being. Now, should this not be enough to make us repose all our confidence in Him?

—SCUPOLI

This thought must have taken strong hold of a certain servant of God in Rome, who, as it is recorded, once addressed this prayer to Him: "O Lord! I desire that there may be no delay; think of the matter Thyself, for I mean to be heard. Thou art my Father, and if Thou wilt not do this for me, there is no one else who

can do it. Consider, if through the merits of Thy Christ I do not deserve it, do not grant it, and I will be content."

St. Francis de Sales was filled with so much confidence in God that he was in perfect tranquillity amid the greatest disasters; for he could not persuade himself, as he often said, that anyone who trusts in a Providence infinite in all respects, has not cause to hope for a good result from whatever it permits to happen to him.

The Lord once appeared to St. Gertrude and said to her: "When anyone has complete confidence in Me and believes that I have the power, the wisdom, and the desire to aid him on all occasions, this ravishes My heart, and does Me such violence that I cannot help favoring such a soul, on account of the pleasure I experience in seeing it so dependent upon Me, and to satisfy the great love I bear to it."

2 God certainly desires our greatest good more than we ourselves desire it. He knows better than we by what way it can come to us; and the choice of ways is wholly in His hands, as it is He who governs and regulates all that occurs in the world. It is, then, most certain that in all chances that can befall, whatever may happen will always be best for us.

—ST. AUGUSTINE

St. Francis de Sales, knowing that all events succeed one another according to the disposal of Divine Providence, rested upon it more tranquilly than an infant upon its mother's bosom. He said that the Lord had taught him this lesson even from his

youth, and that if he were to begin life again, he would despise worldly prudence more than ever, and allow himself to be governed entirely by Divine Providence.

3 Do you desire security? Here you have it. The Lord says to thee, "I will never abandon thee, I will always be with thee!" If a good man made you such a promise, you would trust him. God makes it, and do you doubt? Do you seek a support more sure than the word of God, which is infallible? Surely, He has made the promise, He has written it, He has pledged His word for it, it is most certain.

—ST. AUGUSTINE

It is related in the Life of St. Rose of Lima that she had inherited from her mother, who was very timorous and apprehensive of danger, such great timidity that she did not dare, in the night, to go from one room in the house to another without a candle, except for prayer, for the sake of which she conquered every terror. One evening she lingered longer than usual in the little arbor which had been built for her oratory in the garden. Her mother, afraid that some harm might have come to her, resolved to go in search of her; but not having courage to go alone, she asked her husband to accompany her. When Rose saw them, she immediately ended her prayer, and went to meet them; then excusing herself for her tardiness, she went back with them to the house. But on the way, she began to say to herself: "How is this? My mother, who is as timid as I, feels safe in the company of her husband. And am I afraid, accompanied by my Spouse,

who without ever leaving me, is continually at my side and in my heart!" This reflection made such an impression on her mind that it banished every terror, so that from that time she was no longer afraid of anything; and in any appearance of danger, she would say: *"Non timebo mala, quoniam Tu mecum es—*I will fear no evil, for Thou art with me."

Surius relates of St. Hugo, Bishop of Lincoln, that he was one night grieved and disturbed by the thought of a disaster which he believed to be impending. Then recollecting himself, he smote his breast and said: "Wretch that thou art! God has promised to aid us in all tribulations, and art thou afraid of anything that may happen?"

4 We are firmly convinced that the truths of faith cannot deceive us, and yet we cannot bring ourselves to trust to them; nay, we are far more ready to trust to human reasonings and the deceitful appearance of this world. This, then, is the cause of our slight progress in virtue, and of our small success in what concerns the glory of God.

—ST. VINCENT DE PAUL

St. Anthony and St. Francis arrived at the highest perfection only by confiding obedience to these words of the Gospel: "If thou wilt be perfect, sell what thou hast, give to the poor, and then follow Me."

5 Both for our own profit and the salvation of others, it is absolutely necessary to follow in everything the

bright light of faith, which is accompanied by a certain unction secretly diffused in our hearts. Truly, there is nothing but eternal truth capable of filling our hearts and leading us in a safe path! Believe me, it is enough to be well established upon this divine foundation, to be sure of quickly reaching perfection, and being able to do great things.

—ST. VINCENT DE PAUL

St. Philip Neri always prefaced any business of importance by prayer, by means of which he acquired such great confidence in God that he used to say: "As I have time for prayer, I have sure hope of obtaining from the Lord whatever grace I ask of Him; for I rest entirely upon the promise of the Lord, that we shall receive whatever we ask in prayer with lively faith."

It is told of St. Francis that his brother, seeing him barefooted and thinly clothed in the depth of winter, sent a boy to ask him, in mockery, to sell him a drop of his sweat. The Saint replied joyously: "Tell my brother that I have already sold it all to my God and Lord, and at a very good price."

Father d'Avila took a vow of poverty, that he might preach the Gospel more freely, and said that he found great support in this promise of Christ: *"Quaerite primum regnum Dei et haec omnia adjicientur vobis—Seek the Kingdom of God, and all these things shall be added unto you"*—for it had never deceived him.

6 O Lord of my soul, who can find words to tell what Thou givest to those who trust in Thee, and how much,

on the other hand those lose, who though they may have attained to ecstasies and rapture, yet confide in themselves!

—ST. TERESA

This Saint said she had known persons eminent in virtue and who had even attained to the prayer of union, who afterwards fell into the power of the demon because of their overweening self-confidence. For when the soul sees herself so near to God and perceives the vast difference between the good things of Heaven and those of earth, and experiences the great love the Lord manifests for her, there springs up from these favors such security of nevermore falling from the happiness she enjoys, that it seems to her impossible that so delightful a life should ever be exchanged for the baseness of sensual delights. With this confidence she begins to expose herself to labors and dangers, without discretion or regard to proportion, not considering that she is not yet in condition to leave the nest and fly, as her virtues are not confirmed and she has no experience of danger.

7 To rely upon our own talents is a cause of great loss. For when a Superior, a preacher or a confessor places confidence in his own prudence, knowledge and intelligence, God, to make him know and see his insufficiency, withdraws from him His help, and leaves him to work by himself. Whence it happens that all his plans and labors produce little or no fruit. This is often the cause why our undertakings fail.

—ST. VINCENT DE PAUL

This is clearly seen in the crossing of the Red Sea by the Israelites and the Egyptians. The former placed all their confidence in God, and crossed successfully. The latter placed theirs in their horses, and were drowned.

St. Francis de Sales managed all the affairs that God entrusted to him, with success. The cause of this was that he trusted never to his own ability, but wholly to Divine Providence; and he never hoped to succeed in a business if he had any other reliance than this.

St. Philip Neri used to say: "If a person voluntarily puts himself in the way of sin, saying, 'I shall not fall, I shall not commit it,' it is an almost certain sign that he will fall to the ruin of his soul."

8 Let us endeavor to conceive a very great diffidence of ourselves, and to establish ourselves firmly in this virtue; for, of ourselves we are good for nothing, except to spoil the designs of God. This will keep us in entire dependence upon His guidance and make us have recourse constantly to His help.

—ST. VINCENT DE PAUL

The venerable Father Daponte said of himself that those things that frequently furnish a motive for dejection, such as human frailty, or one's own weakness and sins, rather produced in him a greater confidence, for he fixed his eyes upon the goodness and mercy of God, to whom he had entirely committed himself and his interests.

St. Vincent, King of Bohemia, was asked how he felt when his army had been routed and he himself had been taken prisoner. He replied: "I never felt more encouraged than I do now.

When I was well provided with human aids, I had not time to think of God. Now that I am quite destitute of them all, I think only of God, and that He will not abandon me."

St. Philip Neri exhorted his penitents to follow his example in sometimes saying to God: "O Lord, do not leave anything to me, for if Thou help me not, I shall surely fail"; or, "O Lord, expect nothing from me!" He also said that in speaking of future contingencies, we ought never to say, "I *shall* do," or "I *shall* say"; but rather, with humility, "I know what I ought to do or say, but I do not know what I shall do or say."

9 Be careful not to depend or rely much upon the friendship and protection of men. For they cannot sustain us by themselves; and when the Lord sees us leaning upon them, He withdraws from us.

—ST. VINCENT DE PAUL

This holy man not only refrained from seeking human support, but even refused it when spontaneously offered to him. One day the governor of a city asked his influence at court, in favor of a certain affair, and promised that he would in return protect his missionaries against any who might molest them. But the Saint made this reply: "Whenever I can do it with justice, I will serve you willingly. As for the interests of my Congregation, I beg you to leave them in the hands of God and justice." It was a rule with him not to seek anything by the influence and favor of men.

St. Jane Frances de Chantal was of the same opinion. Her brother, the Archbishop of Bruges, once wrote to her that

in an interview he had just had with the Queen of France, she showed a desire for her prayers and those of her Order. He urged her, therefore, to write to the queen, who, he said, would be much pleased with the attention. The same advice was given her by many persons, both inside and outside of the convent; but she would not receive it and wrote to her brother a letter of excuse, begging him to assure the queen that she and all her nuns would not fail to recommend her to the Lord. She spoke of the matter in this way to her Religious: "I cannot and must not do it, for we ought to keep ourselves too much abased and hidden, to seek by human invention to retain a place in the hearts of the great. If we study to do our duty in regard to them before God, by praying for their safety, their prosperity and above all, their salvation, God, who has undertaken the charge of us, will bring us to their minds when we need their help, and will incline their hearts towards us."

St. Teresa once said: "I am very sure that there is no safety in relying upon men; for they are all like so many stalks of dried rosemary—they break under the least weight of disappointment or contradiction. The true friend in whom alone we can trust is Jesus Christ. When I rely upon Him, I am conscious of such power that I feel able to resist the whole world, were it opposed to me."

10 Whoever manages his affairs with artifices and subterfuges offends the providence of God and renders himself unworthy of His paternal care.

—ST. VINCENT DE PAUL

This glorious Saint kept always at a distance from all artifice in everything he said and did, and left scheming, as he often said, to the prudent of this world.

The same is true of St. Thomas, St. Bonaventure, St. Charles, St. Mary Magdalen de' Pazzi, Sister Maria Crucifixa and others, as we have elsewhere shown. All of these prospered in their affairs and were much esteemed and favored for their frankness, not only by God, but also by men.

11 When one puts all his care on God, and rests wholly upon Him, being careful, meanwhile, to serve Him faithfully, God takes care of him; and the greater the confidence of such a one, the more the care of God extends over him; neither is there any danger of its failing, for God has an infinite love for those souls that repose in Him.

—ST. FRANCIS DE SALES

The same thing was once said by Our Lord to St. Catherine of Siena: "Think of Me, and I will think of you, and take care of all your interests."

St. Hugo, the Bishop, said that it was his experience that the more he attended to performing well and diligently all that pertained to the worship of God, the more God provided for him in all necessary things.

More than any other, St. Francis manifested, and still manifests, this truth, by the wonderful protection of Divine Providence which he experienced and which sustains his sons even to this day. And so, the Viaticum which he gave his companions

when they were going to a distance was this verse of the Psalms: *"Jacta super Dominum curam tuam, et ipse te enutriet*—Cast thy care upon the Lord, and He will sustain thee." And when the Pope asked him about his means of living, he replied: "Holy Father, we have a mother truly poor, but a very rich Father."

Taulerus relates that a servant of God, being often asked by various persons to pray for different objects, promised to do so, but sometimes forgot—and in such cases these people always obtained what they desired, and came back to thank her. Astonished at this, she said one day to the Lord: "How is it, O Lord, that Thou grantest these favors which I never asked?" And the Lord replied: "See, My daughter, on the day you gave Me your will, I gave you Mine, so that sometimes if you do not ask for a particular thing that I know you would be pleased with, I do it as if you had asked Me."

12 Whoever serves God with a pure heart, and setting aside all individual and human interests, seeks only His glory, has reason to hope for success in all he does, and especially under circumstances when, according to human judgment, there is no help; for the Divine works are above the sight of human prudence, and depend upon a loftier principle.

—ST. CHARLES BORROMEO

This holy Cardinal was accustomed to have recourse to God in all his affairs, and commenced, continued and completed all his undertakings with prayer. The more arduous and important anything was, the more prayer he gave to it. And if it

happened that something appeared not only difficult but even hopeless, he did not recoil in the least, but urged himself forward with greater spirit and redoubled prayers. It was thus that he succeeded, to the wonder of all, in so many great affairs that seemed to human judgment impossible. The Saint was once talking with a person of rank, whom he was trying to persuade to have confidence in God in all circumstances, because He never abandons even in the smallest things those who put their trust in Him; and by way of proof, he related the following incident, which had happened to him a little while before. He said that his house-steward complained of being without money and did not know how to provide for the urgent needs of the house, and therefore requested him to be more sparing in alms and pious works, as it was by expenditure of that kind that the house was reduced to such extremity. But he replied only that he ought to trust in God, and hope for help from His Divine Majesty. This advice failed to satisfy him, and he went away much discontented. Within two hours there arrived a bundle of letters, among which was a bill of exchange for three thousand crowns remitted to the Saint, from Spain. Sending for the steward, he gave them to him, and said: "Take them, O thou of little faith! Behold! the Lord has not abandoned us." He added that this was truly a work of Divine Providence, for he was not expecting such a remittance, nor should it have been sent until two months later.

We read also in the process of his canonization that at the time of the great conflicts with the king's ministers on the question of jurisdiction and on account of the excommunications fulminated against them, the Governor of Milan, with some of

the secret council opposed to the Cardinal, often thought of taking rigorous measures against his person, as they knew no other way to hinder him from defending the rights of his Church. But every time that they assembled in the king's council to settle upon something, the thoughts changed in their minds, and the words upon their lips, so that they could come to no resolution against him. They themselves were bewildered and greatly amazed at this, not knowing to what they should ascribe their change of purpose. But doubtless it was the result of his great confidence in God, in reward of which God blessed all his enterprises, removed all obstacles and brought them to a happy ending. It ought, however, to be noticed, as the writer of the Life well observes, that this confidence of the Saint was altogether regulated by Christian prudence. He was most watchful in keeping himself from the vicious extreme of presumption. He never exposed himself to unnecessary dangers, or entertained extravagant plans of little advantage to the service of God and not weighed deliberately and wisely. He employed due diligence and precaution, and on certain occasions he did not refuse human aid, not taking it, however, as his chief reliance, but in subordination to Divine Providence. All this is clearly to be seen in the prudent regulations that he made when the city of Milan was desolated by the plague, and on a thousand other well-known occasions.

13 The pressure of necessity gives occasion to show whether we truly trust in God. Believe me, three strokes will do more than ten ordinarily, if God puts His hand to the work; and He always does when He

takes away human help, and obliges us to perform work above our strength.

—ST. VINCENT DE PAUL

When this Saint was once told by his house-steward that he had not a sou for daily expenses without considering the special ones for approaching ordinations, he replied with a tranquil heart and cheerful face, full of confidence in God: "What good news! Blessed be God! Now is the time to show whether we trust in Him. Oh, how infinite are the treasures of Divine Providence, which we dishonor by our want of trust!"

King Josaphat, finding himself assailed by a great number of enemies, turned to his men and said: "We have no power to resist so many; let us, then, raise our eyes to God, and trust in Him, and all will be well with us." And so, indeed, it was.

14 If a dry stick could possess humility and self-annihilation, and then be chosen to office, God would give it sensitive and intelligent life, rather than permit His servants to be without good government.

—ST. JANE FRANCES DE CHANTAL

The story of the Blessed Berengaria, a Poor Clare, furnishes an illustration of this. She lived for a long time in a Portuguese convent, employed in the lowest offices in the kitchen; for, on account of her love of humility, she made herself appear like a peasant and a half-idiot, so that she had become the laughing stock of the Sisters and was considered unfit for anything but the meanest position in the Order. After a time the Abbess

died, and all the nuns assembled to choose a successor. They had no decided preference for any of their number, and thought the first ballot would show who was most likely to obtain the place. Each of them, therefore, without informing anyone else, gave her vote to Berengaria, considering that this would afford her the desired opportunity, as she was sure not to be chosen. And so, when the Father presiding at the ceremony had received and read the folded ballots of the nuns, he found that Berengaria had been legally elected. Therefore he bade her, in the name of God, take the seat of the Superioress, to receive from the others, according to custom, the first token of homage. The humble maiden was constrained, though with very great repugnance, to take this position. But still greater repugnance was felt on the part of the nuns, who murmured against such an unexpected election and refused to recognize as their Superior one who was quite inexperienced and wholly unfit for such an office. Seeing this the new Abbess, interiorly moved by the Holy Spirit, turned towards the tomb, there placed in the center of the chapter house, and called upon the dead nuns to rise and render her the prescribed homage, to teach their living sisters what obedience they owed. And behold! the sepulcher instantly opened, and seven nuns came forth, one after another. Kneeling, they offered homage and obedience to Berengaria, and then remained on their knees at her feet, in presence of the whole convent, until she bade them return into the sepulcher and rest in peace, which they reverently did. Amazed and affrighted at this sight, the nuns all threw themselves at the feet of their Mother, humbly asked her pardon for their fault and promised and always observed most perfect submission and obedience to her.

15 When we are to undertake anything for the service of God, after invoking His holy light and discovering His will, though we should employ the human means which we consider necessary and suitable in carrying out the orders of Divine Providence, yet we should not depend on them, but on the Divine assistance alone, and from it expect success, with the firm persuasion that whatever happens will be best for us, whether it appears good or bad according to our individual judgment.

—ST. VINCENT DE PAUL

This Saint, when someone asked to be remembered in his prayers, once answered thus: "I have been occupied in business all this morning, so I have spent very little time in prayer, and that with many distractions. You may judge how much can be hoped for today from my prayers. But this does not discourage me, for I put my trust in God, not, certainly, in my preparation, nor in all my efforts; for I am sure that the throne of God's goodness and mercy is raised upon the foundation of our miseries."

Whatever business St. Ignatius Loyola undertook, he did everything as if all depended upon himself, and trusted in God as if all depended upon God.

16 In attending to ordinary business and daily needs, we should not allow ourselves to be transported by eagerness and anxiety, but take reasonable and moderate care—and then leave everything completely and entirely to the disposal and guidance of Divine

Providence, giving it scope to arrange matters for its own ends, and to manifest to us God's Will. For we may consider it certain that when God wills that an affair should succeed, delay does not spoil it; and the greater part He takes in it, the less will be left for us to do.

—ST. VINCENT DE PAUL

Before making use of human means, though honorable and necessary, it was the usual custom of this Saint to have recourse to the Divine, and while recommending the matter to God he would remain quiet and wait until God should give it an impulse to His own ends and for His greater glory. He used to say that Providence gives good success to the plans of those who are willing to follow it, and not run in advance of it. For example, when many charitable ladies importuned him to search for some young girls with whom he might lay the foundation of his Congregation of the Sisters of Charity and he found it difficult to meet with suitable ones, he was not at all discouraged, but contented himself with having recourse to God in prayer and waiting until His Providence should deign to reveal to Him some method of providing for this need.

17 So much earnestness and trouble in seeking means and helps to fortify ourselves in advance against the accidents of this life, and to remedy its ills, is a great failure in confidence towards God. For by this going in advance of the order of His providence, we show that we trust more in our own devices than in His

holy guidance, and that we rest more upon human prudence than upon His holy word.

—ST. VINCENT DE PAUL

When Father Alvarez was rector of a poor college, he had a steward who often came to tell him of the daily wants and what was necessary to support the house. Once he asked him whether he had recommended the matter to God. The steward replied that he had no time to pray. "This," rejoined the good Superior, "ought to be the first thing. Go into some room, and make a little prayer to the Lord. Do you think this flock has no master, or such a one as has no regard for their lives? Go in peace, and remember that this depends not on your efforts." The steward obeyed, and often afterwards found means of support which he considered miraculous.

18 When the will of God is clearly seen in any affair, no matter how difficult, it should be undertaken with intrepidity and pursued with constancy even to the end, however many and great may be the obstacles which oppose it. For the providence of God never fails those things that are undertaken by His order.

—ST. VINCENT DE PAUL

When this Saint had begun an undertaking and felt sure that it was the will of God he never abandoned it for any opposition that might intervene. Instead of becoming disheartened, he only showed the greatest constancy and resolution, the more he was harassed and opposed by creatures.

When St. Charles had weighed any enterprise he was about to commence, prudently and maturely, and judged it good for the service of God—though it might seem to others sure to fail—he began and prosecuted it with great courage, and always with success.

St. Francis de Sales says that St. Jane Frances de Chantal showed a most courageous and generous soul in continuing undertakings with which God had inspired her.

When St. Francis Xavier saw that the honor of God called him, he went without fearing difficulties or dangers of any kind. And so he attempted nothing which he did not continue, and began nothing which he did not pursue to the end.

19 Let us put our confidence in God and establish ourselves in an entire dependence upon His providence. Then we need not fear whatever men can say or do against us, for all will turn to our good. Nay, were all the world to rise against us, nothing would come of it except what was pleasing to God, in whom we have placed our hopes.

—ST. VINCENT DE PAUL

One of his priests having written to this Saint that plans were on foot to supplant his Congregation and that persons of influence were supporting these evil designs, he gave this reply: "Let us establish and settle ourselves firmly in total dependence upon God's providence, and then not allow our minds to be overshadowed by these useless apprehensions, for nothing will happen contrary to His holy will."

While St. Gregory the Bishop had gone down one night into the choir for Matins, some of his rivals placed a woman in his bed, and after the office made some excuse for accompanying him to his chamber. Then the woman, as had been preconcerted, began to cry out and accuse the Bishop of sacrilege. By this he was disgraced through all the city and condemned to imprisonment by the Pope. But God took care of him, for the holy Apostles Peter and Paul visited and consoled him in his prison, and he performed many miracles. The woman, meanwhile, was possessed and tormented by the devil, until she appeared before a council of bishops and revealed the plot. She was then cured by the Saint, the wicked accusers condemned to the severest penalties, the Bishop exonerated by the Pope, and his holiness publicly declared.

20 Souls that are weak and too much attached to their own reputation make a great stir and commotion, and can have no peace if any calumny is spread against them. It is not thus with generous souls who aim at nothing except to please God. They know very well that He sees their innocence and has it at heart more than they themselves, and therefore He will not neglect to defend them as their greatest good requires.

—ST. AUGUSTINE

In a letter to Monsignor Camus, St. Francis de Sales says: "I hear that they are all tearing me to pieces in Paris, but I hope God will patch me up again as good as new, if it is necessary for

His service. I do not care for any more reputation than I need for this. For, provided God be served, what does it matter whether it be by good or evil report, by the exaltation or lowering of our reputation? Let Him dispose of my name and honor as He will, since all is His. And if my abjection increases His glory, ought I not to rejoice in being cast down?" At another time, when an enormous calumny had been invented against him, his friends, seeing that he made no attempt to justify himself, said that he ought to do so because his reputation was most necessary to his ministry. But he told them that the Lord knew how much credit he required for his ministry, and he did not wish for more.

Bishop Palafox, having been accused of maladministration in his office, would not defend himself when an examination into his methods was ordered, but left his cause entirely in the hands of God, saying that He well knew his good intentions and that he expected to be defended by His providence as the glory of God required, whom he desired to serve. And in this way he prospered.

21 When anyone reposes all his confidence in God, God continually exercises a special protection over him, and in this state of things he can be assured that no evil will happen to him.

—ST. VINCENT DE PAUL

For this reason, St. Vincent de Paul was never cast down or discouraged in all the afflictions, crosses, and vexatious accidents which befell him or his priests; but he remained always full of confidence in God, with a perfect evenness of temper and

constant abandonment to Divine Providence. And what is more, he rejoiced to find himself in such difficulties, as they gave him opportunity to exercise a more perfect, absolute and total dependence on the Divine Will.

The Emperor Ferdinand II, hearing some remarks about the bad state of the times, said: "Let us do our part, and then leave ourselves and our affairs to the government of God, who will dispose everything well." And when any disaster was feared, he would say, "The Lord will provide."

22 When once we have placed ourselves totally in the hands of God, we have no cause to fear misfortune; for if any should come to us, He will know how to make it turn to our good, by ways which we do not know now, but which, one day, we shall know.

—ST. VINCENT DE PAUL

Two singular events which happened, one to St. Francis de Sales and the other to St. Ignatius Loyola, prove the truth of this statement. When a young secular, St. Francis, once visited Rome, and returning one evening to an inn near the Tiber where he lodged, he found his servants in a dispute with the landlord, who wished them to find some other house, as he hoped to receive more profit from another party whose luggage he had already taken in and for whom he wished to dispossess the holy baron. Nor would the quarrel have ended with angry words alone, if St. Francis, with his usual meekness, had not ordered his servants to do as the landlord wished. He agreed, then, to find another lodging, but scarcely had he done so when a heavy rain swelled

the Tiber and made it overflow its banks, causing an inundation which carried away the unhappy inn and all its occupants, so that not one escaped, nor was there a trace left of the building, which had been considered one of the best of its kind in Rome.

When St. Ignatius had arrived in Cyprus on his return from visiting the holy places, he found three vessels ready to sail for Italy. The first belonged to Turkey; the second was a Venetian ship, strong and well equipped, and apparently able to struggle successfully with the most furious gales; the third was a little old boat, leaky and worm-eaten. Many urged the master of the Venetian ship to receive Ignatius on board for the love of God, praising him and extolling him as a saint. But when the man heard that Ignatius was poor and had no money for his passage, he answered that if Ignatius was a saint, he did not need a vessel to cross the sea, for he could go on foot, as so many other Saints had done. As he would not receive him, Ignatius was obliged to take the old ship, where they welcomed him freely and with much liberality. The three vessels set sail on the same day; but after they were all well out at sea, in the darkness of the night a fierce tempest arose in which the Turkish ship foundered with all its crew on board, the Venetian ran aground, her passengers barely escaping with their lives, and the old craft alone gained the port. We see in these two examples how the Lord gave His protection to two faithful servants, making use even of the wickedness of men to expel one, and exclude the other, from places doomed to disaster.

It is true that Joseph and Job in the Old Testament suffered great trials, but how incredibly greater were the advantages they derived from them!

23 When we find ourselves in any danger, even a grave one, we ought not to lose courage, but to trust much in the Lord; for where the peril is greater, there also is greater aid from Him who chooses to be called the Helper in dangers and tribulations.

—ST. AMBROSE

St. Ignatius Loyola was once on board a ship in a severe storm when the mast was broken off and all were weeping and trembling in expectation of death. He alone was cheerful and fearless, remembering that the winds and sea obey God and that without His permission, tempests rise not, neither can they sink any ship, and choosing for himself whatever fate God might choose for him.

24 There are some who so cling to their confidence in God that they cannot abandon it even in extreme cases which appear quite hopeless. Oh how dear they are to God, and how much help they receive from Him!

The Emperor Ferdinand II once saw the whole North combined against him. But when he was informed of defeats and of the loss and devastation of provinces, he was not at all disturbed and answered always, "God will deliver me from this tempest." Nor was he mistaken, for when the case appeared desperate he gained a signal victory, by which he discomfited all his enemies.

What could be more desperate than the situation of Susanna, accused, condemned and led out to death? Yet she trusted in the Lord and was set free.

25 Whoever does not lose courage in unexpected difficulties, but immediately has recourse to God with confidence, shows that this virtue is well rooted in his heart.

—ST. ALPHONSUS RODRIGUEZ

We read in the Lives of the Fathers that St. Columban, standing one day without any thought of danger, suddenly saw twelve wolves coming up to him. They surrounded him, and finally began to nibble at his garments. He was not, however, at all alarmed, and did nothing but invoke God in these words: "*Deus, in adjutorium meum intende. Domine, ad adjuvandum me festina,*" upon which the wolves immediately fled.

The Abbot Theodore was asked whether he should be afraid if he heard on a sudden a loud crash and a terrible tumult. "No," he answered, "if the world should fall in ruins, and earth and sky be blended together, Theodore would not be afraid."

26 The confidence of the Christian soul rests in perfect abandonment to God, above and beyond every consideration of human prudence. Oh, what happiness to walk in this perfect dependence upon a sovereign providence, remaining continually under the Divine protection!

—ST. JANE FRANCES DE CHANTAL

Such was the confidence of Abraham, who hoped that his posterity would spread over the whole world, according to the Divine promise, though by the order of God Himself he should

sacrifice to Him the life of his only son at a time when he could not expect to have another.

Equally great was that of holy Job, who afflicted in body, bereft of his sons, deprived of his property and ridiculed by his friends, still said, "Though He should slay me, yet will I always hope in Him."

27 Whoever casts himself into the arms of God's providence and allows himself to be ruled, is borne to Heaven in a chariot with all his crosses, so that he scarcely feels their weight. He who acts otherwise goes on foot, dragging them with labor and weariness.

—ST. BERNARD

The Emperor Ferdinand II said of himself: "Trials and troubles would have worn me out long ago, if I had not abandoned all my affairs, and myself as well, to Providence."

In a city of Italy there lived a poor young girl who was bedridden and afflicted by many infirmities; yet, those who visited her found her always cheerful, and even the report of a threatened famine caused her no alarm. Being asked how she kept up her cheerfulness in the midst of so many miseries, she replied that all her thoughts rested upon God; that she was like a little bird under the wings of Divine Providence, and therefore she was neither afraid nor anxious about anything.

28 The servant of God ought to fear nothing and to give himself but little concern even as to the devils

themselves; for every time they fail to terrify us they lose strength, and the soul masters them more easily. If the Lord is powerful and they are His slaves, what harm can they do to those who are servants of so great a King and Lord?

—ST. TERESA

This Saint testifies of herself that she was so timid that she often did not dare to go into a room alone, even in the day. But finally she began to consider what a shame it was for a soul to be alarmed and affrighted at anything but offending God, when we have so great and powerful a Lord, who rules everything. Then she thought how all creatures, even the devils, are subject to Him, and how she desired to serve this Lord, and aimed at nothing but to please Him and do His will. In conclusion, she said to herself, "What am I afraid of? What do I fear?" and, taking a cross in her hands, she began to challenge the demons, saying, "Come now, all of you, for I am a servant of God: I wish to see what you can do to me!" After that, she said that she felt full of courage, and all her fears vanished; so that though she saw the demons many times afterwards, she had no fear of them at all and it seemed to her, on the contrary, that they feared her, because she felt such superiority over them that she regarded them no more than so many flies.

A servant of God who was much tormented by the devils constantly sang with joy the Psalm, *Laudate, pueri Dominum.* The devils, being angry at this, increased her torments. But she mocked them, and said: "I count you as nothing, vermin! I have my Lord with me, and do not fear you in the least."

29 Though one should fall into many and grievous sins and imperfections, he ought never to despair of his salvation nor lose confidence in God, for the Divine clemency is infinitely greater than human malice.

—ST. JOHN CHRYSOSTOM

When St. Bernard was severely ill, he had a rapture in which he seemed to be led to judgment and there tempted to despair by the devil, to whom he gave this answer: "I confess that I do not deserve Paradise for my works, for I know that I am unworthy of so great a good. Nevertheless, my Lord has two claims to it— one, that He is the Son of God, the other, that He died upon the Cross. The first is sufficient for Him, and the other He gives to me. For this reason I have hope."

St. Vincent Ferrer was remarkable for his confidence in God, which was strikingly illustrated by the following incident. One day he was informed that a dying man had fallen into despair through considering his great sins, and that he had therefore refused to make his confession. He hastened to his bedside with much hope of winning him over. "My brother," he said to him, "will you who know that Jesus Christ died for you, despair of His mercy? You would thus grievously slight the great kindness He has shown you." These words made the sick man very angry, and he answered, "Just for that I mean to be damned—in spite of Christ!" "And in spite of yourself you shall be saved," replied the Saint. Then, turning to the bystanders, he said: "Let us recite the Rosary to the Blessed Virgin, to obtain from her the conversion of this most obstinate sinner." The Lord was pleased to show how acceptable to Him was the generous confidence of His servant,

for before the Rosary was ended, the room was filled with a brilliant light, and the great Mother of God appeared with the Infant upon her arm all stained with blood. The hardened sinner was moved with love, grief, and compunction at this sight. He made his confession with heartfelt contrition and a little while after, with a look of heavenly joy upon his face, breathed forth his spirit into the hands of God.

Blosius relates of St. Gertrude that she was one day considering which, of the many things she had learned from the Lord, she might most usefully reveal to men, when she heard His voice in her heart speaking in this manner: "It would be of the greatest use to them to know and remember that I am continually interceding before My Father for their salvation, and that as often as they stain their hearts through human frailty by evil thoughts, I offer to Him in expiation My most pure heart; and when they commit sinful deeds, I offer to Him My pierced hands; and so, however they err, I instantly seek to appease the Divine Father, that they may obtain pardon on their repentance."

30 Finally, if we wish to perform our actions well and to provide for all our needs, we ought from time to time to look to God in imitation of the example of navigators, who direct their course to the point they seek rather by looking upwards to the sky than downwards where they are floating.

To prove the truth of this sentiment, it is sufficient to cast a glance upon the example of so many Saints already cited for this month, without referring to any new ones.

31 We have yet to speak of the confidence to be practiced in temptations and spiritual aridity. But since this is a point of the highest importance, which cannot be treated briefly, it seems more desirable to make it the subject of a separate treatise which will afford much consolation and help to those who suffer from such trials.

NOVEMBER

Charity

This is the first and greatest commandment:
Thou shalt love the Lord thy God with thy
whole heart; but the second is like unto it: Thou
shalt love thy neighbor as thyself.—MATT. 22:38

---

1 My God and my Lord! what need was there of commanding us to love Thee? Art Thou not most lovely in Thy infinite perfections? And for the infinite love Thou bearest to us, dost Thou not deserve our love? How, then, is it possible that anyone should not love Thee? If there is such a person, it must be because he has not deserved to know Thee. For, a soul that knows God, cannot help loving Him, and loving Him in proportion to his knowledge of Him; so that if he loves Him but little, it is a sign that he knows Him but little; and the more his knowledge increases, the more his love will go on growing.

—ST. TERESA

A very elevated soul once gave her director the following account of her interior: "A great flame of love springs up in my heart, Father, when I clearly perceive, in the time of meditation, how the most holy Humanity of the Lord shows how much He deserves our love, by that which He bears to us, while He loves us even as He loves Himself. He manifests this to us: 1.) By the great things He has done, and is doing, for us. 2.) By the great desire He has to be loved by us, which He proves by so many extraordinary devices of love, and by remaining, as it were, in a state of violence, because He wishes to communicate Himself and make Himself known to us, that He may be loved by us; but as He finds no access, by reason of our want of proper dispositions, He cannot do it. 3.) By the patience with which He bears the coolness He meets with from creatures He has loved so much, and which has no effect upon His unalterable constancy of love.

"Under these beams of light, the soul sends forth various affections—sometimes of wonder that the Divine Majesty should be willing that the creature be loved with an infinite love, and the Creator and Lord with a finite and limited love; sometimes of love, but an excessive love, which devours and consumes it, and it would desire the heart of a Seraph to blaze and burn with the love of its God; nay rather would desire to love Him with that same love with which it sees itself loved by Him; and again of insufferable affliction at seeing itself destitute of the knowledge and love of God, which are the height of its perfection, and which would raise it to the Divine Majesty whom it so earnestly desires. This pain is increased by the new perception with which the Lord makes it understood that not loving Him is a positive slight to His power, wisdom, love, goodness, and so many

admirable things which He has done and suffered for it. Oh, where can it rest and how not sink into nothingness beneath this light! I assure you, Father, that when God placed before my eyes the great contempt I had shown to my Love, when I did not love Him, I do not know how I remained alive. Surely, if He had not suspended my consciousness, I should have died on the spot.

"Finally, the soul is enkindled with ardent longings and desires that its Beloved may be known, and sends up aspirations and ejaculations to that Infinite Goodness, that it may make itself known in order to be loved. It professes its readiness to cooperate in the aid and advancement of souls, in whatever way may be pleasing to the Divine Majesty. It was thus that the loving Lord revealed Himself to me, His most vile and unworthy servant. And when He mercifully imparted to me any of these graces outside of the time of prayer, as when I was conversing with others, or at work, I fell into a trance and was so far unconscious that when the Sisters spoke to me I did not know what they said, though I always understood the Superioress if she required anything as matter of obedience."

The blessed Jacopone was so much affected at seeing so many lose their souls by offenses against God in the Carnival time that he went about crying, "*Amor non amatur, amor non amatur, quia non cognitur*—Love is not loved, Love is not loved, because it is not known."

St. Philip Neri, too, often exclaimed: "O Lord, I do not love Thee, because I do not know Thee."

2 When one has succeeded in placing his heart wholly upon God, he loses his affection for all other things,

and no longer finds consolation in anything, nor clings to anything except God, forgetting his own honor and every interest of his own.

—ST. TERESA

"While there is any created thing which can give me consolation and delight," says St. Bernard, "I do not dare to say that the love of God is ardent and fervid in my heart."

Holy Queen Esther, in the midst of her regal pomp and splendor, could say: "O Lord, Thou knowest well that I have never taken delight in dignity and royal apparel, nor in the banquets of the king, nor in anything have I found consolation until this day, save in Thee, my Lord and God."

St. Catherine of Genoa, after she had been struck by the arrow of divine love, often cried out, "No more world! no more pleasures!" And if she had been mistress of a thousand worlds, she would have thrown them all away, to give her whole heart to God.

St. Ignatius Loyola went so far as to have lost all attachment to anything that was not God, and he had nothing at heart but to please Him and to gain His love. He said one day that if God should give him the choice of going that moment directly to Paradise, or remaining longer in the world to serve Him and advance His Kingdom, even with the uncertainty of his own salvation, he would choose the latter alternative.

3 Alas! we have not as much love as we need! I mean that it would require an infinite amount to have enough to love our God according to His due; and yet, miserable

that we are, we throw it away lavishly upon vile and unworthy objects, as if we had a superfluity.

—ST. FRANCIS DE SALES

This good Saint could not endure to have an affection for anything remain in his heart. He once said: "Truly, if I knew that there was one thread of affection in my soul, which was not of God or for God, I would instantly sever it. I would rather be nothing than not belong wholly to God without any exception."

St. Philip Neri, burning with these flames of love, often cried: "How is it possible that anyone who believes in God can love anything but Him!" and then addressing to God a loving complaint, he would exclaim: "O Lord! since Thou art so lovely and hast commanded me to love Thee, why didst Thou give me but a single heart, and that so small?"

St. Augustine, to animate his soul to center all its love upon God, employed such incentives as these: "What can please thee in this world, O my soul, or what can gain thy love? Wherever thou turnest, thou seest only Heaven and earth. If in both thou findest what is worthy of praise and love, of how much praise and love must He be worthy, who has made these things thou praisest and lovest? My soul, till this time thou hast been long occupied and tossed hither and thither by many and various desires, which have ensnared thy heart and divided it among many loves, leaving thee always disturbed and never secure. Recollect thyself now a little and ask those things that please thee, who is their maker; and since you admire the form, love its Former, and do not lose thyself in what is made, so as to forget Him who made it. Indeed, indeed, my God, Thou art truly worthy

to be revered and loved above everything on earth or in Heaven. Nay rather, all transitory things do not deserve to be loved at all, lest we should lose Thy love."

4 When a soul that truly loves God knows that a thing is of greater perfection, and more for God's service, it pursues it immediately and without difficulty, on account of the pleasure it finds in pleasing Him. Ah my God, what else is needed but to love Thee truly, and truly abandon everything for Thy love, for then Thou wilt render all easy!

—ST. TERESA

Such was the conduct of St. Teresa herself, and so she once said: "Though I desired the new reform (of the Carmelite Order), that I might be apart from everything and follow my vocation with more perfection; yet I desired it in such a way that if I had clearly perceived it was more for God's service to abandon it, I should certainly have done so with perfect peace and tranquillity. For when I am sure that a thing is more perfect and more for God's service, I am at rest; and in the contentment which I experience in pleasing Him, I instantly lose the pain of leaving something which had given me satisfaction." This was so true that in order never to fail in it, she wished to bind herself by a vow to do whatever she might know to be most perfect and most pleasing to the Lord. A similar vow was also taken by St. Andrew Avellino and by St. Jane Frances de Chantal.

In regard to St. Ignatius Loyola, it is well known that he sought in everything not only the glory of God, but His greatest

possible glory. For this reason, the Church, in the prayer assigned for his Feast, sets it down as his distinguished mark, that God chose him to spread His greater glory.

5 When the love of God obtains the mastery of a soul, it produces in it an insatiable desire to labor for the Beloved; so that, though it may perform many and great works and spend much time in His service, all seems nothing, and it constantly grieves at doing so little for its God, and if it could annihilate itself and perish for Him, it would be well pleased. And so it considers itself unprofitable in all that it does and regards its life as idle; for, as love teaches it what God merits, by this clear light it sees all the defects and imperfections of its actions, and thus derives confusion and grief from them all. And as it feels that its work is very poor to be offered to so great a Lord, it is at the greatest distance from vainglory and presumption, and from condemning others.

—ST. JOHN CHRYSOSTOM

St. Vincent de Paul was equally unwearied and insatiable in laboring for God and rendering himself acceptable in His sight; nor did he think he had ever done enough for so great a Lord. In imitation of the Apostles, he forgot the good works which were behind him in the past, and put all his thoughts and efforts upon advancing daily in God's service.

St. Charles was remarkable for this virtue. As long as he lived, he had an insatiable desire to honor God and to spread

and promote His worship, which spurred him on to labor without weariness. He seemed to grow fresher every day, under labors that succeeded one another without intermission. While those who attended him were often prostrated by fatigue, he never gave the least token of it, as if labor were rest and recreation to him. What is more, after all the great undertakings he performed in the service of God, he was never satisfied with what he had done, but was always inventing new methods; nor did he ever think or speak of anything but God, and what might conduce to His service and honor.

6 When one has arrived at the perfect love of God, he becomes as if he were the only man on earth. He cares no more for glory or ignominy; he despises temptations and sufferings; he loses taste and appetite for all things. Finding no support, consolation, or repose in anything, he goes constantly in search of his Beloved, without ever being weary; so that at work or at table, waking or sleeping, in every employment or conversation, his whole thought and his whole aim is to find the Beloved, for his heart is where his treasure is. In one word, he is like a lover who sighs only for the sight of his love, and whose love is his all.

—ST. JOHN CHRYSOSTOM

Zeno the Monk, being absorbed in contemplation, went about one day crying aloud like a madman. He happened to meet the Macedonian emperor, and being asked by him what he was doing, he returned the question. "I am going to hunt," said

the emperor. "And I," replied Zeno, "am going to seek God, and I will not stop until I have found Him." With these words he turned away and left him.

The blessed Raymond Lullo was so absorbed in divine love that his sole concern was love, and he could think and speak of nothing else. If anyone said to him: "Whose are you?" he answered: "Love's." "Whence do you come?" "From Love." "Whither are you going?" "To Love." "Who has brought you here?" "Love."

St. Honoratus the Abbot was so full of the love of God and so desirous to serve and glorify Him, that not only by day but even by night, all his thoughts and affections were directed to Him. While asleep he made short and fervent instructions upon the obligation and the manner of loving God, and his very dreams were filled with the love of God, piety, and devotion.

Similar was the course of life of the glorious St. Vincent Ferrer, whose heart and mind were full of God. He was always thinking of God; he never spoke but of God, or with God. Whether walking, sitting still, studying, or conversing, he always seemed absorbed in God, whose love appeared upon his lips, in his face, in his eyes, in all his sentiments, in all times and places, even when he was asleep; so that, through the cracks in his door, his room was often seen illuminated by the splendor that beamed from his face as he slept.

The excessive heat which many souls suffered from this sacred flame, would seem incredible. St. Aloysius Gonzaga experienced it to such a degree that his face appeared all on fire; St. Catherine of Siena, so that natural fire seemed to her cold rather than warm; St. Peter of Alcantara, so that if he plunged into an icy pond, the water would boil as if red-hot iron had been put into

it; St. Francis di Paula, so that he could light lamps with a touch of his finger, as well as with a blazing taper; the Venerable Sister Maria Villani, so that on turning her thoughts interiorly to God or her eyes exteriorly towards some object of devotion, she would feel as if on fire, and she drank upwards of twenty quarts of cold water a day, without being able to extinguish this flame; and the water, as she swallowed it, seemed as if falling upon glowing iron. She was obliged, on this account, to give up vocal prayers and her usual private devotions, as they all served to fan this interior conflagration. St. Philip Neri, on one of the nights which he passed in the catacombs, threw himself on the ground, exclaiming, "I cannot, I cannot bear it any longer!" when he recovered a little, he found that two of his upper ribs were bent as if by heat.

Two remarkable incidents deserve special mention at this point. St. Mary Magdalen de' Pazzi frequently experienced this holy ardor, and one day she was unusually inflamed by it. She began to hurry through the corridors and the garden, and seizing the hands of the Sisters whom she met, she clasped them closely, and said: "Sisters, do you love our Love? How can you live? Do you not feel yourselves consumed by love?" She next went to the bell-tower, and began to ring a great peal upon the chimes. The Sisters came in a crowd, and asked her why she was ringing. "I am ringing," she answered, "that people may come to love that Love, by whom they are loved so much."

The second occurred in the time of St. Louis of France. One of his ambassadors met one day, in a city to which he had been sent, a woman who was going through the streets with a vase of water in her right hand, and a lighted torch in her left, and

who cried out with deep sighs, "Oh God! oh God! is it possible!" When the ambassador asked her what she wished, she answered: "I would wish, if it were according to the will of God, to extinguish the fires of Hell with this water, and to burn up Paradise with this torch, that God might be loved purely for love's sake."

7 It should be observed that perfect love of God consists not in those delights, tears, and sentiments of devotion that we generally seek, but in a strong determination and keen desire to please God in all things, and to take care, as far as possible, not to offend Him, and to promote His glory.

—ST. TERESA

St. Jane Frances de Chantal showed how well she understood this great truth, by a letter she sent to the Superior of a Religious who was looked upon as a soul filled with the love of God, because she enjoyed extraordinary consolations. "This good girl," she wrote, "greatly needs to be undeceived. She believes herself highly elevated in the love of God, yet she is not much advanced in virtue. I believe that these fervors and exaltations which she feels are the work of nature and self-love. Therefore, she should be shown that the real strength of love consists not in enjoying the divine sweetness, but rather in exact observance of the Rules, and the faithful practice of solid virtue—that is, in humility, the love of contempt, patient endurance of insults and adversities, self-forgetfulness, and a love that seeks not to be known except by God. This alone is true love, and these are its unerring tokens. May God preserve us from that sensible love

which allows us to live in ourselves, while the true leads us to die to ourselves."

Such was the love of St. Thomas Aquinas, of whom it is recorded that he kept his soul always as pure and true as that of a child five years old.

8 The love of God is the tree of life in the midst of the terrestrial paradise. It has, like other trees, six parts— roots, trunk, branches, leaves, flowers and fruit. The roots are the virtues by which love itself is acquired, and the principal are nine in number: 1. True penitence, and reception of the Sacraments; 2. Observance of the Commandments and Rules; 3. Fear of God; 4. Mortification of the passions and appetites; 5. Retirement, and avoidance of the occasion of sin; 6. Examination of conscience; 7. Humility; 8. Obedience; and 9. Charity to our neighbors. The trunk of the tree is surrender of self-will to the will of God. We may discover what the branches are by those words, "*Sub umbra illius quem desideraveram, sedi*—Under the shadow of Him whom I had longed for, I rested." The first of these is lively faith, by which the soul can view the Sun of Justice closely without being dazzled. The second, true confidence in the Divine protection, by means of which one can escape being cast down in the midst of adversities. The third, ardent desires and firm resolutions and other interior acts, continually directed towards obtaining true love. The fourth, constancy in remaining seated beneath this tree. The leaves are: 1. New

graces freely given; 2. Interior sweetness, joy, spiritual gladness, tenderness, or tears; 3. Raptures and ecstasies, referred to in those words: "*Introduxit me rex in cellam vinariam*—The King brought me into the wine cellar." All these things are called leaves, because they serve as an ornament to the tree, and help to mature the fruit; and in the winter of aridity and tribulation they fall, as the leaves do from a tree, while the love of God remains. The flowers are the works and heroic virtues which the loving soul produces, and are what the Bride asked for in the words, "*Fulcite me floribus*—Sustain me with flowers." The fruits are the trials, afflictions, and persecutions which the soul bears with patience, when God gives them to her, or which she even procures for herself of her own accord, to serve Him better, or to imitate Jesus Christ in suffering.

—ST. TERESA

It is no wonder that the Saint knew so well how to describe this holy tree, for she kept it planted in her heart, and well developed in every respect.

The same idea of love was entertained by a good nun of Naples, called Sister Maria de Santiago, in whose life we read that she thought it resembled a beautiful tree planted in the good soil of the souls that possess it, and producing abundantly the flowers and fruits of holy works. One of the principal of these, she said, was love of our neighbor, for which she was herself remarkable, because she kept this fair tree of divine love rooted in her soul.

9 Some torment themselves in seeking means to discover the art of loving God, and do not know—poor creatures—that there is no art or means of loving Him but to love Him—that is, to begin to practice those things which are pleasing to Him.

—ST. FRANCIS DE SALES

St. Vincent de Paul devoted himself nobly to this holy practice, observing God's law with so much exactness, that those who watched him closely assented that no one who was merely a man could fail less than he. He was constantly elevated above himself, upright in his judgments, circumspect in his words, prudent in his conduct, punctual in the practices of piety, and so perfectly united to God, so far as could be judged from the exterior, that it was plain that the love of God was what animated his heart and ruled in all the powers and sentiments of his soul, to regulate every motion and act. It might be said that his whole life was a sacrifice to God, not only of honors, comforts, pleasures and all other earthly blessings, but even of what he had received more directly from His most liberal hand, such as lights, affections and holy desires. Nor did he ever wish for anything except that God should be known and glorified, in all times and places, and by all kinds of people. To this end alone he directed all that he thought, said, and did.

10 The love of God is acquired by resolving to labor and suffer for Him, and to abstain from all that displeases Him, and by carrying this resolution into practice as

occasion arises. But to be able to do it well in great things, it is necessary to attend to it in small.

—ST. TERESA

When this Saint was much opposed in regard to her Foundations, she said that she never did anything without the advice of experienced persons, that she might not in any degree fail in obedience. "For," she added, "rather than commit the least of those faults they charge me with, I would most certainly have abandoned not one, but a thousand convents."

St. Vincent de Paul was remarkable for this virtue. Because he would not consent to anything in the least contrary to justice, simplicity, and charity, he was obliged to bear many unfavorable remarks, indiscreet questions, reproofs, affronts, importunities and other unpleasant treatment from members of his own Order, as well as from others. In such cases he was never observed to give a sign of impatience or to utter a word of complaint, but rather, in order to show the strength of his love for God, he spoke and acted with more than his usual sweetness and tranquillity.

11 A very good way of exercising ourselves in the love of Christ is to acquire the habit of keeping Him present to our minds as far as possible. This may be done in three ways: 1. When we have to perform any action, to represent to ourselves the manner in which He did it while dwelling in the world, as well as the spirit and intention with which He animated it, that we may imitate Him. 2. To think how He is continually looking down upon us from Heaven, and

shedding upon us the abundance of His graces and counsels. 3. To recognize Him in the person of our neighbor. In this way, we shall perform our actions with more ease and perfection; we shall avoid many faults as well as much anxiety and impatience, and in every service that we perform for our neighbors, we shall merit as much as if we did it to Our Lord Himself.

—ST. VINCENT DE PAUL

This was St. Vincent's own practice, and it raised him very high in the love of Jesus. He undertook no business, gave no advice, performed no action, without first fixing his eyes mentally upon the example or words of Christ, and on the rewards which He keeps prepared, and freely dispenses to such as labor well. And in his dealings with others, he beheld in each the very person of Christ. Phrases like these were often on his lips: "As Christ said"; "As Christ did"; "We ought to recognize Christ in all men."

12 Would you know how you stand in regard to the love of God? Here are the signs by which you may discover: As much as the soul grows in divine love, so much do the desires of suffering and of being humbled grow in it. These are the sure tokens of the sacred fire; everything else is but smoke.

—ST. VINCENT DE PAUL

St. John of the Cross proved how firmly he was persuaded of this. When Jesus Christ appeared to him one day and asked

him what reward he desired for the many trials and labors he had borne for love of Him, "No other, O Lord," he replied, "but to suffer and be despised."

One day while they were chanting the words of the Gospel, "*Simon-Joannis, diligis Me plus his?*—Lovest thou Me more than these?" St. Matilda fell into an ecstasy, and heard Christ saying to her: "Matilda, lovest thou Me more than all things in the world?" She replied: "Thou knowest, Lord, that I love Thee." Christ continued: "But lovest thou Me so as to be willing to bear all sorts of trials, sufferings, and humiliations for My sake?" "Thou knowest well," she answered, "that no torments can separate me from Thee." Then Christ said: "But if these torments were terrible, would you bear them gladly and readily for love of Me?" And Matilda replied, "Yes, Lord, most readily!" This great love pleased God so much that it gave her the same merit as if she had suffered all in reality.

13 A sure proof that we love God alone is that we love Him equally in all cases. For, as He is always equal to Himself, the inequality of our love for Him can arise only from the consideration of something which is not Himself.

—ST. FRANCIS DE SALES

By this test we may perceive how pure was the love of this Saint; for, it never increased in prosperity, nor diminished in adversity, but in everything was directed equally to the Lord, and through everything he thanked and blessed Him.

St. Jane Frances de Chantal also gave this excellent proof of her perfect love of God, by feeling equally contented in consolations

and in desolations, of which she suffered many, and for a long time. The reason was, as she said, because in both she desired and sought only the fulfillment of the Divine Will, by which she knew that both prosperity and adversity were sent to her.

"True lovers of God," said a holy soul, "are like the sun, which, though it is sometimes covered with clouds, yet always possesses in itself the same light and the same warmth."

14 The measure of charity may be taken from the want of desires. As desires diminish in a soul, charity increases in it; and when it no longer feels any desire, then it possesses perfect charity.

—ST. AUGUSTINE

St. Francis de Sales used to say of himself: "I wish for very few things, and those few I wish for very little. I have almost no desire, and if I were to begin life again, I should wish to have none at all."

St. Teresa was so fully persuaded of this truth that she exclaimed: "Oh Love, that lovest me more than I love myself, and more than I can understand! How shall I be able, O Lord, to desire more than Thou art willing to give me?"

15 The surest way to discover whether we have the love of God is to see whether we love our neighbor, for the two things are never separated. Be sure, too, that the more you perceive yourself to advance in the love of your neighbor, the more you will do so in that of God. To see how much we love our neighbor is the surest

rule by which to find out how much we love God. It is important, then, to notice with great attention how we walk in this holy love of our neighbor; for if it is with perfection, all is done. And so we ought to examine ourselves carefully as to the little things that are constantly happening, without making much account of certain high-flown ideas about the great things we mean to say and do for our neighbors, which sometimes come to us in prayer, but which are never put into execution.

—ST. TERESA

The blessed Angela di Foligno prayed to the Lord to give her some sign by which she might know whether she truly loved Him, and was loved by Him. "The clearest sign," He answered, "of mutual love between Me and My servants is that they love their neighbors."

Tertullian relates that the mutual love of the first Christians was so manifest that even the heathens were much astonished at it, and said among themselves: "See how these Christians love one another! how much respect they have for each other! how ready they are to render any service, or even to suffer death, for each other's sake!"

St. Jerome says that in his old age St. John the Evangelist was not able to come to the sacred assemblies, except supported by the arms of his followers; nor could he preach long sermons, on account of the weakness of his voice, but he would constantly repeat these few words: "Little children, love one another." After a time, those present became weary and asked him why

he always gave them the same instruction. "Because," he replied, "this is the precept of the Lord; and if you observe this, it alone will be enough."

In order that her nuns might be sure whether their actions proceeded from the spirit of charity, St. Jane Frances de Chantal kept inscribed upon the wall of a corridor through which they were constantly passing, a list of the distinguishing marks which the Apostle assigns to this sublime virtue: "Charity is patient, mild, without jealousy, without ambition, without self-interest, without aversions. It believes all, hopes for all, bears with all." When anyone in chapter accused herself of a fault against charity, she sent her to read these sentences, which she called the mirror of the convent. She often read them herself, in presence of her daughters; then, turning towards them with a glowing countenance, she would add: "Though I speak with the tongue of angels and have not charity, I am nothing; and though I give my body to torture and to fire, and have not charity, this profits me nothing."

16 It is worthwhile to reflect that God, who has commanded us to love our neighbor, has also prescribed the manner in which we are to love Him, that is, as ourselves. This is the rule which cannot be transgressed without fault; and it is so essential that unless our love comes up to this measure, it is not sufficient.

St. Wenceslaus spent a great part of his wealth in purchasing the children of heathen parents, whom he afterwards caused to be brought up in the Catholic Faith.

17 Fraternal charity is the sign of predestination. It makes us known as the true disciples of Christ, for it was this divine virtue that moved Him to live a life of poverty and to die in destitution upon the Cross. Therefore, when we find opportunities of suffering for charity, we ought to bless God for them.

—ST. VINCENT DE PAUL

St. Euphrasia, a nun in the Thebaid, was so full of charity that she spent whole weeks without taking food, on account of her excessive occupation in the service of others, and because she devoted to prayer any little time she had left. It was noticed that for a whole year she never sat down; and her active kindness made her dear and lovely in the eyes of the whole convent, so that she seemed to them not an earthly creature, but an angel incarnate. Finally, God revealed to the Abbess that He should soon take Euphrasia from her. When this came to the ears of one of the Saint's companions, she wept day and night, and Euphrasia, discovering the cause, was herself grieved at the prospect of losing the opportunity of serving God in her neighbor.

Eulogius, a very learned man, resolved to abandon study and give himself entirely to the divine service. He first distributed the greater part of his property among the poor, but not knowing what kind of life to choose in which he might best please God, he went into the public square and there found a leper without hands or feet. Touched with a lively compassion, he made a sort of compact with God that he would take care of this man, and support him till death, in the certain hope of obtaining mercy from the Lord. He took him then to his house, and took care

of him with his own hands, for fifteen years. At the end of this time the man, instigated by the devil, began to insult Eulogius, saying that he must have committed many thefts and rascalities, and so made use of him as a means of expiating his sins, but that he did not wish to stay with him any longer, and desired to be carried back to the square, for he was tired of a vegetable diet and wished for meat. Eulogius brought him some meat, and tried to quiet him. But he would not be pacified, saying that he liked to see plenty of people, and nothing would suit him but to be carried back to the square. Eulogius, not knowing what to do, took him, by ship, to see St. Anthony, who first reproved them both, and then said that God had visited them with this temptation because they were near the end of their days; therefore, they must be patient for a little while, and not separate, for the Lord had permitted this trial, that they might receive a greater reward. They returned home, and at the end of forty days Eulogius died first, and then his patient.

18 God loves our neighbors so much that He gave His life for them; and He is glad even to have us leave Him to do them good. How grateful to Him, then, may we believe the services we render them! Ah, if we understood well how important is this virtue of the love of our neighbor, we should give ourselves entirely to the pursuit of it.

—ST. TERESA

St. Vincent de Paul showed how fully he was persuaded of this truth, for he took this practice so much to heart that he

seemed to have nothing else to do. And it may be truly said that there was never a miser who took so much advantage of opportunities to preserve and increase his wealth, as he to do good to his neighbors. This charity, too, had neither restriction nor limitation, but extended to all times and places and to all persons capable of enjoying its effects.

One morning, before Communion, St. Gertrude was grieving that the lateness of the priest prevented her from confessing some slight faults, when the Lord comforted her by a sight of her own soul decked with rich and resplendent jewels, and said to her: "Why are you sad about this, when you are adorned with the mantle of charity, which, you know, covers a multitude of sins?"

Moses asked to be blotted out of the Book of Life, if so he might obtain from the Lord the pardon of his brothers; St. Paul was ready to be an anathema; and St. Paulinus even became a slave in place of another.

19 Oh, how great must be the love that the Son of God bears to the poor! for He chose the state of poverty. He wished to be called the teacher of the poor, and counts most especially as done to Himself whatever is done for His poor.

—ST. VINCENT DE PAUL

Though this Saint loved all men, yet it may be said that He loved the poor above all; he bore them all in his heart; he had more than a father's love for them so that this most tender affection gave rise in him to a keen sympathy with their miseries, and a constant effort to relieve them. When he met with any case

of want, his heart was immediately filled with compassion, and without waiting to be entreated, he thought of some method of relief; so that his chief care seemed to be to help the needy and assist the poor. He showed this while talking, one day, about the bad weather, which threatened to cause great scarcity of food. "Ah!" he exclaimed with a sigh, "how anxious I feel, not so much for my Congregation, as for the poor! We will go out and ask food for our houses, or serve as vice-curates in the parishes; but what will the poor do? Where can they go? I say with truth, that this is my greatest affliction and trial."

The same may be said of St. Francis de Sales, with the addition that he showed a positive preference for the poor over the rich, in both temporal and spiritual things, for he looked upon them, as he said, as people abandoned by the Lord to our care. Many other Saints were remarkable for their tenderness to the poor. Sister Maria Crucifixa often told her Abbess that if it should ever be necessary to refuse alms to the poor, she would contrive not to be present, as she could not bear it. St. Margaret, a Dominican nun, put so much refinement, delicacy and courtesy into her acts of charity, that the expression "This is not a leaf from Sister Margaret's book" became a proverb to characterize anything that was not well arranged. St. Hedwig, Queen of Poland, served the poor on her knees and washed their feet. St. Stephen, King of Hungary, and others did the same.

20 We should love the poor with peculiar affection, beholding in them the very person of Christ, and showing them the same consideration that He did.

—ST. VINCENT DE PAUL

The venerable Monseigneur de Palafox, after he was a bishop, gave a dinner every Thursday to twelve poor men and was present at it himself. But one day, reading the Life of St. Martin, he found that that Saint gave food to the poor with his own hands, and washed their feet. He decided to do the same, and carried out his plan inflexibly on every Wednesday and Saturday, distributing to all who came the contents of two large pots and doing this with his own hands, remaining in the meantime on his knees, and with his head uncovered. At the close of the distribution, he washed the feet of the poor; and he did all this with the same pleasure and earnestness that he would have felt in doing it to Jesus Christ visibly present. This produced in his heart a great respect for the poor, for he thought every time he met a poor man that he beheld God Himself.

21 To visit and relieve the sick cannot fail to be a thing very pleasing to God, since He has so greatly commended it. But to do it with the greatest ease and merit, we must regard the sufferer not simply as a man, but as Christ Himself, who testifies that He receives in His own person all such service.

St. Mary Magdalen de' Pazzi showed wonderful charity towards all the sick. She visited them every day, and in severe cases many times a day, remaining as long as necessary and serving them in all their needs, for which she provided herself, or through the Superioress or others in charge. By first tasting it herself, she sometimes encouraged them to take food. She bathed them, arranged their beds and swept their rooms, performing

the humblest offices of her own accord. She read spiritual books to them, exhorted them to patience, or gave them consolation, and did everything with so much affection and cheerfulness that she was of the greatest assistance. This charity was universal, free from self-interest, prompted solely by the love of God, regarding the sick now as temples of the Holy Ghost, now as sisters of the angels, and herself always as serving God alone. When medicine was to be given at inconvenient hours, she offered to help the infirmarian. When any required unusual care, she took the whole charge of serving them. She did this in the case of a blind consumptive, of a leper, and of one who had a frightful ulcer, to which she more than once applied her lips. She waited on them all with as much attention as if she had been their servant, bathing them, washing their clothes, and performing all other services through the whole course of their illness, which, in the case of the consumptive, lasted for a year. When the sick were near their end she remained with them all night, without lying down, sometimes staying beside them for fifteen days and nights in succession, now praying for them, now encouraging them with so much feeling and charity that she gave them the greatest comfort. And so all the dying wished to have her present at their passage from this world.

St. John Berchmans bestowed similar care upon the sick, in whatever house he was living. He visited them many times a day and consoled them with spiritual conversation. In summer, he brought them cool water from the fountain at the hottest part of the day to moisten their lips and hands. However numerous they might be, he went to see them all every day, and spent most time with those who required the most aid, or received the

fewest visits. From the rooms where he found many gathered he quickly hastened, to go to those who were alone. He always told some anecdote of the Blessed Virgin to the sick lay-brothers, who watched eagerly for the hour of his visit, and if anything had hindered him they asked the Father in charge to send him later, so much were they consoled by his presence. When he was not able to visit any brother, he did not fail to inquire of the infirmarian in regard to him.

St. Felix the Capuchin showed no less pity for the sick of his Order. At his return to the convent, when he had been out to solicit alms, he went around distributing among them any little delicacies and refreshments he had obtained, consoling them at the same time with amiable words, and showing his readiness to render them whatever service they required.

Many, too, even persons of high rank, have had a vocation for visiting and serving hospitals. St. Stephen, King of Hungary, went to them by night, alone and in disguise. St. Louis, King of France, served the inmates on his knees and with uncovered head, looking upon them as members of Christ and united with Him upon the Cross. And so with many others.

When St. John Gualberto was Abbot, he was so rigorous in regard to the observance of the Rule that he had no mercy on the sick, but desired them to keep it like the well. But this was not pleasing to the Lord, so He permitted him to fall grievously ill, and learn from his own experience how to compassionate sufferers.

22 To have that love for our neighbor which is commanded by the Lord, we must entertain good and

amiable feelings towards him, especially when he is disagreeable and annoying to us on account of any defect, natural or moral; for then we find nothing in him to love, except in God. The maxim of the Saints was that in performing works of charity and kindness, we ought to consider not the person who receives them, but Him for whose sake they are done. Nor let us be discouraged if we sometimes feel repugnance; for an ounce of this solid and reasonable love is of much greater value than any amount of that tender and sensitive love which we share with the animals, and which often deceives and betrays our reason.

—ST. FRANCIS DE SALES

St. Jane Frances de Chantal possessed this love in abundance, for as we read in her Life, she never lost an opportunity of showing it for anyone, whatever faults and deficiencies she might observe in him. She often exhorted her Sisters to do the same, saying to them: "We ought to bear with our neighbors, miserable and ill-conditioned though they may be, even in their follies and trivialities, supporting their tediousness and those little vexations which do no harm beyond wearying us; their want of harmony, too, their weakness, and thoughtlessness occasioned by their deficient knowledge, and all those defects which only regard the person who suffers from them. It is certainly necessary to suffer something, and if our neighbor had no defects and gave us no trouble, how could we have occasion to bear with him?" Having heard that one of her Religious found it very difficult to

bear with the imperfections of another, she wrote thus to her: "My daughter, often consider how it is said in the Gospel that Jesus Christ loved us, and washed us in His blood, and observe that He did not wait to love us until after we were washed from our impurities; but He loved us when we were vile and impure creatures, and then washed us. Let us, then, love this dear neighbor of ours without examination, though he be poor and ill-conditioned, and whatever he may be. And if it were possible to wash away his imperfections with our blood, we should desire to give even the last drop of it for this purpose."

The venerable Sister Maria Crucifixa loved all her neighbors, but she showed special kindness for those who were of an unhappy disposition or who exhibited any dislike to her. Once she was much disobliged by a person in minor orders, who, as she afterwards heard, could not receive ordination because he had not sufficient fortune. She thereupon prevailed upon his mother, who was a duchess, to make a settlement of this requisite amount of property upon him.

23 Let us beware of complaints, resentments and evil-speaking against those who are ill-disposed to us, discontented with us, or hostile to our plans and arrangements, or who even persecute us with injuries, insults, and calumnies. Rather let us go on treating them as cordially as at first, or more so, as far as possible showing them esteem, always speaking well of them, doing them good, serving them on occasion, even to the point of taking shame and disgrace upon ourselves, if necessary to save their honor. All

this ought to be done, first, to overcome evil with good, according to the teaching of the Apostles; and secondly, because they are our allies rather than our adversaries, as they aid us to destroy self-love, which is our greatest foe; and since it is they who give us an opportunity to gain merit, they ought to be considered our dearest friends.

—ST. VINCENT DE PAUL

It was thus that he himself treated those who offended him. He not only pardoned them willingly, and obtained pardon from the government for them when required, but compassionated them, excused them, showed for them the same esteem, affection and respect as if nothing had happened, and did them all the good that was in his power. Still more, as he was very sensitive regarding fraternal charity, he took care to extirpate from their hearts the root of rancor and to gain their affection by exonerating them, humbling himself, and bending to them so much that they were obliged to yield to his humility and charity. He was never heard to complain of anyone, whatever offense he had given, and still less to blame or accuse any, so long as his own interests were the only ones involved. One day a missionary of his Congregation told him that some people, moved, as he thought, by envy, were putting obstacles in the way of the ordination of some new priests. "Yes," he answered, "this function frequently excites emulation and envy. But those who are now in opposition, may have a good and upright motive. So, we ought to preserve all our esteem and respect for them, and believe with them that we are unworthy of such a charge, and that others would execute it

better than we. Let us profit by this sentiment, and give ourselves to God in truth, to serve Him faithfully."

St. Francis de Sales was once talking with an intimate friend, who said that, in his opinion, one of the most difficult precepts of Christianity was that of love towards enemies. "For my part," said St. Francis, "I do not know what my heart is made of, or whether God has been graciously pleased to give me one quite peculiar. For I do not find the fulfillment of this precept in the least difficult; on the contrary, I experience so much pleasure in it, that if God had forbidden me to love my neighbors, I should have the greatest difficulty in obeying Him." The following incident shows how truly he spoke.

A lawyer of Annecy hated the holy prelate for no visible cause and was constantly speaking ill of him, injuring and persecuting him, so that he even tore down one of his notices which was fastened upon the church door and scrawled a thousand disgraceful figures on his confessional. The Saint, who knew all this, met him one day and made him a friendly bow; then taking him by the hand with great politeness, he said whatever he thought most likely to make him change his course; but seeing that his words produced no effect, he added: "I clearly perceive that you hate me, though I do not know why. But assure yourself that if you were to put out one of my eyes, I would look at you with the other as amicably as if you were my best friend." His heart, however, was not softened by this, nor by the efforts of his friends to lead him to reconsider his actions. On the contrary, after firing pistol shots at his windows, he one day fired at the Bishop himself in the street, but by mistake wounded his vicar. For this act he was imprisoned by the senate, and not withstanding the

interposition of the Saint, he was condemned to death. But the holy Bishop, having obtained a reprieve, used his influence with the king so successfully as to obtain his pardon. He went himself to the prison to bring the good news, and to entreat him to abandon a hostility for which he had no just cause. Finding him hardened as ever and ready with calumnies and insults, he knelt and asked his pardon. Finally, perceiving that nothing would move him, he left by his side the pardon he had obtained for him and took leave, saying: "I have rescued you from the hands of man's justice, and you are not converted. You will fall under the justice of God, from which you cannot escape." This soon happened; for a little while after, his life came to an unhappy end.

In the Lives of the Fathers we read of a monk who, when he knew that another was speaking ill of him, was much pleased, and often visited him when such a one was in the neighborhood, and sent him presents when at a distance.

There was also another, who always showed the greatest love to any who insulted him, saying to those who were astonished at it: "Those who insult us give us the means of perfecting ourselves; and those who praise and honor us put stumbling blocks before our feet, and give us subjects of pride."

An old monk, too, is mentioned, whose cell was often entered secretly by another monk, who robbed him of anything good that he had, particularly in the way of food. This the good old man noticed in silence, and worked harder than before, and ate less, saying to himself, "This poor brother must be in want." When the holy old man lay on his deathbed, surrounded by the monks, he saw among them the robber, and begging him to approach, he clasped his hands and kissed them, saying: "Dear

hands! how much am I obliged to you! I thank you with all possible earnestness, for by your means I am now going to Paradise!"

St. Teresa was accustomed to redouble her charity towards those who offended her.

St. Francis Borgia used to call those who brought upon him any mortification or trial his assistants and friends.

A certain good nun, whenever she received an injury from anyone, always hastened to the Most Holy Sacrament and made an offering of it, saying: "O Lord, for love of Thee I pardon her who has done me this wrong! Mayest Thou pardon her for love of me!"

One of her nuns once told St. Jane Frances de Chantal that another Sister had revealed some of her faults, but she had resolved, for the love of God, not to do the same to her in return. The good Mother embraced her tenderly, saying: "May it please my God that this resolution shall never pass away from your mind! I should consider myself most happy if I could find it in the hearts of all our Sisters."

24 Let us endeavor to show ourselves full of compassion towards the faulty and the sinful. If we do not show compassion and charity to these, we do not deserve to have God show it towards us.

—ST. VINCENT DE PAUL

This Saint was never astonished at any fault that he saw committed; for he said that to commit faults was the characteristic of man, as he was conceived and born in sin. This acquaintance that he had with the common miseries of man was what

made him behave with so much sweetness and compassion to all sinners. He avoided harshness and used only mild and compassionate words and ways, even with the most guilty, endeavoring to conceal and make little account of their faults with a marvellous prudence and charity, and desiring to have his missionaries follow the same course.

When St. John Berchmans had charge of the Novitiate, if the Father Rector ordered him to impose a penance upon any novice, he felt such great compassion that he would kneel and ask the favor of performing it in his place. But when this was not granted, he imposed it with such suavity, that no one ever showed any hesitation about accepting it.

St. Francis once said to the Blessed Cataneus, his General: "By this I shall know whether you love God and me, His and your servant; that is, by your showing mercy to delinquents. When you find one, do not let him go without his feeling the effect of your kindness; and if you see him fall a thousand times, love him always more than myself, that you may attract him to good, and never fail to be merciful to all such."

St. Francis de Sales had a heart so tender towards evildoers that he often said, "There is no one but God and myself who truly loves wicked men." He gave proof of extraordinary charity towards them by ascribing their misdeeds to human frailty.

25 Among all those who are included under the title of neighbor, there are none who deserve it more, in one sense, than those of our own household. They are nearest of all to us, living under the same roof and eating the same bread. Therefore they ought to

be one of the principal objects of our love, and we should practice in regard to them all the acts of a true charity, which ought to be founded not upon flesh and blood, or upon their good qualities, but altogether upon God.

—ST. FRANCIS DE SALES

St. Vincent de Paul bore great love to all the members of his Congregation. He showed esteem and veneration for all, and welcomed them all with such tokens of affection that each felt sure of being tenderly loved by him. He provided for their needs with great solicitude, for he could not bear to see any of them suffer. He was often seen to rise from the table to set aside dishes for the lay-brothers, who came after the rest, and if it happened that the cook had nothing for any one, or delayed in serving him, he would give him his own portion and constrain him to take it. He was most attentive in providing relief and comfort for the sick, often going himself to inquire into their condition and their needs; he advised the infirmarians to take all possible care of them, and the Superiors of houses to spare no fatigue or expense in providing for them. He tried to soothe their sufferings by special marks of love and attention, and offered his prayers to God on their behalf. If he perceived that any one of them had a particular desire to speak to him, he left everything to listen to him and gave him all the time he needed. When he belonged to the king's council, the importance of the business there transacted prevented him from leaving it in the midst to go to them, so that he deferred this work of charity until the evening, after the general examen, and denied himself the necessary repose that he

might not deprive them of this satisfaction. When he saw that anyone was troubled by interior trials or temptations, he made every effort to free or else to relieve him; and if anyone seemed hardened, he did his best to win him by gentleness and mildness, sometimes even throwing himself at the feet of such and begging them not to yield to their besetting sin. Prostrating himself once before one who was unwilling to yield, he said to him: "I will not rise from this spot till you have granted what I am asking for your good, nor am I willing that the devil should have more influence with you than myself."

St. Jane Frances de Chantal had great charity towards all her neighbors. Greater, however, more intense and more tender, was that which she bore to her Religious, and she strove to have them feel the same towards one another. In an exhortation which she made one day to lead them to this, she said: "Observe, that when Jesus Christ gave the commandment of fraternal charity to His Apostles, He did not speak in the same way of the love which they were to bear to all men and of that which they were to bear to one another. Speaking of the former, He said, 'Love your neighbors as yourselves'; but of the latter, 'Love one another as I have loved you, and as My Father loves Me.' Now, the love with which Jesus Christ has loved us, and still more, that love with which His Divine Father loves Him, is a disinterested love, a love of equality, a love of inseparable union; therefore, you ought to love one another with this love, to fulfill to perfection the divine commandment."

She herself loved her daughters in this way, with a disinterested love, which had no advantage or pleasure of her own for its aim; with a love of equality, which made her equally affable

and kind to all, accommodating herself to the feelings, desires, and inclinations of each, and making herself all things to all with admirable condescension, as far as she lawfully could; and finally, with a love of inseparable union, for no defect, imperfection, or bad quality of theirs could remove them a hair's breadth from her loving heart.

26 God sometimes gives a certain union of heart and tender love for our neighbor, which is one of the greatest and most excellent gifts that His divine bounty bestows on man.

—ST. FRANCIS DE SALES

The Saint himself had received this beautiful gift. One day, conversing with a confidential friend, he spoke thus: "I think there is not a soul in the world that loves more cordially, more tenderly, or, so to speak, more amorously, than I, for so it has pleased God to form my heart."

St. Ambrose relates how this love was shown by a holy contention which took place between St. Theodora the Virgin and a soldier. The Saint was put in a position of great danger on account of her faith in Christ, when the soldier came to her and begged her to change clothes with him, that she might escape and save her honor. This she did; but when the holy virgin saw her preserver led to martyrdom, she could not endure the thought that her rescue should cost him his life, and publicly exclaimed that it was she who had been condemned, not the one in custody, who was in reality not a woman, but a man. The soldier, on the contrary, asserted that the judge had not condemned

her to death. This friendly struggle to save each other from death
ended in both receiving the grace of martyrdom.

27 It is not enough to have love for our neighbor—we
should notice of what sort it is, and whether it is
true. If we love our neighbor because he does us
good, that is, because he loves us, and brings us some
advantage, honor, or pleasure, that is what we call a
love of complacency, and is common to us with the
animals. If we love him for any good that we see in
him, that is, on account of beauty, style, amiability or attractiveness, this is love of friendship, which
we share with the heathens. Therefore, neither of
these is a true love, and they are of no merit, because
purely natural and of short duration, being founded
upon motives which often cease to exist. In fact, if
we love anyone because he is virtuous, or handsome, or
our friend, what will become of this love if he should
cease to be virtuous, or handsome, or to love us, or,
still worse, if he should become our enemy? When
the foundation upon which our love rested, sinks,
how can it support itself? The true love which alone
is meritorious and lasting is that which arises from
the charity which leads us to love our neighbor in
God and for God; that is, because it pleases God,
or because he is dear to God, or because God dwells
in him, or that it may be so. There is, however, no
harm in loving him also for any honorable reason,
provided that we love him more for God's sake than

for any other cause. Yet the less mixture our love has of other motives, the purer and more perfect it will be. Nor does this hinder us from loving some, such as our parents and benefactors, or the virtuous, more than others, when such preference does not arise from the greater good they do to us, but from the greater resemblance they have to God, or because God wills it. Oh how rare is the love of this sort, which deserves to be called true love!

Nolite amare secundum carnem, sed secundum spiritum sanctum—Love not according to the flesh, but according to the Holy Spirit.—*St. Francis de Sales*

For this reason, he entertained great love and universal respect for all his neighbors—because he saw God in them, and them in God; and this made him very exact in all the duties of courtesy, in which he was never known to fail towards anyone. He felt, indeed, great tenderness for his friends; but because he loved them with relation to God, he was always ready to deprive himself of them. Writing to the Superioress of a convent, he gave her this warning: "Hold the balance evenly among your daughters, that their natural gifts may not cause you to divide your affection and your good offices unjustly. How many persons are there exteriorly polished, who are very pleasing in the eyes of God? Beauty, grace, agreeable conversation and manners, suit the taste of those who still live according to their inclinations. Charity regards true virtues and beauty of soul, and diffuses itself over all without partiality."

St. Vincent de Paul made it one of his chief practices to regard God alone in all men, and to honor in them the divine

perfections; and from this most pure sentiment there sprang up in his heart a respectful love for all, and especially for ecclesiastics, in whom he most clearly recognized the image of the power and holiness of the Creator. Therefore, he charged his missionaries to love and honor them all, and never to say anything but good of them, especially in preaching to the people. He provided for their needs with particular care, as he was unwilling to see the dignity of the priesthood lowered in their persons.

Among the acts of charity which St. Mary Magdalen de' Pazzi resolved to perform was this—that she would reverence and love creatures only because God loves them, and that she would rejoice in the love He bears them, and the perfections He communicates to them. At the point of death, she said that though she had borne great love to all her Sisters, she had loved them only in fulfillment of the precept of love left us by Jesus Christ, and because He had loved them so much, and that outside of this, she had never had the slightest attachment to any creature.

28 Ah! when shall we see ourselves steeped in sweetness and suavity towards our neighbors! When shall we see their souls in the sacred bosom of Jesus! Whoever looks upon his neighbor in any other position, runs a risk of loving him neither purely nor perseveringly, nor impartially; but in such a place, who would not love him? Who would not bear with him? Who would not be patient with his imperfections? Who would consider him an object of dislike? Now, our neighbor is truly there in the bosom and within the heart of the Divine Saviour. He is there as one most

beloved and altogether amiable, so that the loving Lord dies from pure love of him.

—ST. FRANCIS DE SALES

This was the principal reason why this holy prelate was so mild, so tender, so respectful, so patient, to everyone—because he saw them all in the heart of Jesus. He manifested this one day when Monsignor di Bellei, his penitent, complained to him of the great respect he showed him. "What respect," he answered, "do you show Jesus Christ, whom I honor in your person?"

It was one of the chief maxims of St. Vincent de Paul not to regard his neighbor according to exterior appearance, but as he was in the sight of God. "I must not regard," he said, "a poor peasant or country girl as to their exterior or their natural gifts, for often one can hardly recognize in them any resemblance to a rational creature, so rude and earthly are they! But when we look upon them with the eye of Faith, we shall find them so deeply graven on the heart of the Son of God, that He even gave His life for each of them. How desirable it is to view our neighbor in God Himself, that we may make the account of him which Christ our Lord made!"

29 When Raguel saw the young Tobias without knowing him, he exclaimed: "Oh how much this young man resembles my cousin!" And when he heard that he was the son of that cousin, he embraced him warmly, and gave him a thousand benedictions, weeping over him for love. Now, why was this? Not, certainly, on account of his good qualities, for he did

not yet know what his disposition was; but because, as he said, "Thou art the son of an excellent man, and resemblest him greatly." See what love does, when it is true. If we loved God truly, we should do as much for all our neighbors, who are all sons of God, and resemble Him much.

—ST. FRANCIS DE SALES

This reflection made the Saint show great respect to all. One day someone criticized him for showing too much honor to the servant of a nobleman, who had brought him a message. "I do not know how to make these distinctions," he answered. "All men bear the image and likeness of God, and that furnishes me with a sufficient motive for respecting them." When he met persons or even animals heavily loaded, he stood aside that they might pass more easily, and never permitted his servants to make them stop or go back, saying, "Are they not men like we? And do they not at this moment deserve more consideration than we?"

St. Mary Magdalen de' Pazzi often looked upon the image of God as seen in her Sisters, which excited in her heart great love for them; and when any one of them seemed to her imperfect and unworthy, she thought perhaps she had some hidden gift which caused God to find pleasure in her.

A holy Religious once wrote this resolution: "I will love God for Himself, and for love of Him I will serve those who bear His image. I will give my heart to Him, and my hands to my neighbor, that he may be united to God."

The Venerable Maria Seraphina di Dio said of herself that she consoled herself under trials, in associating with her neighbors,

by the thought that she was beholding in them the image of God, and that therefore she could not do less than treat them with benevolence and cordiality.

When Theodosius was extremely provoked and resolved to punish severely the inhabitants of Antioch, who had insulted the statue he had raised to Flacilla, whom he had greatly loved for her rare virtues, St. Macedonius begged one of his courtiers to say these words to him in his name: "O Emperor, truly you would do right in punishing these insolent men, but I pray you, remember that they are the loving images of God; and if you dare to let loose your rage against the images of the Lord, you may draw down upon yourself His anger. For, if ill-treatment to the image of your dear consort displeased you so much, how can you suppose that God will not be equally displeased with what you may inflict upon His images, so dear to Him that to re-cast them He had not spared to shed all His blood?" These words, uttered with great simplicity and reported to the emperor, did much to pacify him.

30 Among the means best fitted to acquire and preserve union and charity with God and our neighbor, none can be found better and more efficacious than holy humility, in abasing ourselves beneath all, esteeming ourselves the least, the worst, and lowest of all, and thinking evil of no one. For, self-love and pride are what lead us to sustain our opinions against those of our neighbor, and thus cool the love we owe him.

—ST. VINCENT DE PAUL

A Franciscan preacher once severely reproved in a sermon a vice of which a marquis present in the congregation was guilty. The latter went to the monk after the sermon, loaded him with insults, and ended by saying, "Do you know me?" "Yes," replied the Father, "and I consider it a great honor to be acquainted with such a nobleman, for me, whom am but a rustic by birth, and the humblest of men," adding other things in his own disparagement. The marquis was pacified by this reply, and went away with tears in his eyes and full of veneration for the priest.

The Abbot Motues removed to a cell in a place called Eradion. But being much troubled there by another monk and fearing that there could be no harmony between them, he returned to his former abode. The monks of Eradion grieved much at his departure, and after a while went after him, taking with them the one with whom there had been difficulty. When they came near the Abbot's cell, they took off their outer garments and left them in charge of this brother. Motues, on seeing the monks, welcomed them kindly and asked what had become of their cloaks. Hearing that they were near at hand, in the care of his former companion, he was much pleased, and instantly hastened out to meet him. Then, throwing himself at his feet, he asked his pardon and embraced him, and took him to his cell with the rest. He kept them all for three days and afterwards went back with them to Eradion.

DECEMBER

Union

---

*Qui manet in charitate, in Deo manet, et
Deus in eo—Who abideth in charity, abideth
in God, and God in him.*—1 JOHN 4:16

---

1 The object of all virtues is to bring us into union with
God, in which alone is laid up all the happiness that
can be enjoyed in this world. Now, in what does this
union properly consist? In nothing save a perfect conformity and resemblance between our will and the will
of God, so that these two wills are absolutely alike—
there is nothing in one repugnant to the other; all
that one wishes and loves, the other wishes and loves;
whatever pleases or displeases one, pleases or displeases the other.

—ST. JOHN OF THE CROSS

The Blessed Virgin possessed this perfect union, and St. Bernard says of her that she kept her eyes on the watch and her consent fully prepared for every token of the Divine Will.

The Venerable Mother Seraphina di Dio had advanced far on this road, for in an account which she gave of herself to her director, she was able to say: "My soul seems to be so much in harmony with Our Lord, that whatever He operates in it always appears most fitting, for it is the very thing which it wills for itself. Whatever comes to my soul is a sweet morsel made on purpose for it, and it seems unable to desire anything else, so that it never experiences bitterness or trouble." Once when she accused herself of want of conformity to the Divine Will, she received at that moment a ray of light by which she saw how beautiful is the will of God so clearly that she remained for some time overcome with astonishment that a creature, sprung from nothing, should fail to love the most holy and beautiful will of its Creator.

2 Those deceive themselves who believe that union with God consists in ecstasies or raptures, and in the enjoyment of Him. For it consists in nothing except the surrender and subjection of our will with our thoughts, words and actions, to the will of God and it is perfect when the will finds itself separated from everything, and attached only to that of God, so that every one of its movements is solely and purely the volition of God. This is the true and essential union which I have always desired, and which I constantly ask of the Lord. Oh, how many of us there are who say this, and who think

we desire only this! But, wretched that we are, how few are ever to attain it!

—ST. TERESA

This Saint never ceased to wonder at the great privilege which man possesses in being able to unite himself to his Creator, and at the wonderful desire which so great a sovereign entertains to see him united to Himself. This, therefore, was the object of her keenest desires, and for this she strove more ardently than for anything else.

St. John the Baptist abode in the desert for twenty-four years. God knows how his heart was touched with love for his Saviour even from his birth, and how earnestly he desired to enjoy His presence; and yet, devoted to the simple will of God, he remained there discharging his duty, without even once seeing Him. And after he had baptized Him, he did not follow Him, but continued in his office. What can we say of all this, if not that his was a spirit detached from all things and from God Himself, to perform His will? "This example," said St. Francis de Sales, "overwhelms my soul with its grandeur."

3 Union with God takes place in three ways: by conformity, by uniformity, and by deiformity. Conformity is a complete subordination of our will to the Divine Will in all our actions, and in all occurrences and events, so that we will and accept all that God wills and sends, however painful and repulsive it may be. Uniformity is a close union of our will with the Divine Will, by which we will, not only all that God wills, but

we will it solely because He wills it, and so all repugnances are banished. Deformity is a transformation which renders our will one with that of God, so that it is no longer conscious of itself, as if it were no longer in existence, but only feels in itself the Divine Will, and, as if it were changed into it, no longer desires in any of its acts and operations anything, even what is most holy, with or through the created will, but only in the uncreated, made its own by transformation.

—FR. ACHILLE GAGLIARDI

St. Mary Magdalen de' Pazzi attained to all three degrees of union. As to the first, she often said with great feeling: "If I should see Hell open, and believe that it was the Lord's will that I should suffer eternally in those flames, I would plunge into them instantly, of my own accord, to accomplish His Divine Will." For the second, she said in an ecstasy that she had at Pentecost, "I protest that I do not seek or desire the Holy Spirit, except according to the will of God. I desire His presence, and I do not desire it, because I do not wish to desire it of myself as of myself; so that if God should give it to me to do my will, and not His as His, but as mine, even though His will were to be found in this, yet not primarily and totally His, I should be in no wise content. So much does it concern me not to wish to possess or make my own, what I have given to Him, and what I wish should be wholly His, that I may be able to say with perfect truth in everything, *Fiat voluntas Tua*." For the third, she lived as one dead to herself, without any intention or will of her own. In another ecstasy, the Lord showed her her own soul in this

condition, under the form of another soul, which she described in these terms: "She follows her Spouse without understanding, without speaking, without hearing, without tasting, and, so to speak, without acting, and as if dead. She thinks only of following the interior attraction of the Divine Word, that she may not offend Him."

4 Conformity to the Divine Will is a most powerful means to overcome every temptation, to eradicate every imperfection, and to preserve peace of heart. It is a most efficacious remedy for all ills, and the treasure of the Christian. It includes in itself in an eminent degree mortification, abnegation, indifference, imitation of Christ, union with God and in general all the virtues, which are not virtues at all, except as they are in conformity with the will of God, the origin and rule of all perfection.

—ST. VINCENT DE PAUL

St. Vincent de Paul was himself so much attached to this virtue that it might be called his characteristic and principal one, or a kind of general virtue which spreads its influence over all the rest, which aroused all his feelings and all his powers of mind and body and was the mainspring of all his actions. If he placed himself in the presence of God in his prayers or other exercises, his first impulse was to say with St. Paul, "Lord, what wilt Thou have me do?" If he was very attentive in consulting and hearkening to God, and showed great circumspection in distinguishing between true inspirations proceeding from the Holy Spirit and false ones which

come from the devil or from nature, this was in order to recognize the will of God with greater certainty and be in a better position to execute it. And, finally, if he rejected so resolutely the maxims of the world and attached himself solely to those of the Gospel, if he renounced himself so perfectly; if he embraced crosses with so much affection, and gave himself up to do and suffer all for God—this, too, was to conform himself more perfectly to the whole will of his Divine Lord.

The blessed Jacopone being astonished that he no longer felt any disturbances and evil impulses, as he did at first, heard an interior voice saying: "This comes from your having wholly abandoned yourself to the Divine Will, and being content with all it does."

5 So great is the delight which the angels take in executing the will of God, that if it were His will that one of them should come upon earth to pull up weeds and root out nettles from a field, he would leave Paradise immediately and set himself to work with all his heart, and with infinite pleasure.

—BL. HENRY SUSO

He himself was so satisfied with the will of God, so completely attached and submissive to it, that he said, "I would rather be a bat at the Divine Will, than a seraph at my own."

So great was the love and tenderness which St. Mary Magdalen de' Pazzi entertained for the Divine Will that at the mere mention of it, she would be lost in an ocean of spiritual joy, and sometimes rapt into ecstasies. One evening, after most of

the others had retired to sleep, someone said of a certain Sister that she had a great desire to do the will of God. The Saint replied joyously, "She is right, for to do the will of God is a thing most lovely"—and with that she remained bereft of sense, for she could not bear the flood of sweetness that flowed over her at the thought of the loveliness of the Divine Will. She then ran through the dormitory, exclaiming, "How amiable is the Divine Will!" and calling upon the rest to come and confess this with her. She excited such a tender emotion in them all, that they arose and went with her to the chapel, where they all unitedly confessed with a loud voice that the Divine Will was worthy of all love, and the hearts of all were deeply stirred.

6 A soul truly resigned to God has no affection for any created thing, for it sees clearly that all its possessions, except God, are vain and a nullity. So its single object and aim is to die to itself, and to resign itself actually and always in all things.

—BL. HENRY SUSO

St. Vincent de Paul excelled in this, for he lived quite apart from all creatures, and even from himself, taking no care but to depend in everything upon the will of God and the disposal of His holy providence.

The soul of the Venerable Mother Seraphina had arrived at this happy state, as appears from an account she gave of herself to her director in these terms: "The state in which I find my soul at present is that I wish for nothing except what God wills. The will and pleasure of God has so penetrated me, and has become

so wrought into my own will and pleasure, that it has made itself mine and I desire that alone which God wills, and not only do I will it, but I am not able to will otherwise, nor to have any pleasure or will but His. This is my sole and complete will, nor have I need to produce or repeat acts of it, for I have it deeply impressed upon my soul; I love and esteem it, and rejoice in it supremely."

7 As the Lord knows for what we all are adapted, He gives to all their positions as He sees to be most for His own glory, for their salvation, and the good of their neighbors. Our mistake, then, is in not submitting ourselves totally to whatever He wishes to do with us.

—ST. TERESA

When her director expressed a doubt as to the spiritual course she was following and bade her try another, St. Teresa was only able to place herself in the hands of God, that He who knew what was best for her might wholly accomplish His holy will in her heart.

The Lord one day gave St. Francis Borgia the choice of life or death for his wife, who was seriously ill. But he replied with emotion, "Why, O Lord, commit to my judgment what lies solely in Thy power? What concerns me is to follow Thy holy will in all things, since no one knows better than Thou what is best for me. Do, then, what is most pleasing to Thee, not only with my wife, but with my children also, and with myself. *Fiat voluntas Tua!*"

A blind man earnestly entreated St. Vedastus, on the day of his festival, to give him sight, and obtained it. Then, continuing

his prayer, he said that he would not have asked it except as a help towards his salvation, when it was immediately taken away again. The same thing happened to another, who was cured of a painful infirmity by the intercession of St. Thomas of Canterbury, but who protested to the Saint that if health was not best for him, he did not desire it. Upon this, his previous illness instantly returned, at which he felt no disappointment.

8 We ought to submit to the will of God, and be content in whatever state it may please Him to put us; nor should we ever desire to change it for another, until we know that such is His pleasure. This is the most excellent and the most useful practice that can be adopted upon earth.

—ST. VINCENT DE PAUL

The venerable Father Daponte told an intimate friend that he was glad of all his natural defects of appearance and speech, since it had pleased the Lord to mark him with them; that he was glad also of all his temptations and miseries, both interior and exterior, since God so willed it, and that if it were the will of God that he should live a thousand years, oppressed by far greater trials and in the deepest darkness, provided that he should not offend Him, he would be quite content.

When the news of her husband's death in the war was brought to St. Elizabeth, she instantly raised her heart to God, and said: "O Lord, Thou knowest well that I preferred his presence to all the delights of the world! But since it has pleased Thee to take him from me, I assent so fully to Thy holy will, that if

I could bring him back by plucking out a single hair from my head, I would not do it, except at Thy will."

9 Never believe you have attained such purity as you should, whilst your will is not freely and gladly submissive to the holy will of God, as to all, and in all, even in things the most repugnant.

—ST. FRANCIS DE SALES

St. Jane Frances de Chantal said that he arrived at such purity, as she knew from himself, for in his deepest afflictions he experienced a sweetness a hundred times greater than usual. This came from the intimate union with God that he enjoyed, which made the bitterest things most delicious to him.

The Congregation of St. Vincent de Paul met with a serious loss of property. He informed a friend of it in this way: "As you are one of our best friends, I cannot do less than let you know of the loss we have met with—not, indeed, as a misfortune that has befallen us, but as a favor which the Lord has bestowed on us, and in the intention that you may help us to render Him due thanks. Favors and benefits are the name I give to the afflictions that He sends us, especially when they are well received. And as His infinite goodness has ordained this loss, He has made us accept it with perfect and entire resignation, and, I can safely say, with as much gladness as we should have felt at any prosperous event."

10 One act of resignation to the Divine Will, when it ordains what is repugnant to us, is worth more than

a hundred thousand successes according to our own will and pleasure.

—ST. VINCENT DE PAUL

How much, in the midst of all his disasters, did holy Job merit before God by his "*Dominus dedit, Dominus abstulit*—The Lord hath given, and the Lord hath taken away!"

11 Perfect resignation is nothing else than a complete moral annihilation of thoughts and affections, when one renounces himself totally in God, that He may guide him as He wills and pleases, as if one no longer knew or cared for either himself or anything else except God. It is thus that the soul, so to speak, loses itself in God, not, indeed as to its nature, but as to the appropriation of its powers.

—BL. HENRY SUSO

St. Catherine of Genoa was one of those happy souls who attained to a share in this holy annihilation in which, as she herself attests, she had no longer thoughts, affections or desires as to anything, except to leave God to do with her, and in her, all that He might will, without any choice or resistance on her part, and that this gave her in all circumstances and occasions a delight like that of the blessed, who have no will but that of their God. And so she was able to say: "If I eat, if I drink, if I speak, if I am silent, if I sleep, if I wake, if I see, if I hear, if I meditate, if I am in the church, if I am in the house, if I am in the street, if I am sick or well, in every hour and moment of my life, I would

do only God's will and my neighbor's for His sake; or rather, I would not wish to be able to do, to speak, or to think anything apart from the will of God; and if anything in me should oppose itself to this, I would wish that it might instantly become dust and be scattered to the winds."

A young girl, whom she had never seen, once appeared to St. Aldegonde and told her, in the name of the Blessed Virgin, that she might ask what she chose, and it would be given her. But the Saint replied cheerfully that she desired nothing, except that in all things the holy will of God should be accomplished, to which she would be resigned with all possible satisfaction and pleasure.

12 When shall it be that we shall taste the sweetness of the Divine Will in all that happens to us, considering in everything only His good pleasure, by whom it is certain that adversity is sent with as much love as prosperity, and as much for our good? When shall we cast ourselves unreservedly into the arms of our most loving Father in Heaven, leaving to Him the care of ourselves and of our affairs, and reserving only the desire of pleasing Him, and of serving Him well in all that we can?

—ST. JANE FRANCES DE CHANTAL

When St. Peter was about to hold a disputation with Simon Magus, he received word from his opponent that on account of important business, he should be obliged to defer the debate for three days. St. Clement, who had just been converted and who

was with St. Peter, was grieved at this delay. But St. Peter consoled him by saying: "My son, it is to be expected of the heathens that they will be troubled when things do not turn according to their wishes; but for us, who know that the Lord guides and disposes all things, we ought in all cases to abide in great peace and consolation. I will show you that this event which displeases you is in reality for your good, for if the discussion had taken place now, you would have understood but little of it; but later you will understand it better, for in the meantime I will instruct you so that you will be able to derive greater advantage from it. So, for the future, beware of separating yourself from the Divine Will, and always be sure that whatever happens will be for the best."

We read of the wife of a soldier, who used to say when a misfortune happened to anyone, "It will be the best thing for him." She made the same remark on the occasion of her husband's losing an eye. Some time after, it happened that the king was near death, and, according to the custom of the country, someone was chosen to honor his death by dying with him. It happened that this soldier was chosen, but when he was informed of his ill-fortune, he immediately said: "But no! It is not proper that so great a king should have a one-eyed man for his companion in death!" This was approved by all, so that the loss of an eye was no evil, but a great piece of good fortune.

13 To lose ourselves in God is simply to give up our own will to Him. When a soul can say truly, "Lord, I have no other will than Thine," it is truly lost in God, and united to Him.

—ST. FRANCIS DE SALES

The venerable Father Daponte made this prayer, and repeated it every day: "*Fiat, Domine de me, in me, pro me, et circa me et omnia mea, sancta voluntas Tua, in omnibus et per omnia et in aeternum*—Concerning me, in me, for me, in regard to me, and all that I have, may Thy holy will, O Lord, be done, in all things, and through all things, and to eternity."

The Lord appeared one day to St. Gertrude and said to her: "Daughter, behold I bring you in one hand health, and in the other sickness. Choose which you please!" The Saint, throwing herself at His feet, with her hands crossed upon her bosom, answered: "O Lord, I pray Thee not to consider my will at all, but solely Thine own, and to do with me whatever will result in Thy greatest glory and satisfaction; for I have no desire except to have whatever Thou wishest me to have." The Lord was much pleased with this reply, and added: "Let those who desire that I should often visit them give Me the key of their will, and never take it back." Instructed by these words, the Saint composed for herself this aspiration, which she frequently repeated ever after: "*Non mea, sed Tua voluntas fiat, Jesu amantissime!*—Not my will, but Thine be done, O most loving Jesus!"

14   There are many who say to the Lord, "I give myself wholly to Thee, without any reserve," but there are few who embrace the practice of this abandonment, which consists in receiving with a certain indifference every sort of event, as it happens in conformity with Divine Providence, as well afflictions as consolations, contempt and reproaches as honor and glory.

—ST. FRANCIS DE SALES

St. Vincent de Paul was a brilliant example of this. In all places, times, occupations, and circumstances, in tribulation and consolation, in illness, in cold and heat, in encountering reproaches, calumnies, the loss of friends or property, he was never troubled or disturbed; but, as if all these events had been similar, he remained in great peace and tranquillity of soul, which he manifested by the sweetness of his words and the serenity of his countenance; for he never lost sight of his maxim that nothing happens to this world except as ordained by Divine Providence, into whose hands he had entirely abandoned himself. This once made a priest say in astonishment, "M. Vincent is always M. Vincent!"

Particular examples may be of use to illustrate this. When he received news that parties were endeavoring to bring lawsuits and disturb his missionaries in their possessions and in houses and lands which they had acquired, his usual reply was that nothing would succeed except what God pleased, and that as He was master of all their goods, it was just that He should dispose of them according to His Divine Will. When one of the most important and useful members of his Congregation was seriously ill, he wrote thus to a person who was much grieved at the misfortune: "It seems as if Our Lord wished to take His portion of our little company. It is, I hope, entirely His, and so He has a right to make use of it as He sees best. For myself, the chief desire that I have is to wish nothing except the fulfillment of His Divine Will."

In fact, though the preservation of his Congregation was so dear to him, he never desired either that or its increase and progress, except insofar as he was sure that God willed it—so

that, as he once said, he would not have taken a step or uttered a word to that end, except in entire dependence on the Divine Will. His practice was the same in what regarded himself personally, for he bore his many and great infirmities with much peace and tranquillity of soul. In the last year of his life he perceived clearly, and often said, that he was gradually failing, but always with a perfect indifference, which proved that living and dying, suffering and relief, were the same to him. He was indifferent as to the food and the remedies given him, and though he would sometimes express the opinion that one thing or another did him harm, still he always took what the physicians ordered him, and seemed as well pleased with bad results as with good. In everything he regarded only the accomplishment of God's good pleasure as the sole object of his desire and of his joy; nor was there ever observed in him, either in sickness or health, the least token of a feeling opposed to this holy disposition.

St. Jane Frances de Chantal had attained the same height, for we read of her that she received with equal indifference whatever occurred, whether adverse or prosperous, as she had no desire but that God would do with her and in her regard whatever He might please. For this reason, she never cared to think about what might happen to herself or others in the future; that is, about what she should do in such or such circumstances; as, for example, if she were in extreme want, whether she would go out and beg, or wait for help from Divine Providence; she said that in such a case, she would ask the Lord with fresh confidence what she was to do, leaving herself, meantime, in His hands. She was once asked whether, in the various dangers she had encountered by land and water in her frequent journeys, she had always

hoped that God would rescue her from them. She replied that she had hoped not for rescue, but only that the Lord would do what might be for His greater glory, by freeing her from the danger or by leaving her to perish in it, and that in this total dependence on the divine disposal, her heart remained peaceful, tranquil and at rest.

To conclude, a holy and learned man said that a soul perfectly resigned is like a body that forms a perfect square, which stands firmly on whichever side it may be thrown.

15 If you give yourself to the practice of holy abandonment, though you may not perceive that you gain at all, you will, in fact, advance greatly, as it is with those who sail upon the open sea with favorable winds, trusting wholly to the care of the pilot.

—ST. FRANCIS DE SALES

There was in a certain monastery a Religious whose power of working miracles was so great that the sick were cured by merely touching his garments or his cincture. The Abbot wondered at this, as he saw nothing remarkable about him, and one day asked him for what cause God worked so many miracles by his means. "I do not know," he replied, "for I do not fast, nor use the discipline, nor watch, nor pray, nor labor any more than others. This only I perceive in myself—that nothing which happens disturbs or disquiets me, but my soul remains in equal tranquillity in the midst of all events, however unfortunate they may be for myself or others, because I have left everything in the hands of God. And so, whether it be prosperity or adversity, whether it be

little or much, I take all as coming from His hands." "Then were you not troubled the other day," rejoined the Abbot, "when the enemy burned our granary?" "Not in the least," was his answer. "Here, then, is the cause of your miracles," returned the Abbot.

A farmer who always had larger and better crops than his neighbors was once asked the reason by one of them. "Why, I always have the weather to suit me," he answered, "for I always wish it to be as God wishes it, and not otherwise."

16 One of the principal effects of holy abandonment in God is evenness of spirits in the various accidents of this life, which is certainly a point of great perfection, and very pleasing to God. The way to maintain it is in imitation of the pilots, to look continually at the Pole Star, that is, the Divine Will, in order to be constantly in conformity with it. For it is this will which, with infinite wisdom, rightly distributes prosperity and adversity, health and sickness, riches and poverty, honor and contempt, knowledge and ignorance, and all that happens in this life. On the other hand, if we regard creatures without this relation to God, we cannot prevent our feelings and disposition from changing, according to the variety of accidents which occur.

—ST. FRANCIS DE SALES

Taulerus relates that there was once a great theologian who for eight years in succession prayed to God to show him someone who would teach him the way of truth, and that finally,

when he was one day offering this prayer with great fervor, he heard a voice from Heaven saying to him, "Go to the temple, and there you shall find him!" He went, and found a poor beggar on the church steps, half-clothed with a few rags, and covered with sores. Moved with compassion, he saluted him kindly with the words, "God give you good day, my good man!" "I never have a bad day," said the beggar, with a cheerful look. "God give you good fortune!" went on the theologian. "I have never experienced any misfortunes," answered the other. "How is this!" exclaimed the theologian; "you have never had bad days, and never experienced misfortunes, loaded as you are with woes and miseries!" "I will tell you," replied the mendicant. "I have cast myself wholly upon the Divine Will, to which I so conform my own that whatever God wills, I will also. So when hunger, thirst, cold, heat or sickness molest me, I do nothing but praise God, and whatever happens to me—whether it be prosperous or adverse, whether it be pleasing or unpleasant—I take all from the hand of God with great gladness, as that which can but be good, since it comes from a Cause which can produce only what is best." "But," went on the theologian, "if God should choose to send you to Hell, what would you do?" "I would immediately plunge into it," returned the beggar. "For, see! I have two arms: one is humility, by which I keep myself always attached to His most sacred humanity; the other is love, which attaches me to His divinity. Now, if He were to cast me into Hell, I would cling to Him so tightly with these two arms, that He would be obliged to come with me, and with such companionship it would not grieve me much even to be in Hell." "Who can you be?" wondered the theologian. "I am

a king" was the answer. "And where is your kingdom?" "In my soul, for I know so well how to rule my faculties, both interior and exterior, that all the powers, inclinations, and affections of my soul are completely subject to me." "Tell me, how did you learn such great perfection?" "By recollection, meditation, and union with God. I was never able to find peace in anything less than God before I succeeded in finding Him, and since then I enjoy continual peace." "And where did you find Him?" "Where I left affection for all other things."

17 In this holy abandonment springs up that beautiful freedom of spirit which the perfect possess, and in which there is found all the happiness that can be desired in this life; for in fearing nothing, and seeking and desiring nothing of the things of the world, they possess all.

—ST. TERESA

One of these beautiful souls was that of St. Francis de Sales. In whatever happened to him, he always showed as much satisfaction as if all had gone according to his wishes. For example, when a fierce persecution had been raised against him and the Order he had founded, he wrote thus to St. Jane Frances de Chantal: "I leave all these opposing blasts to the providence of God. Let them blow or cease, as shall please Him; tempest and calm are equally dear to me. If the world did not speak ill of us, we should not be the servants of Christ."

The Emperor Ferdinand II made this prayer every day: "O Lord! if it be indeed for Thy glory and my salvation that I

retain the position in which I am, keep me in it, and I will glorify Thee. If it be to Thy praise and my good that I sink to a lower place, abase me, and I will glorify Thee."

Father Alvarez never thought about what was to happen to him, and if any thought of the kind offered itself, he would say, "It will be as God wills." Then, raising his heart to God, he would add: "O Lord, I wish for nothing but to please Thee and satisfy Thee!"

18 How beautiful it is to behold a person destitute of all attachment, ready for any act of virtue or charity, gentle to all, indifferent as to any employment, serene in consolations and tribulations, and wholly content if only the will of God be done!

—ST. FRANCIS DE SALES

Behold how this Saint, without intending it, has depicted himself to the life! For he was precisely such a person as is here described, as may be seen from many incidents recorded in this work.

19 When we have totally abandoned ourselves to the pleasure of God, submitting without any reserve our will and affections to His dominion, we shall see our souls so united to His Divine Majesty that we shall be able to say with that perfect model of Christians, St. Paul: "In myself I no longer live, but Jesus Christ in me."

—ST. FRANCIS DE SALES

This Saint, according to the testimony of one who knew him intimately, in the last years of his life had reached such a point that he desired, loved, or regarded only God in all things. As a result, he seemed always absorbed in God and said that there was nothing in the world which could satisfy him except God. He frequently uttered with ecstatic feeling these words of the Psalmist: "Lord, what is there in Heaven for me, or what do I desire upon earth save Thee? Thou art my portion and my inheritance forever." All that was not God was nothing for him, and this was one of his principal maxims.

20 When one seeks to unite himself to God, he should endeavor to discover, by self-examination, whether there is anything which forms a barrier between his soul and God, and whether in anything he seeks himself or turns back to himself.

—BL. HENRY SUSO

St. John Berchmans, after examining himself to see whether he had an attachment to anything whatever, found that there was nothing on earth for which he felt or could feel affection. This he expressed in a sentence found among his manuscripts: "*Nulli rei sum affectus, et nihil habeo cui afficiar.*"

A gentleman of very high family who had passed most of his life at court, guiding himself by the maxims of the world, was finally gained over for God by St. Vincent de Paul and applied himself so earnestly to the pursuit of perfection that he became a model to all. Desiring still to advance, and feeling sure the more he separated himself from creatures, the more he would

be united by God, he often examined himself as to whether he had any attachment for relatives, friends, honors, property or comforts, and whenever he discovered anything that was an entanglement to him, he immediately broke or cut it away. One day he made his usual examination while riding on horseback, and could think of nothing for which he specially cared until he finally perceived that he had a fondness for his sword, which had saved his life in many duels. Instantly springing from the horse, he went up to a large stone, upon which he shivered it to pieces. Afterwards he told the incident to St. Vincent and assured him that this act gave him such complete freedom that he never after felt affection for any perishable thing.

21 The condition of union seems to be nothing else than dying, so to speak, entirely to all the things of the world, and living in the enjoyment of God.

—ST. TERESA

This was the blessed state of St. Catherine of Genoa, who confessed that she once had a vision in which it was shown her how all good proceeds from God, without any previous cause except His pure and simple goodness, by which He was moved to do us good in so many ways and forms. "From that sight," she said, "there rose in my heart such an interior flame of love that I lost all understanding, thought, wish or love for anything except God; so that my soul neither knows nor can wish for anything more or other than it is enjoying at present, and is more pleased and satisfied with this than with anything it could obtain by all its efforts and exertions. And if I should ask myself what I desire

or aim at, I could only answer, 'Nothing except what Love gives me!' He keeps me so occupied and satisfied with Himself that I have no need to plan or seek for anything to sustain my powers, supported and sustained as they are."

22 The soul which remains attached to anything, even to the least thing, however many its virtues may be, will never arrive at the liberty of the divine union. It matters little whether a bird be fastened by a stout or a slender cord—as long as he does not break it, slender as it may be, it will prevent him from flying freely. Oh what a pity it is to see some souls, like rich ships, loaded with a precious freight of good works, spiritual exercises, virtues and favors from God, which, for want of courage to make an end of some miserable little fancy or affection, can never arrive at the port of divine union, while it only needs one good earnest effort to break asunder that thread of attachment! For, to a soul freed from attachment to any creature, the Lord cannot fail to communicate Himself fully, as the sun cannot help entering and lighting up an open room when the sky is clear.

—ST. JOHN CHRYSOSTOM

It is related in the Life of St. Gregory that a rich man left the world and retired into a wood, taking with him, to afford him some recreation in that solitude, only a little cat, as he loved it and often caressed it. After living thus for some years in a constant

course of prayers and penances, he prayed the Lord to be pleased to show him what reward was prepared for him. Then God revealed to him that he might hope for a place in Heaven equal to that which Pope Gregory would receive. The good hermit was much grieved at this information and could not understand why one who had left all he had for God, and had served Him with such austerity, should not receive a greater reward than one who was living in the midst of riches and luxury. But the Lord opened his eyes by showing him that he was more attached to his cat than Gregory to all the riches and honors he enjoyed; and that perfection consists precisely in detachment from all that is not God.

The nuns of the Visitation make special profession of detachment from everything, as they cannot appropriate to themselves the smallest article, not even a needle. To maintain this excellent spirit in its full vigor and prevent them from becoming attached to any object, their Rule requires them to exchange with one another every year the articles of which they make use—their rooms, books, furniture, everything—even the crosses they wear upon their bosoms.

23 See why we never arrive at sanctification after so many Communions as we make! It is because we do not suffer the Lord to reign in us as He would desire. He enters our breasts and finds our hearts full of desires, affections and trifling vanities. This is not what He seeks. He would wish to find them quite empty, in order to render Himself absolute master and governor of them.

—ST. FRANCIS DE SALES

The Saint himself possessed a heart of this latter kind. His confessor testifies of him that he would permit no affection to remain in it that was not of God and for God. And so, if he saw anything alien to this springing up, he was ready to extirpate it, as it were, with steel and fire.

The Lord once said to a good soul that the best disposition for receiving abundant graces in Holy Communion is to empty the heart of everything. For if a great noble goes to the house of one of his retainers with the intention of filling all his boxes and chests, but finds them full of chaff and earth and sand, he is forced to retire with regret.

This is the reason why holy souls have been so earnest in making good Communions. The Empress Leonora, who received three times a week, spent two hours in previous meditation, and wore a girdle of hair-cloth and chains, with sharp points wound several times about her arms. After receiving, she remained for a quarter of an hour prostrate with her face upon the ground, conversing with her Divine Guest in sweet and tender welcome. Then, to retain the warmth of devotion through the day, she remained in silence and solitude in her room. St. Aloysius Gonzaga gave the whole week to his Communion. He offered the actions of the three days preceding it as a preparation, and so endeavored to do them well; and those of the three following days he intended for a thanksgiving.

The venerable Monseigneur de Palafox, after his conversion and while still a secular, communicated often, that is, once a week. He took up the practice of asking God for one virtue at each Communion, and resolving to extirpate some particular fault, occupying in this sometimes days, sometimes whole weeks.

He thus endeavored, by the aid of divine grace, to conquer his evil inclinations and to change his long-established habits, with a success that could be noticed from day to day.

St. John Berchmans was unwilling to receive Communion on holidays, because, as he said, he could not preserve the necessary quiet and devotion on such days; and if he was to Communicate, he asked permission to remain in the house. He said on one occasion that each time he received Holy Communion he felt his soul perceptibly revived and invigorated.

24 To arrive at perfect union, there is needed a total and perfect mortification of the senses and desires. The shortest and most effectual method of obtaining it is this: As to the senses whatever pleasing object may offer itself to them, unconnected with pure love to God, we should refuse it to them instantly, for the love of Jesus Christ, who in this life neither had nor desired to have any pleasure except to do the will of His Father, which He called His food. If, for example, there should arise a fancy or wish to hear or see things which do not concern the service of God or lead especially to Him, we should deny this fancy, and refrain from beholding or hearing these things; but if this is not possible, it is sufficient not to consent with the will. Then as to the desires, we should endeavor to incline always to what is poorest, worst, most laborious, most difficult, most unpleasant, and to desire nothing except to suffer and be despised.

—ST. JOHN OF THE CROSS

Such, in truth, was the life of this Saint, which he passed in the continual exercise of interior and exterior mortification, of which he never seemed to have enough—and in this way he attained to great union with God.

St. Francis Borgia often prayed the Lord to make all the pleasures of this life painful to him, and he strove to render them so himself, as far as he was able. And so he desired with avidity, sought with solicitude and embraced with gladness all that was contrary to self-love, in food, clothing and habitation. By this means he made great progress in virtue and holy union.

25 If you desire to arrive at union with God, let your conversation and manner of life be as interior as possible. Do not reveal yourself, or come forth from yourself, either by words, gestures or manners, but strive to keep yourself within yourself, turning to God alone, who is present within you, and excluding from your heart all that you shall see or hear.

—BL. HENRY SUSO

Father Alvarez, being asked the reason why he had seemed unusually thoughtful for some days, answered: "I am trying to live as if I were in the deserts of Africa, and to keep my heart as much at a distance from all creatures as if I were really in a desert." And in this he succeeded.

St. Rose of Lima made unusual efforts to conceal not only the good works and penances that she performed, but even the spiritual gifts which she received from the Lord—never revealing them without necessity, even to her directors. A person of high

rank once had a great desire to know the special favors this Saint enjoyed, and pressed her spiritual Father to elicit an account of them from her. Though he foresaw that it would be very difficult, yet he was so desirous to grant the favor that he tried to accomplish it under various pretexts, and with much persuasion. The pious maiden soon perceived the object of these artifices, and in the humblest words entreated him not to question her about the matter. She said that from her earliest years she had most frequently supplicated her Spouse that no one might ever discover what He had wrought in her out of His pure goodness; and as the good God had granted this, His minister should not take away a favor which He had bestowed.

St. Thomas Aquinas, from his earliest youth, was constantly seeking to know God. When he had become a Religious, his sole gratification was to think, to speak and to hear of God; so that if anything was introduced in general conversation which was not connected with God, he paid no attention to it, as a matter which did not concern him. He so directed to God and His good pleasure all his works and actions, that when the Lord Himself asked him what reward he would desire for the many works he had written for Him, "No other," he replied, "but Thyself alone, my Lord and my Love!"

26 Be immovable in this resolution, to remain simply in the presence of God, by means of an entire renunciation and abandonment of yourself into the arms of His most holy will. Every time that you find your spirit outside this dear abode, lead it back gently, this love of simple confidence, and this reliance and

repose of the soul upon the paternal bosom of the Divine Goodness, includes all that can be desired to please God.

—ST. FRANCIS DE SALES

This was the favorite exercise of St. Jane Frances de Chantal, which she practiced by means of a simple glance towards God, a simple acquiescence in His most holy will, by resting simply in it, as a little child in the arms and upon the bosom of its mother, without seeking to do anything else or trying to examine what the Lord was working in her, or why He was doing it. In this she found her most complete repose, as she confessed in an account that she gave of herself to her director. "I feel my soul," she said to him, "much inclined to sustain itself by a simple glance raised to God and His Divine Goodness. Though I no longer feel that total abandonment and sweet confidence which I once felt, and though I cannot even make an act of it, yet it seems to me that by this glance alone these virtues become more firm and solid than ever, and if I were to follow my interior impulse, I should practice nothing else." To check any disposition to a redundancy of words, she wrote upon a card a long prayer, including many petitions, praises and thanksgivings for her friends and relatives, and all for whom she was under obligation to pray, whether living or dead. She hung this card around her neck and wore it night and day, having previously stipulated with Our Lord that whenever she pressed it to her bosom she should be considered as offering all the prayers it contained.

Among the many practices of devotion which the venerable Sister Maria Crucifixa employed in thanksgiving after Communion,

one was to place Jesus in the Blessed Sacrament at rest in her soul, as if He were sleeping there, while she stood at His side, watching Him in humble silence, and obliging all her faculties, both interior and exterior, to refrain from all exercise which was not directed to Him, and from every act except such as showed reverence for Him, that by an ill-timed activity they might not awake her Beloved. Thus she kept all her powers long abased in silent reverence, occupied only with Jesus lying in her heart. She confessed that she had derived greater profit from this exercise than from any other. She took care, however, in her previous preparation, to furnish the place well for Him, with devout affections and various acts, that He might rest with less discomfort.

27 When I see some persons very anxious about being attentive in prayer, and keeping their heads bowed while occupied in it, as if they did not dare to stir in the least, or to move even in thought, that the joy and sensible devotion they have may not leave them even in the slightest degree; this shows me how little they understand the road which leads to union, while they imagine that the whole affair consists in keeping their thoughts fixed. No, no, the Lord desires works. Therefore, when things present themselves to be done, to which obedience or charity obliges you, do not at all regard losing that devotion and enjoyment of God, that you may give Him pleasure by doing these things; for they will lead you more quickly than the others to holy union.

—ST. TERESA

The blessed Clara di Montefalco willingly employed herself in the work of the convent, and said that in it the gift of prayer even comes to its perfection.

When St. Mary Magdalen de' Pazzi was a novice, she sometimes had permission from the Mistress to spend in prayer the time which was allotted to her companions for work. But she did not accept this favor, saying that she was more willing to be occupied in any exercise of obedience, however laborious and humble, than in the very loftiest contemplation. When asked the reason, she replied: "Because in performing the duties of the Order and of obedience, I am sure of doing the will of God, of which I am not sure when I engage in prayer or other exercises, no matter how good and holy, which have been chosen by my own will." She had the same feeling in regard to charity to her neighbor, and preferred it to contemplation, dear as that was to her. For to aid her neighbor in spiritual or temporal employments, she was ever ready to leave prayer, contemplation and every other spiritual delight.

28 Self-will, as God says by the Prophet, is what spoils and corrupts our devotions, labors, and penances. Therefore, not to lose time and trouble, we must endeavor never to act from the impulse of nature, interest, inclination, temper, or caprice, but always from the pure and single motive of doing the will of God, and accustom ourselves to this in all things. This is the most effectual, nay rather the only means of arriving safely and quickly at union with God.

—ST. VINCENT DE PAUL

It was the great and only anxiety of this Saint not to undertake anything to which he might not seem impelled by the Divine Will. And so he made it a rule never to engage by himself in new enterprises even for the glory of God, which he had so much at heart, but always waited until the will of the Lord should be manifested to him by Superiors, or at least by the opinion of others, or the prayers which he made or asked; for his humility made him always distrust his own light, and fear to be deceived.

This most important truth was well understood by St. Catherine of Genoa, who spoke thus on the subject: "There is no pest more malignant than that of self-will, which is so subtle, so malicious, so deeply seated, which conceals itself in so many ways and defends itself by so many reasons, that it seems indeed a demon. When it cannot gain direct obedience, it knows well how to win its way in some other form and under various excuses and pretexts, such as health, necessity, charity, justice, perfection, suffering for God, giving good example, finding spiritual consolation, condescending to the weakness of others, while we are all the while seeking, contriving and cherishing our own interests. I behold in it a sea of malice so envenomed, so opposed to God, that He alone can rescue us from it, and since He sees this better than we He has great compassion on us and never ceases to send us inspirations, contradictions, and helps of all sorts to deliver us."

29 To attain union with God, all the adversities that He sends us are necessary; for His only aim is to consume all our evil inclinations from within and from without. Therefore, slights, injuries, insults,

infirmities, poverty, abandonment by friends and relatives, humiliations, temptations of the devil and many other things opposed to our human nature—all are extremely needed by us, that we may fight until by means of victories we have extirpated all our evil inclinations, so that we may feel them no longer. Nay more, until all adversities no longer seem bitter to us, but rather sweet for God, we shall never arrive at the divine union.

—ST. CATHERINE OF GENOA

"That such is the truth in this matter," added the Saint, "I have proved by my own experience. For Divine Love sees that we hold so tenaciously to what we have chosen, because it seems to us good, and right, and beautiful, and that we will not listen to a word against it, as we are blinded by self-love; and so it makes a ruin of all that we love, by means of death, illness, poverty, hatred, discord and detractions, together with scandals, lies and disgrace falling upon our relatives, our friends, or ourselves, so that we do not know what to do with ourselves, as we are thus drawn away from everything we had cared for, and receive from all only pain and confusion and know not why the Lord permits these events, which seem quite contrary to reason, both as regards God and the world; therefore, we torment ourselves, and strive and seek and hope to escape from so many ills, but can find no outlet.

"When Divine Love has held the soul for a time in this suspense, and in despair and disgust with all she had hitherto loved, then He reveals Himself to her with a countenance full of beauty

and splendor. And as soon as the soul, stripped and destitute of every other help, beholds Him, she casts herself into His arms, and after considering the divine operations of pure love, she says to herself: 'O blind one! with what wast thou occupied? What didst thou seek? Seest thou not that here is all thou seekest and desirest, and all the delights thou wouldst possess? Dost thou not find here more than thou couldst ever desire? O Divine Love! with what sweet art Thou hast drawn me to put aside all love of self, and to clothe myself with a love pure and full of all true joys. Now that I see the truth, I no longer complain except of my ignorance and blindness. And now I leave to Thee all care of myself, seeing clearly that Thou doest for me far better than I have the skill or power to do for myself. I no longer wish to regard anything but Thy operations, which only aim at what the soul truly wishes and desires, though from her blindness she knows not how to gain it.'"

St. Elizabeth, daughter of the King of Hungary, after being left a widow was expelled from her home, abandoned by all and tried by detraction, affronts and contempt. She endured all with much patience, or rather, she was most happy to be able to bear such sufferings for the love of God, who rewarded her abundantly with the most precious gifts.

30 To acquire perfection in general and all the virtues in particular, even to attaining union with God, it is necessary to set before ourselves an example which may serve as a guide for all our actions and all our progress. Now, it is certain that we can find no safer or grander example than that which God Himself

has offered us in the person of His Divine Son, and happy is he who shall make the best copy of it. This, then, should be our book and our mirror, in which we ought to look, whatever circumstances may occur; that is, we should consider in what manner Our Lord behaved in similar cases, and what instruction He has left us in regard to them, and then follow generously His sentiments and example.

—ST. VINCENT DE PAUL

It was the constant practice of this Saint to guide himself thus in all affairs, by the example and teaching of the Saviour, which he kept before his eyes as a pattern in every action; so that when he had to make any decision, to give any advice or recommendation, he instantly sought in the life and words of Christ some ground upon which to base it. And so he scarcely ever spoke without bringing in some word or action of the Son of God, which he would introduce in a wonderfully apposite manner. But if he could think of nothing which had any bearing upon the point, he would meditate a little before acting, and say to himself, "How would Christ speak or act in this case?" and then immediately did what he thought the Lord would have done.

In the Chronicles of St. Francis we are told that one of his Religious had a vision in which he saw a path thickly set with briars, and at the opening of it stood St. Francis with many of his followers. In their midst was Jesus Christ, who said to them, "This is the way we must go," and He immediately began to advance into it. The Religious were alarmed, and considered the

undertaking too difficult; but the Saint encouraged them, saying that it should be enough for them to walk in the footprints of the Lord. He then set the example, and they all followed with much ease.

31 Oh what remorse we shall feel at the end of our lives, when we look back upon the great number of instructions and examples afforded by God and the Saints for our perfection, and so carelessly received by us! If this end were to come to you today, how would you be pleased with the life you have led this year?

—ST. FRANCIS DE SALES

St. Vincent de Paul used often to say: "Oh wretched me! what an account I shall have to render at the tribunal of God, where I am so soon to appear, of the many graces His Divine Goodness has bestowed upon me, if I have derived no fruit from them!"

St. John Berchmans was so attentive to his own perfection that whatever he learned in regard to it remained impressed upon his mind, and he put it into practice with the greatest exactness.

Thomas à Kempis tells of a pious person who one day fell into great anxiety in regard to his final perseverance. Prostrating himself before an altar, he raised his eyes, and exclaimed: "Oh, if I only knew that I was to persevere in good to the end!" He instantly heard an interior voice that replied, "Well, if you knew, what would you do? Do now what you would wish to have done in that hour, and you will be in perfect security." Consoled by

this, he abandoned himself entirely into the hands of God, without further inquiry as to the good or bad state of his conscience, and rather endeavored to discover and fulfill the will of God to the best of his ability.

In the Lives of the Fathers we read of an old monk who, when asked what exercise should be employed to attain perfection, made this answer: "From the day I left the world, I have said to myself every morning: 'Today thou art born again! Begin now to serve God, and to live in this holy place! Commence thy life each day as if the following one were to end it!' This I have done without missing a day."

Monseigneur de Palafox, as we read in his Life, at the very beginning of his conversion had a light from on high by which he understood that he ought to live day by day, that is, to take all possible care to live as if he believed each day that he was then to die and render his account to God. He acted in this manner through the whole remainder of his life, and he confessed that a method so sure to give him satisfaction at the hour of death had also been of great value during his life. It is thus that we should profit in our lives by the lights that God gives us, if we desire in death to rejoice at having received them.

CPSIA information can be obtained
at www.ICGtesting.com
Printed in the USA
BVHW031617160721
612130BV00003B/218